Living by GOD's Master Plan

Living by GOD's Master Plan

Michael Lawson

Christian Focus

ISBN 1 85792 541 6

Published in 2000 by Christian Focus Publications, Geanies House, Fearn, Ross-shire, IV20, 1TW, Great Britain. Previously published in 1987 as The Unfolding Kingdom by Kingsway Publications, Eastbourne, Great Britain.

Cover design by Owen Daily

Printed and bound in Great Britain by
The Guernsey Press Co. Ltd., Guernsey, Channel Islands

Contents

FOREWORD by William Taylor 7

INTRODUCTION 9

1. THE GOD WHO REIGNS 13

2. THE GOD WHO ACTS 29

3. THE GOD WHO SAVES 47

4. TEACHING THE KINGDOM (1) 67

5. TEACHING THE KINGDOM (2) 93

6. TEACHING THE KINGDOM (3) 107

7. COMMUNICATING THE KINGDOM 129

8. KINGDOM PEOPLE 147

9. KINGDOM RESPONSIBILITIES 171

10. KINGDOM EXPECTATIONS 193

11. THE MASTER PLAN 219

Appendix – A case study: ASSESSING
CONTEMPORARY CLAIMS OF THE
COMING OF THE KINGDOM 243

SUBJECT INDEX 267

SCRIPTURE INDEX 269

FOREWORD

In the last minutes of Robert Zemeckis' film *Forrest Gump*, Tom Hanks watches a feather floating down from the sky. He remarks: "I don't know if Momma was right or if it's Lieutenant Dan. I don't know if we each have a destiny or if we're all just floating around accidental-like on a breeze."

In that brief Hollywood scene Hanks captures the great uncertainty of our age, which has long since lost confidence in there being clear answers to the big questions about where we have come from and where we are going; let alone how to live in the light of the elusive answers.

The biblical reality of the Kingdom of God provides an authoritative answer to this confusion. With his expert grasp of the Old Testament, his remarkable ability to communicate with simplicity and clarity, and his deep pastoral and theological insight, Michael Lawson manages to root this big Bible idea firmly in the context of God's revealed plans for His people.

In doing so, Michael has turned what is often seen as a vague and slippery idea into a concrete and deeply attractive reality. He enables us to understand the reality of the Kingdom of God. And above all he makes us want to engage actively here and now in God's eternal purposes as we seek to shape our lives in the light of God's Ruler and King, Jesus Christ.

This is an excellent book for the turning of the Millennium. It lays out God's Master Plan. It enables us to understand our part in that plan. And it straightens out much of the popular confusion and misunderstanding surrounding that plan.

William Taylor
Rector,
St Helen Bishopsgate,
London

INTRODUCTION

The kingdom of God has always been a talking point. What is it? When will it come? How will life change? Such questions concerning the coming rule of God were as hotly debated among Jews at the beginning of the first century A.D. as they are among Christians today – in fact, far more so. When Jesus announced the imminence of the kingdom in his first major public statement, 'The time has come. The kingdom of God is near. Repent and believe the good news!' (Mark 1:15), ripples of Messiah fever and kingdom speculation pulsated through the entire land of Palestine. Kingdom talk was upon everybody's lips; imaginations were fired and political hopes kindled. In consequence, Jesus found himself face to face with ideas and claims about the kingdom which often were as wild, extravagant and man-centred as they were filled with enthusiasm for God's promised salvation. Against this background, Jesus proclaimed the Lord's supreme purpose: to re-establish the rule of God in the lives of men and women everywhere, and bring heaven down to earth. In short, he proclaimed the coming of the kingdom of God.

Millennium expectations
Today, as the dawn rises on a new millennium, kingdom talk is again upon our lips. Yet the shapes and forms of the kingdom are as varied as the choices now offered by Digital TV. In this new, sometimes alarming age, the choice of futures is bewildering. In the years to come, what will shape our lives? Will it be new age hopes and the coming age of Aquarius? Or will global economic and environmental pessimism line up centre stage? Is confident talk about world-wide revival, or an imminent second coming to be taken seriously? Once the Eiffel Tower's Millennium Countdown Clock started ticking, many believed the conclusion was at last in sight. The Millennium Bug may not have destroyed the planet, but what of the future? Who holds the key? Who is worthy to break the seals and open the scroll?

God's master plan

It is the assertion of the Bible that Jesus of Nazareth alone holds
the future in his hands. 'I will give you the keys of the kingdom,'
he told his disciple, Peter (Matt. 16:19); 'I am alive for ever and
ever! And I hold the keys of death and Hades' (Rev. 1:18); 'He is
able to open the scroll and its seven seals' (Rev. 5:5). In the
Palestine of the first century, Jesus encountered every kind of
speculative assertion about the shape of the coming future of God.
Yet the kingdom Jesus spoke of was far more radical than the
radicals could ever dream. For though the good news of the kingdom of God makes its clear appearance in the first three Gospels,
providing the major burden of the teaching of Jesus, it is in no
sense *new* news.

The theme of the kingdom of God unfolds right from the
beginning of the Bible, from the covenant God made with Abraham
onwards. Jesus did not inaugurate something essentially new. The
kingdom of God is God's master plan to reunite heaven and earth,
to usher in to individual lives, and human society as a whole, the
rule and direction of the living God as a tangible reality for
everyday life and experience. Most of all, Jesus came to fulfil
what had been promised for many hundreds of years, and in him
the purpose of history finds its climax.

So today, faced with increasing claims and counterclaims about
the activity of God in our world and future, a Christian's first
responsibility is to look back to the Jesus of history, and the
particular way he faced the kingdom claims of first century
Palestine. For Jesus often encountered a mindset similarly
preoccupied with a narrow parochial agenda, where grace was
squeezed from the picture. His strategy was to spend much of his
ministry *correcting* wrong ideas about the kingdom and its Messiah
– in particular those misplaced ideas which had emerged during
the period between the Testaments. By drawing on the rich heritage
of God's teaching already revealed in the Hebrew Scriptures –
our Old Testament, he aimed to clarify truth and revive hopes
based on the authentic expectations voiced by Moses and the
prophets.

Living in the light of God's rule

It is for this reason Jesus regarded the Old Testament as the basis and backdrop to all his teaching. God had spoken, and was speaking, once more, finally and completely, through his Son. To grasp the fullness of this revelation as Jesus taught about the kingdom, we need to inform ourselves about the kind of controversies to which Jesus was responding. With many similarities in our situation today, we will not unravel claims about the future and the kingdom of God unless we immerse ourselves in the full richness of the Bible's thinking, and its response to both controversy and untruth.

As we begin upon this path we discover that the kingdom of God was not dreamt up for the sake of the New Testament. God carefully planned and prepared its unfolding. The kingdom is dynamic; each stage of its reality has only been unveiled at God's chosen moments in salvation-history. Yet while the teaching on the kingdom has been fully revealed by God, its reality unfolds still, and is moving gradually and unquenchably towards its climax – though none can tell when. Jesus was direct: 'It is not for you to know the times or dates the Father has set by his own authority' (Acts 1:7).

We face many of the same questions in our time as the Jews of the first century did in theirs. It is natural we should aspire to know the nature of the kingdom, yes, and when it will appear – as well as the extent of its impact upon our lives. But we must not exclude what was for Jesus the final and most lastingly important question when contemplating the kingdom of God. If it is a fact that God is coming to rule – if he *is* bringing in his kingdom – how should we ourselves live in the light of that reality?

As Jesus addresses both the people of his time and us today, we will discover he makes us live with a paradox. *The kingdom has arrived – in him – but the best is yet to come.* His passionate concern is the same as it was for his disciples: kingdom people must learn to live lives fit for a King's rule. Privileges and responsibilities belong together. Radical discipleship, signs and wonders, social responsibility, personal spirituality – all are subservient to the grand design. The Lord of history, who is the

Lord of glory, wants a people for himself, to be agents of his blessing to the whole earth. This is the purpose of the unfolding kingdom. By it, the future of the whole world is assured, and God's master plan will finally come to completion. In that day, finally it will be said in triumph: 'The kingdom of the world has become the kingdom of our Lord and of his Christ, and he will reign for ever and ever' (Rev. 11:15).

Chapter 1

THE GOD WHO REIGNS

Those who hope in the LORD will renew their strength. They will soar on wings like eagles; they will run and not grow weary, they will walk and not be faint (Isa. 40:31).

There have always been people who find it inexplicable or offensive to believe in a God who reigns. The idea that God has a guiding, over-ruling hand in human affairs, is viewed uncomfortably and seen as a loathsome violation of freedom of choice and man's right to self-determination.

It was over this issue that Moses came into conflict with Egypt's Pharaoh, Rameses II, Elijah confronted the prophets of Baal on Mount Carmel, and the Apostle Paul argued with the Stoic and Epicurean philosophers at the Areopagus in first-century Athens. Today, the assertion of God's sovereign power – his reign – still meets with mystification or rejection. Yet the reign of God is a fundamental biblical truth, and its offence goes deeper than philosophical incomprehension. Such resistance involves deeper questions of individual morality and personal response to God.

Concept or co-operation?

That God desires a guiding role in human affairs is a challenge to our inner selves and the way we live our lives. It is not that we do not understand the ways of God, we would rather be in control of our own lives. Philosophical questions there may be, but the moral ambiguities of human nature are the real barrier to knowing God. The Bible's assertion of the sovereignty of God is a direct challenge to our unregenerate moral outlook – our lifestyles, concerns and priorities. Put at its simplest, it is a question of who rules? It is common experience with the discovery that God desires a decisive part in our lives, that the defences quickly spring up. It is part of our fallen condition to be resistant to the purposes and direction of

13

God, for fallen humanity instinctively aims to go it alone.

The kingdom of God, then, is not so much a concept as a co-operation; not so much an idea to be explored as a relationship to be developed. God wants to co-operate with us, and us to co-operate with him, in a partnership. But it will be a partnership where he takes the initiative and where we must be prepared to open up our lives to him. This is partly what is meant in biblical terms by the reign or sovereignty of God, and what the New Testament describes as the lordship of Christ. Under that sovereign lordship, no longer do we go it alone; we co-operate with the divine King himself – the God who reigns – who has great plans for us, for the church and for the world.

So when we start to think about the kingdom of God, this is where we must begin. The biblical metaphor is clear: every kingdom has a king, and every king reigns. To understand the kingdom biblically, we must therefore ask the initial question, What does it mean when we speak of the God who reigns? If this is the God whose kingdom it is, we need first to know something about him, in his character and his sovereign power, if he is going to have a significant part to play in our lives.

History speaks today
The Bible is an historical book. That is far from implying that it is in any sense irrelevant because it was written a long time ago. By contrast, the historical nature of the Bible lies not only in real events which took place at a specific time and place, but also in the fact that God often taught his people about himself and his concerns for them in the light of those historical situations. As the people lived through an event with God, so their Lord would teach them about himself in relation to that specific happening. This is just one facet of the rich educative process of revelation which the Lord uses throughout the Bible to teach his people about his nature, ways and will.

From the very beginning of the Old Testament it is clear that those events would often be painful moments in the history of God's people. The Bible's great affirmations about God's power and goodness are often made against such a background of pain and suffering. What we are dealing with is not a book of philosophy or poetry which is out of touch with the realities of everyday life. This is a unique book of reality, teaching a living experience of the one true God who lives and moves and is in all kinds of situations past and present. In this precise sense, therefore, history speaks today.

Understanding the Bible

It is for this reason that we will be looking at the Bible's revelation according to the unfolding of some of its major themes. Though Genesis introduces us to the God whose grandeur as Creator towers over all that he has made, the fullest revelation of his grace and strength comes later in the scriptures. In the Genesis drama of Creation and Fall, and the first steps of covenant making, we are quickly introduced to the God who plans a long-term rescue for the human race and the remaking of mankind. This is the God who reigns, whose fullest revelation in Old Testament terms is seen through Israel's greatest prophets, Isaiah, Jeremiah and Ezekiel. Their messages were given during times of national bewilderment and turmoil.

It was into such a situation that the prophet Isaiah was called to be God's spokesman. In the confident yet reassuring words of chapter 40 of his prophecy, some of the most remarkable affirmations in the whole Bible concerning the sovereignty of God, the God who reigns, are made. They form one of the most comprehensive pictures of God's sovereignty in the entire Old Testament.

Both the background and details of Isaiah 40 teach us much about the issues raised by the grand-sounding assertion that the God of Israel is indeed the God who is King and who reigns as the sovereign Lord over all things.

> See, the Sovereign LORD comes with power,
>   and his arm rules for him.
> See, his reward is with him,
>   and his recompense accompanies him.
> He tends his flock like a shepherd:
>   He gathers the lambs in his arms

and carries them close to his heart;
    he gently leads those that have young.

Who has measured the waters in the hollow of his hand,
    or with the breadth of his hand marked off the heavens?
Who has held the dust of the earth in a basket,
    or weighed the mountains on the scales
    and the hills in a balance?
Who has understood the mind of the LORD,
    or instructed him as his counsellor?
Whom did the LORD consult to enlighten him,
    and who taught him the right way?
Who was it that taught him knowledge
    or showed him the path of understanding?

Surely the nations are like a drop in a bucket;
    they are regarded as dust on the scales;
    he weighs the islands as though they were fine dust.
Lebanon is not sufficient for altar fires,
    nor its animals enough for burnt offerings.
Before him all the nations are as nothing;
    they are regarded by him as worthless
    and less than nothing.

To whom, then, will you compare God?
    What image will you compare him to?
As for an idol, a craftsman casts it,
    and a goldsmith overlays it with gold
    and fashions silver chains for it.
A man too poor to present such an offering
    selects wood that will not rot.
He looks for a skilled craftsman
    to set up an idol that will not topple.

Do you not know?
    Have you not heard?
Has it not been told you from the beginning?
    Have you not understood since the earth was founded?
He sits enthroned above the circle of the earth,
    and its people are like grasshoppers.
He stretches out the heavens like a canopy,
    and spreads them out like a tent to live in.

He brings princes to naught
    and reduces the rulers of this world to nothing.
No sooner are they planted,
    no sooner are they sown,
    no sooner do they take root in the ground,
than he blows on them and they wither,
    and a whirlwind sweeps them away like chaff.

'To whom will you compare me?
    Or who is my equal?' says the Holy One.
Lift your eyes and look to the heavens:
    Who created all these?
He who brings out the starry host one by one,
    and calls them each by name.
Because of his great power and mighty strength,
    not one of them is missing.

Why do you say, O Jacob,
    and complain, O Israel,
'My way is hidden from the Lord;
    my cause is disregarded by my God'?
Do you not know?
    Have you not heard?
The Lord is the everlasting God,
    the Creator of the ends of the earth.
He will not grow tired or weary,
    and his understanding no one can fathom.
He gives strength to the weary
    and increases the power of the weak.
Even youths grow tired and weary,
    and young men stumble and fall;
but those who hope in the Lord
    will renew their strength.
They will soar on wings like eagles;
    they will run and not grow weary,
    they will walk and not be faint (Isa. 40:10-31).

Is God in control?

In Isaiah's time, Assyria and Babylon were two of the ancient world's major superpowers. Israel by contrast was a small and relatively powerless nation. Compare any small European country of today with the might and resources of the United States of America to feel the relative insignificance of Israel in relation to these two enormous superpowers. Yet not only was Israel small, she was vulnerable; continually buffeted, she faced the constant threat of attack and war.

Up to this point in the period of which Isaiah speaks, Assyria has been the main threat to Israel's peace and stability. That threat is now behind them. However, it appears there is worse to come. The Babylonian empire is poised to attack – no small threat, since Babylon is a gigantic, powerful and aggressive enemy.

At this stage in Isaiah's prophecy, Jerusalem has certainly been saved from Assyria. But the relief is short-lived. According to Isaiah, the Babylonians are on the war-path. Not only will they sack the city of Jerusalem, the inhabitants of Jerusalem will be carried off into exile as the Babylonians' captives. As Isaiah writes, the dreadful possibility has been set in motion.

It must have seemed as disastrous then, as the Holocaust was for the Jews during the Second World War. Exile, coupled with devastation, a prospect of terrible calamity was unfolding before their very eyes. It is difficult to grasp how disturbing such a threat to their existence must have been to their morale and stability.

Here, then, is a people facing almost crushing pressure. 'Is God in control?' In the circumstances, this is far from an abstract question. The Babylonians were just round the corner. 'Is God King of his people or not?' In like fashion, this was a deeply felt issue, arising out of a situation whose effects were becoming painfully felt by everyone in the nation.

In chapters 40 to 48, through the prophet Isaiah, the Lord declares words which came as strength to the people. Political commentators were pessimistic: it must have looked like the end of their nation. Yet the Lord promised a complete turn-round of events. The outrageous power of Babylon will be overthrown by Cyrus, King of the Persian empire. If that was not indeed remarkable enough, still further help was promised. Amazingly, Cyrus would return the Hebrew exiles to their homeland. Yet in front of their eyes the powerful Babylonians were already carrying their people away. How could God turn the heart of Cyrus, a pagan and despotic ruler, and enable him to set God's people free? If it were to happen, then who could doubt the power in the land?

Those events did take place. The Babylonians were overturned and Cyrus did return the captives. So after all, God is in control. He does reign – in spite of the Israelites' present picture of turmoil and uncertainty. Yet Isaiah is the mouthpiece to an even greater hope: God will step on to the stage of human history in person, to establish his rule for ever.

The coming reign

No time-scale is given for this event. But the certainty is there. He is coming. The King will come to his people. According to Isaiah, this is the goal of history. The God who is in control of the lives of the people of Jerusalem will reveal himself to all men everywhere, as the God who reigns. He is the true King of his divine kingdom.

We have the benefit of living well over two and a half thousand years after the prophet Isaiah. God has already been made known to us in the fullest sense in Jesus Christ. History prepared us for it. Yet for us there is still more to come. Jesus' second coming is confidently proclaimed by Isaiah: 'The glory of the LORD shall be revealed, and all flesh shall see it together, for the mouth of the LORD has spoken' (Isa. 40:5).

The clear implication of Isaiah's prophecy, which was given in response to a specific historical situation, is that God will be seen to reign as the God of the *whole* world beyond the borders of Israel. That is the Lord's pledge in these words. He will make himself known universally. Jesus took hold of that promise and related it to his own return to this world. Therefore, even though God's reign has not yet reached its final consummation, the promise stands and will be fulfilled. The certainty vitally affects our perspectives and objectives today.

The story so far

God is speaking through Isaiah to a calamitous situation in Israel's fortunes. Yet with his overall control of history, the Lord declares not only Israel's distress to be nearing its end – but this same God is on his way, coming to their world and ours. God is neither silent nor passive. History will one day come to an end and God will be there, in control. When the kingdom comes in all its power and glory, it will be the beginning of something altogether new.

But all this could simply be dismissed as so much rhetoric, which is precisely what Isaiah was accused of.

'What kind of God are you talking about?'

That is the question the Israelites were asking. This kind of comment is behind the polemical nature of the prophet's language in Isaiah 40. Here is Isaiah standing up making grand affirmations. What kind of response might he have received?

'Look Isaiah, we're in the middle of a war. What is God really like? Has he any power? Is he in control?'

Under the circumstances, some people must have felt that they were reasonable questions. In response, there are several issues which Isaiah highlights.

Who is God?

'To whom then will you liken God, or what likeness compare with him?' (Isa. 40:18).

Isaiah underlines a primary truth about God's power and compassion:

'Behold the Sovereign LORD comes with might, and his arm rules for him.... He will feed his flock like a shepherd, he will gather the lambs in his arms, he will carry them in his bosom, and gently lead those that are with young' (Isa. 40:10-11).

This is a remarkable statement. There is the confident assertion that God rules. His power over this world is total. And there is an extraordinary, unheard of declaration of God's compassion and care like the shepherd's gentle care for the lambs of his flock.

For a people living in an agrarian culture, such a picture would be a familiar, everyday image. Yet it is none the less remarkable, for Isaiah is saying, 'You may not have realized it – but God is like that.'

So pause and consider. In our experience of national and international politics and government, we do not normally connect absolute power with compassionate care. Yet the extraordinary truth is, God is like *that*. He is powerful and yet he cares. The pictures of the supreme ruler and the gentle shepherd are brought together.

In some ways we share the Israelites' problem today. Consciously or unconsciously we often will attempt to scale God down, and have a much smaller impression of the truth about him than the facts demand.

This is the reason why at this point in chapter 40, from verse 19 onwards, Isaiah speaks about idols. The Israelites were well aware of religious cultures around them whose images of wood and metal were supposed to represent deities. As Elijah pointed out in a different context, such tribal deities were rather on the small side to be of any use! (cf. 1 Kgs. 18).

Isaiah is saying that the moment you scale God down and fail to acknowledge the full reality of these truths about him, your God becomes almost as useless to you as a lifeless, dumb idol.

By implication, then, Isaiah is asking the question, 'What is your vision of God?' The God who reigns is a God who is complete in his power and strength. He is the God who is able to and who longs to respond to the needs of Israel and our needs today with compassion and love. The danger was, and is, of having a reduced vision so that our God is a scaled-down version and a little on the small side to be any use at all. But this kind of God is really no more powerful or compassionate than a dumb idol. The question posed by Isaiah is one for every believer to consider – *what is your real vision of God?* And so Isaiah moves on to make a far-reaching declaration.

The incomparable God

In aiming to correct the defective view of God which confines him to the status of an idol, Isaiah interrogates Israel: 'Have you not known? Have you not heard? Has it not been told you from the beginning? Have you not understood from the foundations of the earth?' (Isa. 40:21). There follows a picture of God as the powerful transcendent Creator who rules the world he has made and to whom earthly rivals are inconsequential. After that bold picture of contrasts, Isaiah asks another question: 'To whom then will you compare me, that I should be like him? says the Holy One' (Isa. 40:25).

So on his own admission, God is incomparable. But *how* is he beyond comparison? Two particular senses are involved: he is the Creator *and* he is the Lord of history.

Isaiah says the reason you can be sure God is in control is because of these two related facts. First, he is the originator of all that there is. He is the Creator. And second, he has, by virtue of that fact, the right to the overall say in the outworking and outcome of history.

Human beings do exercise their God-given freedom, but ultimately the final decisions rest with God. That is why we describe him as the Lord of history. It is the same strength of power as Creator which enables the Lord to be the one who finally calls the tune. All history in its direction and outcome is subject to God. This is what Isaiah affirms: 'It is he who sits above the circle of the earth, and its inhabitants are like grasshoppers; who stretches out the heavens like a curtain, and spreads them like a tent to dwell in: who brings princes to naught, and makes the rulers of the earth as nothing' (Isa. 40:22-23).

God knows when to put his foot down. And when he does, in Isaiah's phrase, he 'brings princes to naught, and makes the rulers of the earth as nothing'. The most powerful, even the most malevolent in their use of power in this world, are nothing before the over-all and over-ruling power of God. However destructive and painful, the system of evil rampant in the world today will never gain the upper hand. The rule of terror will come to a decisive end. It would not be so if there were not a God who reigns.

What is the implication? If God is sovereign, then he is the ultimate authority, the highest court of appeal over all real-life political situations, and the negotiator upon whom the ultimate peace of the world depends. Equally, his sovereignty extends to all the personal situations of turmoil and threat we face in our own lives.

The knowledge of the God who is incomparable in creation and providence, if nothing else, should drive us to our knees, not only out of sheer wonder, but because it would be folly not to trust your life to such a God as this. Isaiah clearly believed so. This is why he continues his message with an imperative.

Open your eyes and expand your vision of God!

> 'Lift up your eyes on high and see: who created these? He who brings out their host by number, calling them all by name; by the greatness of his might, and because he is strong in power not one is missing' (Isa. 40:26).

It is possible to have very little consciousness of God as we go through the day. Yet it is equally possible to learn to see the activity of God as being constantly displayed in the everyday events of our lives. How the Israelites needed reminding that God reigns even in situations of pressure and turmoil.

God does prompt us. He is present in the meetings we have with people, in the unforeseen events and in moments of joy as well as times of sadness and pain.

It is something like the difference between seeing in black and white and seeing in colour. If you have normal eyesight, you won't see things in monochrome, but it is still possible to be totally unaware of the riches of colour around you. Until, that is, you consciously open your eyes to the wonderful variety of the colour there is present all around.

So, in this spiritual sense Isaiah encourages a people under pressure to open their eyes, in a serious, thoughtful and devoted manner, to the presence and activity of God. The same truth still applies. We too should expand our vision of God's power and of his presence in our lives, to see reality – God's reality – in full colour.

It is clear from all this that Isaiah had a personal and pastoral concern for God's people. From the pictures he uses, the questions he asks and the vision of God he encourages, he appears to be interested only in truth which was applied to people's lives. And so Isaiah brings his hearers, both ancient Israelites and his hearers today, to the point of challenge and decision – to a sense of personal application of the great truths about God he has been expounding.

Let God reign!

In their distress and pessimism about the outcome of international affairs, the Israelites were tempted to abandon all hope and become despondent. They felt that God had given up, that he no longer watched over them. But Isaiah rebukes them: 'Why do you say, O Jacob, and speak, O Israel, "My way is hid from the LORD, and my right is disregarded by my God"?' (Isa. 40:27).

When things get rough our attitude can become as defeatist as the Israelites. Perhaps we feel that God cannot see or understand our situation. We echo the sentiment, 'My way is hid from the Lord.' Either that, or we think God does not really care about what we are going through, so we exclaim, 'My right is disregarded by my God.'

But what was Isaiah's response to these attitudes? Again he focuses on God himself:

'Have you not known? Have you not heard? The LORD is the everlasting God, the Creator of the ends of the earth. He does not faint or grow weary, his understanding is unsearchable. He gives power to the faint, and to him who has no might he increases strength. Even youths shall faint and be weary, and young men shall fall exhausted; but they who wait for the LORD shall renew their strength, they shall mount up with wings like eagles, they shall run and not be weary, they shall walk and not faint' (Isa. 40:28-31).

His message is for those who are weak, those who are tempted to give up when the going gets tough. They are the ones in the firing-line. It includes the Israelites who were threatened by the Babylonians, but also us in our personal, national and global anxieties. The God who is in control, the God who does not grow weary or faint, offers a power to overcome. It is a power to transcend the hurdles and obstacles which are an all too regular part of our everyday lives. We are not offered an easy ride, but we will be given strength to overcome in every situation. Our God is the God who reigns, and therefore he is able to strengthen those who want to find his way out of painful or difficult situations.

It is a Bible teaching *and* a fact of experience that God doesn't necessarily take the obstacles away. But he does give strength to cope in the midst of the obstacles. Those who wait for the Lord – that is to say, those who steadfastly put their trust and hope and resolve in the living God – will find in the midst of all their uphill struggles, a renewed strength. In the end they will transcend their problems, as though mounting up with the wings of an eagle. Since God is active in the arena of everyday affairs, there is a promise of renewed physical vigour: 'They shall run and not be weary, they shall walk and not faint.' It is as basic as getting through the day. This sovereign God, precisely because he is the God who reigns, is able to help this happen.

This is Isaiah's magisterial divine vision: the power and compassion of God, the God who is incomparable and who is the Creator, the originator of all things, the Lord, the guiding hand of history. This is who we are speaking of when we offer praise to God, when we sing, pray, think, worship. He is the God who reigns.

Knowing the attributes of God

Fundamental to the mind and understanding of Isaiah is the thought that to be able to trust God in practice, there must be growth in our own understanding of what God is like in himself. As theologians put it, we have to learn about his character and attributes.

If we were speaking of a human being in these terms, we would speak of personality and ability. It is normal practice when you apply for a new job to be asked both for references and to attend an interview. A prospective employer needs to know about our personality and abilities to see whether we are fitted for the task he has in mind. Isaiah's message to the people facing impending calamity, is that God is indeed fitted for the task of their deliverance. They can be sure he is fit to respond in such a way, because of his nature, character and attributes.

So as we begin to think about the God who reigns, the God who in reality is King of his kingdom, this is our starting-point. His purposes are tied in to his character. His activities depend on his attributes. All that God *does* relates to all that God *is* in himself – his holiness, purity, power, strength, goodness and love. He is King of his kingdom.

There is a negative side to all this. Isaiah has equally implied that a God who does *not* reign would be a God not worth knowing. That thought leads us on to the next stage in our examination of the kingdom. For above all, God does want us to know him. As a loving Father he desires a guiding hand in our affairs. Far from seeking to violate our freedom of choice and our self-determination, the God who reigns wants a people for himself – his very own kingdom people. He wants us to belong to him, and be blessed by him – the King – forever.

Summary Points

■ God's rule is revealed as both present and future

■ Isaiah spoke to a demoralized people who needed to relearn truths about God which they had ignored or forgotten

■ The Lord sometimes lets us face difficult times, to help us grow in our trust

For Reflection

It is not that we do not understand the ways of God, we would rather be in control of our own lives ... for fallen humanity instinctively aims to go it alone. (p. 13)

■ How true is this in your experience?

■ What scriptures can you think of which express this truth?

■ If you were trying to explain this to an unchurched person, how would you go about it?

■ Look at Romans 7:15-25. What insight do you gain on this from Paul's experience and teaching?

In our experience of national and international politics and government, we do not normally connect absolute power with compassionate care. (pp. 20-21)

- How do you connect the thoughts of God the ruler, and God the carer?

- What does this mean for society, the church, your life?

- What difference does this teaching make to our evangelism?

- Look again at Isaiah 40, and compare with Ezekiel 34:12-14, 23, 31; Psalm 23, John 10:11, 14-16.

- Note that Jesus is called the good shepherd (John 10:11, 14); the great Shepherd (Heb. 13:20); and the head Shepherd (1 Pet. 5:4).

The knowledge of the God who is incomparable in creation and providence, if nothing else, should drive us to our knees, not only out of sheer wonder, but because it would be folly not to trust your life to such a God as this. (pp. 22-23)

"For this reason I kneel before the Father, from whom his whole family in heaven and on earth derives its name" (Eph. 3:14-15).

- What can you learn from Paul's prayer in Ephesians 3:14-21?

God's purposes are tied in to his character. His activities depend on his attributes. All that God does relates to all that God is in himself. (p. 25)

What difference does this theological key make

- to your praying?

- your daily confidence to live for God?

- any decisions you need to make?

- issues facing your church?

Chapter 2

THE GOD WHO ACTS

Rejoice greatly, O Daughter of Zion! Shout, Daughter of Jerusalem! See, your king comes to you, righteous and having salvation, gentle and riding on a donkey, on a colt, the foal of a donkey (Zech. 9:9. And quoted in Matt. 21:5).

The existence of a king suggests a kingdom. A kingdom implies a people. Central, then, to God's purposes for the unfolding of history is this kingdom – which, rightly understood, is a community concept. The Lord desires a people for himself – a community with a purpose. The God who acts has a purpose for a special people to influence the whole world throughout history and beyond.

We have thought already about the nature and character of the God who reigns. So we turn our attention now to this God who acts – the God who desires a people for himself. This is the God who by the act of covenant-making ties in his creation of a kingdom people with the promise of blessing and restoration to the whole world.

Deep-rooted antagonism

What is the basis upon which entry into the kingdom rests? Is everyone automatically included? Or does our experience of this rebellious world suggest that the King would have some extremely awkward subjects on his hands if that were the case?

When we reflect upon ourselves, and the shortcomings of our moral natures, it can bring the sharp reminder that we are rebellious creatures who suffer from a deep-rooted inner antagonism to the Lord's rule. 'All have sinned and fall short of the glory of God' (Rom. 3:23). There is no distinction among us. Sinful attitudes and behaviour flow from a deep-rooted alienation from God. That spiritual fact is common to all. Biblical estimations of human imperfection are disturbingly precise. Their diagnosis rests on a clear understanding of the root cause.

The remaking of mankind

It is all the more remarkable, then, that the God who reigns – the pure, holy and sovereign Lord of all the earth – desires a people for himself. He wants a kingdom *truly* fit for a King. But with our fundamental antagonism to God's rule and control this makes human beings an odd choice for subjects. If therefore there is to be 'a people for God', some far-reaching changes will be required, so far-reaching that it may be asked, why should God go to so much trouble?

The only possible reason for his endeavours is that behind the creation of a kingdom or a community of people for God, there is a grand design: God plans nothing less than the remaking of mankind.

From the very beginning of the Bible it becomes clear that God has a great purpose for the whole world. That purpose is to reverse the catastrophic effects of the Fall, and to re-establish God's rule in the lives of men and women throughout and for all the ages to come. This is the God who acts decisively in human history to restore to the world the reign of God in the lives of men and women everywhere. The kingdom is a single grand design, bringing salvation and transformation for humanity by the remaking of mankind.

Covenant relationships

A picture of a bride on her wedding day, beautifully dressed for her husband, is an especially memorable sight, full of loveliness and hope for the future. Yet it is a sad fact that marriages do not always turn out to be full of happiness and joy. In the UK four in ten marriages end in divorce.

Such an understanding of human relationships can give us a clearer insight into the biblical thinking behind the biblical concept of covenant. For the question of relationship is at the very heart of the necessity of a covenant.

Central to the meaning of the covenant are two ideas: estrangement and reconciliation. They are the two basic elements. In a sentence: the covenant is to do with the mending of a broken relationship.

Covenant perspectives

Some people insist on reading the last page of a novel or a thriller before they arrive at the end of the book. Perhaps it is either because they cannot stand the suspense, or they feel they need to know how it all turns out in the end in order to make sense of what happens in between. Whatever we may feel about literary cheating, the Bible positively encourages knowledge of the beginning and ending of the story – so the perspective of what comes in between will shine out more clearly.

This is why at the Bible's commencement, in Genesis 3, we learn of the Fall. It is an issue of relationships and estrangement: mankind's estrangement from the God who has created and loved him. But when we turn to the end of the book, to Revelation 21, the 'last page' of the Bible, we see that reconciliation has taken place, and the relationship between God and man has been restored:

> I saw a new heaven and a new earth, for the first heaven and the first earth had passed away.... I saw the Holy City, the new Jerusalem, coming down out of heaven from God, prepared as a bride beautifully dressed for her husband.... Now the dwelling of God is with men, and he will live with them. They will be his people, and God himself will be with them and be their God (Rev. 21:1-3).

These are the essential perspectives of the covenant: the beginning and ending, estrangement and reconciliation. The covenant is God's single-minded agreement to restore the estranged relationship between mankind and himself. This is the essence of salvation. The estrangement began at the beginning of man's pre-history. The reconciliation will be fulfilled in the most complete sense at a point still in the future. Because it is to do with relationships, it involves God with a people, a kingdom for a King.

Before we look at the biblical covenants in action, however, we need to go further into what constitutes a covenant in the Bible and how the parties to a biblical covenant relate to one another.

The nature of a covenant

Forms of covenant-making are a common part of everyday experience. We may use the term 'covenant' relatively rarely, but such agreements are frequently made. Covenant-making is a normal part of our day-to-day transactions with others. There is a principle at work behind all this. It is to do with an agreement which seals a relationship of co-operation. Without that agreement, there is no belonging or working together. Unless you say the words 'I will', there can be no marriage. Unless you exchange contracts, you cannot buy or sell a house. There has to be an agreement: it seals the relationship of belonging and co-operation.

This is the nature of a covenant. But a covenant implies the existence of people, parties to an agreement. How do the parties to a covenant relate to each other? In everyday life, the kinds of covenant or agreement or contract most of us are involved in are two-sided. The bride gets a chance to say 'I will', as well as the groom. When you sign and exchange contracts for a house, those two parties have obligations within those covenants. All these examples of covenants are two-sided.

By contrast God's covenants are one-sided. They are unilateral rather than bilateral. God's covenant is designed to bring us into relationship with himself. It is his decision. It depends on him to make it possible. We have nothing we can contribute. In that sense it is a one-sided covenant – God's unilateral agreement, the King's decree. A contrast may help us to understand this better.

If you order some goods, say from a mail order catalogue or

over the Internet, it's a two sided agreement. The seller agrees to provide the goods, and you agree to pay them whatever the charge is. But God's covenant is on a different basis – it's *one* sided. We have nothing to contribute in payment. He comes up with the goods. We simply accept what he offers us.

There are important questions about how we live in response to this unilateral covenant agreement and we shall come to them later. But for the moment we should note this important issue for kingdom thinking. God's covenant is one-sided. He alone has instituted it and has promised to carry out its obligations. Its effectiveness does not depend on us. It is a unilateral arrangement which brings us the possibility of a relationship with himself. We must willingly enter that relationship, however, because without an agreement there can be no relationship.

Which one did you say?

When we speak of the covenant in the Bible, we have to be careful about exactly which covenant we mean. The Bible has many references to covenants, so it is important to get our bearings straight, otherwise confusion can arise. It would be rather like saying how much you like Strauss waltzes. What you mean would not necessarily be clear. Someone would be bound to ask, 'Which particular Strauss do you mean?' There are three different Johann Strausses, then one Edward and one Joseph all in the same family. Just to confuse matters, there is also Richard Strauss, the famous composer of *Der Rosenkavalier*, who is no relation to the others, and neither did he write waltzes, or not many of them. So, that's six Strausses in all. No wonder music-lovers get confused!

When we come to speak about the covenant, therefore, we equally must ask: which one do you mean? If we stick only to the Old Testament for the moment, there are four: the Covenant with Noah, the Covenant with Abraham, the Covenant with Moses and the Covenant with David. So which covenant do we mean? We will look at each in turn.

The four Old Testament covenants

1. The covenant with Noah reveals the mercy of God

Covenant history begins with Noah. The Noachic covenant is the covenant of mercy, made by God with Noah, and a one-sided agreement. Genesis 9:8-17 records the main details. God promises never again to flood the earth. He pledges himself to replace his wrath and judgement with mercy. This covenant is still in force.

The process has begun. Estrangement is giving way to reconciliation. As the fault is on one side (ours), and the capacity for restoration is similarly one-sided (God's), so this is a covenant of mercy. It reminds us that all God's dealings with man rest upon his mercy, which ultimately finds fullest expression in Jesus' death on the cross. The cross more forcibly than anything else speaks to us of the *cost* of mercy. There is no sense in the Bible in which mercy is seen as a passive act. The covenant of mercy made with Noah committed God to a profoundly sacrificial, costly and painful fulfilment to this covenant promise.

But for this covenant, the history of the world would have taken a different and terminal course. In his mercy God did something about our sin-dominated situation – even though ultimately it cost him the life of his Son.

The covenant of mercy is the foundation for the covenant of grace. This is the next stage in God's dealings with mankind: to restore the relationship; to change it from estrangement to reconciliation.

2. The covenant with Abraham reveals the grace of God

> God said to Abram, 'Behold, my covenant is with you, and you shall be the father of a multitude of nations. No longer shall your name be Abram, but your name shall be Abraham; for I have made you the father of a multitude of nations.... And I will establish my covenant between me and you and your descendants after you throughout their generations for an everlasting covenant, to be God to you and your descendants after you' (Gen. 17:3-5, 7).

In this passage God's self-declaration of what he is going to do is clear. Like all covenant legislation (with one important exception which we shall examine later) the covenant here is unilateral. God himself is declaring what he will do. It reveals his grace, because only he can do it. It assumes an attitude of mercy, because of the covenant with Noah already legislated. And, above all, it shows forth the richness of God's love in its promise that God will bless. 'I will bless you, and make your name great, so that you will be a blessing' (Gen. 12:2).

When compared with their rich Hebrew counterparts, our own everyday use of the words 'bless' and 'blessing' are poor relations indeed. God's promise to bless is a far-reaching, dynamic and saving concept. It is a pity our overworked English use of the terms provides such a watered-down equivalent for so powerful a promised divine activity.

What is it that gives the covenant of grace, with this promised dynamic sense of blessing, its characteristic power – not just in action, but in scope, breadth and vision?

Those who work in marketing or advertising are rarely happier than when they can present a product as being unrestricted in its usefulness and effectively indestructible. 'Useful for the whole family,' they say confidently. 'Virtually unbreakable. Should last for ever.' So run the slogans. In practice, universal application and everlasting power may not be such common characteristics of marketable products; but by contrast, in the realm of grace they are the two distinctive attributes of the covenant with Abraham. They require further exploration.

(a) The covenant made with Abraham is universal

'You shall be the father of a multitude of nations' (Gen. 17:4).

For Abraham to hear those words, and for his descendants to read and meditate upon them for many hundreds of years after, must have come as a mind-expanding thought. What did it mean? To paraphrase it into the simplest terms, we could say God created the Hebrew religion of the Old Testament in order to provide the essential building blocks to create Christianity.

It's sometimes (wrongly) said that Judaism failed, so God dreamt up Christianity instead. This is a subtle distortion of the truth. The facts tell a different story. Judaism today is equally out of tune with the Bible when it claims that Judaism is meant to last as Judaism for ever, and that by and large Judaism has little to do with anyone who is not born a Jew. That is just as much of a serious distortion, and the truth requires clear restatement.

For Christians and Jews of these persuasions, the Old Testament speaks a clearly correcting word. Genesis 17:4 shows in detail the nature of God's promise. Abraham is to be the father of *many* nations. He is the founding father of a long line, stretching beyond Israel to a multitude of nations. The scope is breathtaking. What a vision. To India, Russia, Spain, Great Britain, the United States, Ethiopia, Djibouti, Italy and New Zealand. In fact anywhere where there are true believers in this same God – the God of Abraham, the God and Father of Jesus Christ – this universal promise to Abraham is extended: 'You shall be the father of a multitude of nations.'

The universal nature of this covenant with Abraham was built in from the very beginning. Christians and Jews take note! Here is something important about the economy of God. God does not go in for false starts or failures. The work of salvation is destined to be effective for ever.

(b) The covenant made with Abraham is everlasting

'I will establish my covenant between me and you and your descendants after you throughout their generations for an everlasting covenant, to be God to you and to your descendants after you' (Gen. 17:7).

The covenant which God made with Abraham still stands today – because God designed it to be everlasting. The people of Old Testament times were often wayward, as we are, yet the religion of Old Testament times did not fail. Only the ceremonial practices of Old Testament legislation have been superseded.

Along with the economy of God, at work here is *the educative process of God.* The Lord wants to create a people for himself. Such a people need to learn the ways of God. In this way, God created the religion of the Hebrews in order that Christianity might grow out of a context of God's Old Testament revelation. In the richest sense, Jesus was a Jew. In his life, death, resurrection, ascension and promised coming, he fulfils the promises and prophecies concerning God's saving acts made clearly, educatively and historically in the Old Testament literature.

So it is dangerous ground to carelessly suggest that the old covenant failed. It did not. God's grace never fails. Only people fail. We will return to this point. But for the moment we should take firmly into our thinking the strong language of grace. God's covenant made with Abraham is universal in its significance and everlasting in its power. This is the nature of grace: it is God's ability to change what we cannot change, and to save our very lives.

It is true there is biblical language which speaks of covenant failure. If biblical covenants are unilateral, how can this possibly be? Surely God does not fail? The answer lies in the fact that there is one important covenant which is noticeably *two-sided* – bilateral – in its nature. As such we must learn from it, both in our understanding of God and his requirements of us, and also in our appreciation of the way the unfolding of God's kingdom is progressive and restorative. This is the covenant made at Sinai.

3. The covenant with Moses reveals the holiness of God

For a generation unschooled in the scriptures, the animation film *The Prince of Egypt* has brought the drama of the Exodus to life in a brilliant and compelling way. It shows the extent of the power of the hand of God upon Israel in Egypt. This was no political revolution of the underclass. It was a tremendous saving act of God which enabled the people to leave their Egyptian captivity.

The film ends where the covenant begins. Now in the Sinai desert, through Moses, God is about to reveal his law to the people, summarized in the ten commandments. This is why God speaks about obeying his voice: 'Now if you obey me fully and keep my covenant, then out of all nations you will be my treasured possession. Although the whole earth is mine, you will be for me *a kingdom of priests* and a holy nation' (Exod. 19:5-6).

A kingdom people must learn to keep the King's commandments. Later in the covenant legislation the Lord makes this principle specific. It is to do with the principle that those who belong to the King must share in the family likeness. There is only one set of rules for the whole household: 'You shall be holy, for I am holy' (Lev. 11:45).

This is why, technically, God's laws are called a holiness code. They are household rules. They are rules designed to be obeyed. Obedience to God's ways is a simple principle, but one which teaches further truth about God.

In one of his films on bringing up children, the American psychologist, James Dobson, points out that the values we have as people are the values we want our children to have. So it is with love, kindness and sometimes a firm hand, that we have to teach them to obey, especially in the early formative years. The way we bring up our children reflects the heart of our own values and hopes.

It is the same with God. His commandments reveal his own heart and values, what we call his holiness. If we wish to be part of his covenant people, to be held in relationship to God, it means we have to learn to obey him as our heavenly Father and accept his discipline.

Theologians point out that God's law is an expression of his holiness. Therefore to keep the law is to begin to take on the family likeness. A restored relationship requires a changed lifestyle. The sad fact is that God's people in the Old Testament times did not succeed in keeping that law. So was it the covenant that failed?

The covenant made with Moses is the only bilateral covenant in the Bible. Yet, as we observed, God never fails – it is only people who fail God. The prophet Jeremiah, sometimes known as the 'prophet of tears', expresses the deep burden of this fact as he looks towards the future and records the Lord's promise of a new covenant to come:

> 'Behold the days are coming,' says the LORD, 'when I will make a new covenant with the house of Israel and the house of Judah, not like the covenant which I made with their fathers when I took them by the hand to bring them out of the land of Egypt, my covenant which they broke, though I was their husband' (Jer. 31:31-32).

From the reference to Egypt, it is clear it is the Mosaic covenant referred to here. The question arises: Where was the fault? Was the covenant inadequate or were the people of Israel lacking in some way?

Here's a way to illustrate a response to such questions. Have you ever contemplated going on a diet? Slimming magazines have a fascinatingly effective, if mildly cruel way of revealing the truth to those who want to beat the bulge. Potential slimmers who want to be convinced of their need of a diet are counselled to do some post bath-time assessment.

The instructions are simple. You climb out of the bath. You leave aside the temptation to hide your beauty away with a towel. Then, in front of the mirror, you gaze upon your full glory until the moment when you are fully convinced or perhaps convicted of the truth – new light on 'mirror, mirror on the wall'!

Slimming advice aside, many people forget that this is one of the main functions of the law of God. The law holds up a mirror to the reality of our sinful lives. Only then, when we see our reflection in it, do we see ourselves as we really are. 'I would not have known what sin was except through the law' (Rom. 7:7).

The giving of the law to Moses was never meant to be an end in itself. Neither were the spiritual life of Old Testament times nor Hebrew religious practices in general designed to be an end in themselves or to go on forever. But they *were* meant to highlight the sinfulness of man before a holy God, and reflect a clear need for radical surgery upon man's wayward path.

Many centuries later, coming from a sincere and dedicated Jewish background, the apostle Paul expresses this dilemma about the law:

> When I want to do good, evil is right there with me. For in my inner being I delight in God's law; but I see another law at work in the members of my body, waging war against the law of my mind and making me a prisoner of the law of sin at work within my members. What a wretched man I am! Who will rescue me from this body of death? (Rom. 7:21-24).

The law revealed to Paul, as it reveals to us, that we need the grace of God. 'The law was put in charge to lead us to Christ that we might be justified by faith' (Gal. 3:24). As a people at fault, we need nothing less than the mercy of God if we are to remain in relationship with him.

So through the mirror of the law we see that the Mosaic covenant did reveal the failure of the people to obey God. At the heart of all this lies a deep inability to keep the law. The law was meant to show them the holiness of God. It was meant to be a mirror to their sin, as it is meant for us today. It was never meant to be a means of salvation.

To summarise so far. The covenant made with Noah speaks powerfully of God's mercy. The covenant made with Abraham is everlasting. The covenant made with Moses is simply incomplete. It was always meant to find its completion in Christ himself. Here, then, we must return to the overview of the biblical story. God's strategy, whose outworking we are witnessing in human history, is to return man from estrangement and restore him to fellowship with the Lord himself. He is working to re-establish his rule, the kingdom of God.

However, before we move on to the new covenant, where the fulfilment Jesus brings is made explicit, there is a further important Old Testament covenant which we must examine for the development of our insight into the nature of the unfolding kingdom.

4. The covenant with David reveals the kingdom of God

If David had lived and died in one of the world's great modern democracies, there would be no difficulty in finding statues and memorials to him practically everywhere you looked. In London, Washington, Delhi, Nairobi or wherever it might be, a statue, a library, an institute or a centre of worship – preserving and extolling the great name of David – would be an obvious part of the cultural, political and religious landscape. Such memorials are a measure of esteem. This is a heritage and inheritance which powerfully symbolizes both history and hope: a nation's proud past and a dynamic inspiration for the future.

The age of David was regarded by the Jews who lived after him, and the biblical writers themselves, as nothing short of the Golden Age. Here is the king who put Israel on the map, 'the sweet psalmist of Israel' (2 Sam. 23:1) and 'a man after God's own heart' (1 Sam. 13:14): the king whose zeal for the Lord caused him to reform the religious life of Israel to bring deep and lasting spiritual benefit for many centuries. Such is David's importance that any messianic hope that was to arise from Israel and that promised to herald the age of blessing, would now, inevitably, be seen in Davidic terms. From then on, one might say, the Messiah had been named. He was to be the 'Son of David'.

In the New Testament's fifty-eight references to David, the clearest link is drawn, in precisely this way, between Jesus and David. Paul speaks of Jesus as being 'descended from David according to the flesh' (Rom. 1:3). And Jesus himself is recorded by John as saying: 'I am the root and the offspring of David' (Rev. 22:16). David, the shepherd boy turned king of Israel, is one whose impact cannot be overestimated. Not only is his life a model for all subsequent views on kingship, but as far as messianic hopes were concerned his life and times became a tangible model for the kingdom itself.

(a) Pictures of truth

To understand further how these pictures of God's kingdom gradually unfold and develop, we need to enter into the manner in which God himself has caused the inspired writers of the Bible to use everyday language to picture these truths in intelligible form.

All religious language – language about God and his ways – is analogical. Using language as his means of revelation and communication, God has chosen to use models drawn from human experience to speak of divine truths, events and expectations. So in a famous passage (Isa. 53:1), Isaiah speaks of 'the arm of the LORD' and in the New Testament Jesus, referring to the kingdom, speaks graphically of the finger of God (Luke 11:20), while the apostle Paul can speak of God's right hand (Rom. 8:34). Yet we know that God in himself, in the ancient phrase of the Book of Common Prayer, has neither 'body, parts, nor passions'. Only by extension of thought does human language, drawn from life experience, speak of God's purpose, action and authority. The language is analogical: it communicates by means of analogies drawn from our human experience.

So if I want to speak of God's purposes, I might speak of 'the arm of the Lord'. We all know that when we lift up our arm we give the clear impression of our intention to do something. It is the symbol of intended action. By analogy, then, we are able to speak of God's plans and purposes.

The comparison does not mean that what is being described is limited to the horizons of our human perspectives. Through revelation, God is opening a window on to himself. By analogy, what we know of human authority, and the sense of control and direction which that suggests, can be applied to God. It enables us to speak powerfully of the perfection of his supreme dominion. In biblical language, the human picture – whether it be of sovereignty, fatherhood, love or whatever – is but a model. When that model is applied to our understanding of God, it becomes a jumping-off point, enabling us to enter more fully into the perfection of truth which is the essence of God's nature and being.

Biblical writers freely use the device of analogy. They draw pictures of truth. Analogy underlies the whole process of revelation, and enables us to see the purpose of the Davidic covenant in a far clearer light.

(b) A kingdom in focus

In order for the people of God in Old Testament times to have a hope and an expectation of a kingdom of heaven, they had to have an experience of a kingdom on earth.

In order for Israel to look forward to the coming of a *supreme* king – a Messiah or deliverer – they needed the experience of a *great* king by whom they could measure greatness, wisdom and devotion to the cause of God.

These are reasons why God chose the life and times of David to be his model, both of messiahship and the kingdom: his example brings the kingdom into focus. David's reign was the Golden Age. Everybody knew it. And God wanted to say to Israel then, and for hundreds of years to come, 'When God's Anointed ushers in the kingdom – this is what it will be like.'

However, the correspondence will not be complete. There is a proviso to all biblical analogical language; it is the same principle which is apparent when we see a model in the light of reality. So the kingdom of David bears the same relation of imperfect to perfect, of shadow to substance, when it is seen in the light of the kingdom of God. As the letter to the Hebrews was to point out, looking back on all this many centuries later, the reality is indeed 'far better'. None the less, the model – in this case David's 'Golden Era', along with the promise it embodies – is rightly savoured as a taste of the future. It is something special in its own right. For the time being it is not something to be held too tenaciously, for there is coming a day when the fulfilment will arrive.

2 Samuel 7 is the main passage concerned with this Davidic covenant. Israel had taken on a massively contrasted existence to her earlier history. No longer was she a loosely drawn-together arrangement of desert tribes. Now firmly settled in the land,

she had become a united people, a nation with a great king. At Sinai, having been delivered from Egypt, Israel needed to be constituted into a nation, a holy people to receive and obey the law of God. Now in their settled nationhood, led by a king rather than a prophet, further covenant legislation was called for. Several points need to be borne in mind:

- Neither the Mosaic nor the Davidic covenants alter the people's basic interaction with God, established by the covenant of grace with Abraham.

- These two covenants are for new situations, not new relationships. They fill out the *terms* of God's covenant promises and expectation.

- Particularly in the Davidic covenant, the covenant points firmly in the direction of the future.

- The covenant made with Abraham is still the organizing element in God's dealings with man.

- Both the Mosaic and Davidic covenants legislate for new situations in the life of God's people, while opening up exciting dimensions of promise and fulfilment for a future hope.

Here, in the covenant promises of God to David, we begin to see a picture emerging of God's promised kingdom. God's purposes are unfolding – and his people need to be informed. God promises a place for his people – a place of peace for his people to dwell in (2 Sam. 7:10-11). The Lord promises to establish a kingdom over which a descendant of David's will rule (2 Sam. 7:12). The king will build a house for God's name, and his reign will be eternal (2 Sam. 7:13). The unique covenant relationship of father to son, previously used corporately of the people of God, is individualized and applied to the Davidic king:

'I will be his father, and he shall be my son' (2 Sam. 7:14).

All this gave to the people of God nothing less than a picture of truth, a model upon which to base their understanding of God's promises and ways. Above all, it gave them a clear sense that God is active: he is working his purposes out. It also reinforced the message that, as God's very own covenant people, they indeed had a future and a hope.

Summary Points

■ Estrangement and reconciliation are at the heart of God's initiative in covenant making.

■ The covenant with Noah reveals the mercy of God

■ The covenant with Abraham reveals the grace of God

■ The covenant with Moses reveals the holiness of God

■ The covenant with David reveals the kingdom of God

For Reflection

God created the Hebrew religion of the Old Testament, in order to provide the essential building blocks for Christianity (p. 36).

With reference to God's acts of covenant making, how would you illustrate the truth of this statement?

Judaism failed, so God dreamed up Christianity instead (p. 36).

Is this true, and if not why not?

How would you explain to a Jewish person how Christians see the importance of the Old Testament?

God's grace never fails. Only people fail (p. 37).

Compare Genesis 50:20 with Acts 2:23-24

What practical and realistic encouragement can you take from this statement?

What does this truth say to your church today?

What does it mean to call Jesus, 'the son of David'?

Look at Matthew 21:1-16, and pick out all the references hidden and explicit to Jesus as the promised David-like Messiah.

Chapter 3

THE GOD WHO SAVES

I will give you a new heart and put a new spirit in you; I will remove from you your heart of stone and give you a heart of flesh (Ezek. 36:26).

If the David years were a Golden Age, the years and centuries which followed his death tell a markedly different story. The land of Palestine is a small country (ten thousand square miles overall, smaller than Belgium, about the size of Yorkshire or New Jersey), yet from a political point of view its geographical position makes it highly strategic. Herein lies a clue to the turbulent times which characterized Israel's history from the time of David to the coming of Jesus, and beyond, to the present.

The battleground of the nations
The position of Palestine as a corridor for overland traffic between Egypt, Syria and Mesopotamia has made the Megiddo Pass the scene of many battles and bitter strife.

It was here in the thirteenth century BC, after his triumph over the king of Hazor, that Joshua defeated the king of Megiddo (Josh. 12:21). The Israelite hold on his capital was not to last, for in the twelfth century BC the Philistines, advancing inland from the coast, repossessed Megiddo, and the whole of the Jezreel plain as far as Bet Shean. Sovereignty over the area passed to and fro. Solomon was able to make Megiddo the capital of his fifth administrative area in the tenth century BC, after his father, David, had defeated the Philistines (1 Kgs. 4:12).

Megiddo's heyday as an Israelite stronghold came to an end in 733 BC when it was captured by the Assyrians under Tiglath-Pileser III. Yet the whole area of Megiddo remained the scene of continuing strife which has continued down the years. This

is where King Josiah of Judah fell in battle against Pharaoh
Necho of Egypt; Napoleon defeated the Turkish in 1799, as did
General Allenby in 1917. Again, in 1948, it was here that the
Israelis halted the Arab push towards Haifa. The Megiddo plain
is a striking visual reminder of the turbulent history of struggle
and strife which has dominated the history of Israel through the
centuries.

In Old Testament times, Israel had scant resources when
compared with the Syrian or Egyptian armies. It was a small
nation and not at all an international power. It seems against all
the odds that Israel survived. Yet God preserved his people, not
because of their political ingenuity or resources, but because of
their uniqueness. Israel was a people under the covenant, a
people with a divine purpose, whose God is the God who saves.

Hard times
The people of this covenant-saving God did indeed have a future
and a hope. However, for the majority of the Israelites, that
must have been painful and difficult to believe during the
unsettling years of depression, the years when God's people
languished in exile in Babylon: 'How shall we sing the LORD's
song in a foreign land?' (Ps. 137:4). There were many moments
of spiritual depression for Israel, when their God-promised
future and hope seemed all but shattered by exile, occupation
and oppression.

This was especially the case during the uncertain times of
Antiochus IV Epiphanes (175-164 BC), when it was difficult
to believe Israel had an assured future hope. This notorious
Seleucid ruler scandalized the Jews during his occupation of
their land, and eventually provoked them into open rebellion:
the celebrated revolt led by Judas Maccabaeus in 165 BC.

Antiochus went to extraordinary lengths to provoke the Jews
to fury. He forbade the Sabbath and the practice of circumcision.
He forced the Jews to violate their food laws. He martyred a
family of a mother and seven sons who refused to defile
themselves by eating pork. Antiochus introduced ritual

prostitution into the sacred precincts of the temple in Jerusalem. He saved the worst insult to 167 BC, when he horrified Jewish sensibilities by the sacrifice of a pig in the Jerusalem Temple – on an altar erected to the Greek god Zeus!

Times were truly hard. In 66 BC the Roman leader, Pompey, was given the task of clearing the Mediterranean of pirates. In only three months he completed his work and then, as a kind of triumphant postscript, he marched into Palestine, taking Jerusalem itself in 63 BC. As a sign of Roman domination, and a gesture of defiance to Israel and her God, Pompey strutted into the Temple's holy of holies, where only the high priest was permitted to enter once a year. It was a calculated blow. But it was only the first-fruits: there was far worse to come.

Had not Isaiah prophesied about the supremacy of Israel? Were not all the peoples of the world to come to Jerusalem to worship? The promise was clear: 'Nations will come to your light, and kings to the brightness of your dawn' (Isa. 60:3). Yet the Roman occupation and the legislature of their puppet rulers spoke of a steep decline in the fortunes of Israel, of their future and their hope. Their holy places were desecrated; their laws and customs flouted; their people were ill-treated and forced into slavery by their Roman overlords.

The times are changing....

In a situation such as this who would not long for the Golden Age to be restored? Who would not look eagerly for a Messiah, a deliverer, a David? After all, the Holy Scriptures promised: 'Of the increase of his government and peace there will be no end. He will reign on David's throne and over his kingdom, establishing and upholding it with justice and righteousness from that time on and for ever' (Isa. 9:7).

The expectation developed of one to come who would be a figure even greater than David – someone to put Israel back on the map and establish a kingdom at least as secure as David's rule. This would be a kingdom to last for ever, never again to suffer the insult of foreign domination, and the blasphemy of

God's law violated; never again to be ground into the dust by pagan oppressors. This is God's *chosen* people. 'A kingdom of priests and a holy nation' (Exod. 19:6). The kingdom to come would be one where Israel could fulfil her destiny and be a light to the nations.

In this period leading up to the coming of Jesus' public ministry, there was definitely a sense that the times were changing. There was a sense abroad that a turning-point in history had been reached. Messiah-talk was an everyday occurrence: 'Who will it be?' 'Who will deliver Israel?' The question was on everyone's lips. The leader writers talked of nothing else. It was the No 1 political issue.

As popular feeling grew, aspirations became increasingly militant and nationalistic. Israel needed a king, but not a Roman puppet like Herod. Any king fit for a kingdom in Israel would have to be a king who could bump the Romans on their aristocratic foreign noses and send them packing to the place where they belonged.

Freedom fighters

This ongoing series of interrelated events and expectations forms the political background against which the New Testament is written. Such are the anticipations and concerns to which Jesus had to respond in his three-year public ministry in Palestine.

The world has had its freedom fighters in practically every situation of political occupation and repression. In the first century AD, the most politically active Jews were the Zealots, the freedom fighters of their time. As far as the Zealots were concerned, if Israel were to have a Messiah, then freedom from the despotic Romans would have to be uppermost in his manifesto.

Many of the Zealots' other ideas were right and good. The prophets had made known that God is concerned for justice – for the poor, the under-privileged, for peace and human rights. So in relation to this background, the issue became clearly focused. At the time of Jesus the political temperature was such that in the popular mind the promised Messiah equalled a national hero – one who would boot out the Romans – in short, a God-inspired, but political saviour for Israel.

Root causes

Many years before this depressed era in Israel's fortunes, the prophet Jeremiah made it clear that the God who saves has a different set of priorities altogether. The Lord who had called Israel to be his special people, bound them to himself by a solemn covenant, and revealed to them his law, his name, character and ways – this same ruling Lord's priority was not to re-politicise but to *transform* his people. This priority went back to the root cause of man's disarray, so evident in social and political terms, whose origins lie in man's broken relationship with God. This is where the action was required. The promise of the covenant was to bring repair at this very point. *I will give you a new heart and put a new spirit in you; I will remove from you your heart of stone and give you a heart of flesh. And I will put my Spirit in you and move you to follow my decrees and be careful to keep my laws. You will live in the land I gave your forefathers; you will be my people, and I will be your God* (Ezek. 36:26-28). This was God's priority.

The education process

Christians reading the Old Testament sometimes feel a sense of embarrassment or discomfort when they come across the sacrificial system and the complex paraphernalia of tabernacle and temple worship. Isn't this religion with a capital *R*? Aren't these practices primitive and repulsive? In the light of all that violence and gore, isn't it a relief that Jesus and the love principle has taken over from the God of wrath and the pools of blood of Old Testament times?

A superficial reading of the Old Testament may give this impression. But to enter these times without understanding what lies behind these practices can only result in a distorted view. For here there is a divinely ordained *education process* – one which God used to teach his people about mankind and its relationship to God.

That some of the biblical facts are unpalatable should not therefore surprise us. They reflect unpalatable truths about human make-up and nature which a primitive people had to learn in a language they would be able to understand. What underlies all this is the depth of wrong and disarray at the heart of man. This is why some of the biblical visual aids involved in the teaching process make us uneasy. They speak of our marred human condition. It is not peculiar to our world to forget how marred our human state is – an unwillingness to admit the facts of the human condition has been common throughout human history. If we do not like the shedding of blood, a moment's thought should remind us of its main teaching value – the horror with which God looks upon sin.

Written in blood

What then in broader terms does the sacrificial system teach us? From the very beginning of the Bible and Abel's offering in Genesis 4:4, right through to the death of Jesus (see Heb. 9:11-14), an inter-relationship is taught between the shedding of blood and personal interaction with a holy God. The truth about man and God is written in blood so that its message should be unmistakable.

In Leviticus 17:11 the Old Testament itself provides a key to understanding this principle: 'For the life of a creature is in the blood, and I have given it to you to make atonement for yourselves on the altar; it is the blood that makes atonement for one's life.'

The first teaching point here is that *blood makes atonement* (literally 'at one-ment' – making sinful man 'at one' with the Holy God). The shedding of blood pays off the debt of sin.

The second teaching point is that it does this *by the payment of a life*. The flowing blood was a powerful symbol and demonstration that life had been terminated and taken in substitution as payment for the guilt-stained life of a sinner.

Such was the effectiveness of the sacrifices God provided

that Isaiah can say: 'Though your sins are like scarlet, they shall be as white as snow; though they are red as crimson, they shall be like wool' (Isa. 1:18). Scarlet and crimson are the fast colours used for dyeing white wool. The implication is, since they are fast colours, only God can wash them out. The sacrifices were effective because God provided them: 'I have given it to you to make atonement for yourselves.'

But those sacrifices were only effective because they relied on a greater sacrifice to come. They were educative in that they taught the people about the seriousness of sin, the holiness of God and the necessity of atonement. They also taught the people to look forward to a final deliverance, to the One who would be 'pierced for our transgressions ... crushed for our iniquities', one upon whom the Lord would lay 'the iniquity of us all' (Isa. 53:5-6). That such a deliverance was necessary is one of the main teaching burdens of the Pentateuch, the first five books of the Bible, and especially Leviticus.

The changes God will make

God has made a covenant with his people. He longs to establish his kingdom, the rule of God in the lives of men. In the Golden Age of David, we have already been given a foretaste of what that might be like. But first things first. Root causes must be dealt with. Covenant promises must be fulfilled. Action is required at the points where repair is needed. Only then can mankind be brought into a fit state for the kingdom to come, since, as Jesus pointed out, the kingdom of God begins 'within you' (Luke 17:21) – at the level of motivation and commitment. It is a question of who rules. If the kingdom is to come, then God must rule in the heart. That means changes.

'The time is coming,' declares the LORD, 'when I will make a new covenant with the house of Israel and with the house of Judah ... I will put my law in their minds and write it on their hearts. I will be their God, and they will be my people' (Jer. 31:31, 33).

God's *promise* is declared in the words, 'I will make a new covenant.' The *outcome* of the promise is spelt out in kingdom terms: 'I will be their God, and they shall be my people' (Jer. 31:33). It is clear from this that the notions of covenant and kingdom belong together. The one describes the *privilege* of relationship; the other, *God's rule* which flows from the establishment of that relationship.

The changes God announces through Jeremiah go to the heart of the matter. They show that when God saves, he saves effectively. He is not content to deal with surface matters, rearranging the outward behaviour and circumstances of his people. It is what is underneath which counts. It is thus that God deals with the heart.

It would have been easy for the battered and beleaguered Jews of Jesus' time to forget this, and bypass the need for major surgery. Yet the Davidic covenant, and the coming of God's chosen deliverer, could not be fulfilled until the moral weaknesses revealed by the Mosaic covenant had been righted. When God comes in salvation, this is what he will do; through a new covenant, the Lord will effect a major change that will deal with the root problems of sinful people in relation to a holy God.

The circumcision of the heart

Through Jeremiah, God announced his solution: 'I will make a new covenant.... I will put my law in their minds and write it on their hearts. I will be their God, and they will be my people' (Jer 31:31, 33 NIV).

This is certainly *good* news, but it is not *new* news. The inward transformation promised through the words of Jeremiah is not as though God had experienced a brainwave; that he had decided to shut up shop and dispose of the old covenant – because it had never worked anyway. The new covenant is not *new* news. It was first announced by Moses, and bears powerful witness – that God never does things by halves.

The Shema, the great commandment, is engraved upon the

soul and identity of everyone born a Jew. 'Hear, O Israel: The LORD our God, the LORD is one. Love the LORD your God with all your heart and with all your soul and with all your strength' (Deut. 6:4-5). It would indeed be a strange God who could bring a people into such a privileged relationship with himself, command such whole-hearted and radical response of love, and yet finally fail to provide the ability, strength and power whereby that could be fulfilled. It would be as useless as expecting a car to run without petrol. You might succeed in pushing it down the hill. But you would not stand much chance of getting it down the motorway. When God provides the road map, he in no way neglects the provision of power.

So, later in Deuteronomy, having announced the responsibility of the believers to love God, Moses then makes a remarkable prophecy concerning the future. That the hope is *future* is clear from the context (Deut. 30:1-5), with its talk of the Jews being scattered and dispersed throughout the world. But the promise is definite and explicit: 'The LORD your God will circumcise your hearts and the hearts of your descendants, so that you may love him with all your heart and with all your soul, and live' (Deut. 30:6).

Inward transformation

This is our biggest human need – to be changed from the inside. One of the shortcomings of the reductionist views of human nature and the malaise of society is that external issues are so often uppermost in this kind of thinking. They say our struggles and problems are all to do with externals such as the economic system or unemployment or political strife, or this and that. All these are important issues, yet the Bible insists the true diagnosis lies at a far deeper level. *The outside is only a reflection of what is going on within*. Our untidy and rebellious inner lives need to be changed, radically and lastingly. Such is the promise of the good news first announced by Moses. We will be changed – but from the inside out.

Covenant signs

What did Moses mean by the curious expression 'circumcision of the heart'? It would have been clear to his hearers because they were steeped in this kind of thinking. For us however, coming from a different age and culture, the language presents a greater challenge. The key to understanding is the purpose of covenant signs.

When a couple are married, they join hands and they give and receive a ring or rings. It is a sign of their agreement, their covenant of marriage. In fact 'shaking on it' is an ancient way of both signing and sealing an agreement in a wide range of activities involving two parties. So when God makes an agreement, when he makes a covenant, he provides a sign, which when subsequently observed will bring to mind the *fact* of the covenant, that it stands and is in force.

The earliest covenant sign is the rainbow: 'This is the sign of the covenant I am making.... I have set my rainbow in the clouds.... Never again will the waters become a flood to destroy all life.... I will see it and remember the everlasting covenant between God and all living creatures' (Gen. 9:12-16). It is a visual contract. God has made a covenant of mercy, and he is saying to Noah; 'See, there's a rainbow – every time I see it, and you see it, we'll remember there is an agreement in force between us, a covenant I, unilaterally, have committed myself to. There is the sign for you.'

Covenant signs are unique in that they speak of God's promise – a special kind of promise which will never be broken. This is why in Revelation 4:3, in the vision of the throne in heaven, 'A rainbow, resembling an emerald, encircled the throne.' This is a vivid picture of the future. The rainbow enveloping the place from which sovereignty flows, signifies that the covenant of mercy stands for ever. Just as he first placed it in the sky in Noah's time, so the King has hung up his warrior's bow above his throne – as a constant reminder of his divine mercy to the world. This is the glorious revelation – there is mercy in heaven! The rainbow guarantees it.

Theologically, there is a link between the sign and what is promised. Chocolate boxes in sweet-shop windows are visually just the dummy box, with nothing inside. In spiritual terms, an outward sign without an inner reality is a fraud. So covenant signs are signs of grace. God provides inwardly what the sign signifies outwardly.

When Moses, therefore, speaks about inward circumcision, he is speaking of God providing that grace within. It is a promise of a new ability, a new power to keep God's commandments; it is a power to be different inside, to be transformed so that we may love him with all our heart and with all our soul, and live (Deut. 30:6).

Fulfilment of signs

Circumcision is a sign of the everlasting covenant made with Abraham (Gen. 17:11). So under the new covenant which Jeremiah announces, the inward reality of that sign is fulfilled. What is specifically new about the new covenant is that it *fulfils* what has gone before, it does not *abolish* it. Jesus was insistent on this point: 'Do not think that I have come to abolish the Law or the Prophets; I have not come to abolish them but to fulfil them' (Matt. 5:17).

How does that fulfilment come about? Paul gives the answer:

> In him you were also circumcised, in the putting off of the sinful nature, not with a circumcision done by the hands of men but with the circumcision done by Christ, having been buried with him in baptism and raised with him through your faith in the power of God, who raised him from the dead (Col. 2:11-12).

Baptism is the new covenant sign which replaces the Old Testament sign of circumcision, since, as Paul says, the inward sinful nature has been circumcised by Christ. It has been dealt with by his death and resurrection – the effective payment for sin – with which we identify ourselves, through our baptism. This is where the kingdom begins – it starts within, at the heartbeat, where the real me is crying out to be changed. A new covenant has been instituted; God has fulfilled his promise to put his law in our minds and write it on our hearts. The outward and visible sign has become an inward and spiritual grace.

Announcing the kingdom

When God moved decisively into history to begin the dramatic series of events culminating in the death and resurrection of Jesus, the full reality of the kingdom promise and hope was announced in an extraordinary and prophetic way by Mary, the mother of Jesus.

Down the centuries, we have come to call her words *The Magnificat* (Luke 1:46-55). This song of Mary, one of the New Testament's 'prophetic' passages, is a remarkable statement about the future, focusing on Jesus' part in it. As a high point of revelation, it provides one of the most cogent statements about Jesus and the kingdom in the whole of the New Testament.

Star-gazers

We would all like to know what the future holds. The future is a question which has fascinated mankind since earliest times. As the new millennium unfolds, futurology has once more become especially popular. 'What will the new century hold? Will there be peace? How will life change?' Futurology, like star-gazing, has become a Western passion of mind. Journalists, politicians and religious leaders all excel at the sport. Sometimes they encourage us. More often, they dismay us! But why do they do it? And why do we take notice?

It is only natural to wish to know the direction our lives may take in the future. We want to know the forces governing our lives. Are there any certainties? Is there any hope?

Mary's words provide a powerful response to such questions and concerns. Their power is derived from their subject: Jesus and the kingdom of God. They tell of the coming rule of God, and what he will do when his power is fully implemented in the person of Jesus.

What is in a name?

As the century turns, the most popular names in Britain are Chloe, Emily and Megan for girls, and Jack, Thomas and James for boys. As a sign of Britain's multi-cultural make-up, Mohammed remains a firm favourite, ranked at 34 in the top fifty list of most popular names.

For many parents the choice of a baby's name is undoubtedly linked to some kind of significance in the name itself. But names have a greater and more special significance in the Bible than any names we have today. In the biblical world names are not just labels. We see this especially in the name of the child to be born. The name announced by the angel (Luke. 1:30), 'Jesus', means 'God to the rescue'. This Jesus, according to the angel, will be an even greater king than David – hitherto the greatest king in the whole of Jewish history. This can only mean that Jesus is to be the one in whom all the kingdom hopes are vested – the Messiah.

To Jewish ears this must have been a stupendous claim. So too was the claim about his kingdom – it will last for ever: 'of his kingdom there will be no end' (Luke 1:33). What a message to receive! No wonder it threw Mary into some confusion. Apart from anything else, how could she have a child? Yes, she was engaged. But she and Joseph weren't living together. It was impossible!

In Mary's story, we see God reaching out to rescue his people. He is to be the father of the child. The kingdom and the king are coming: 'the child to be born will be called holy, the Son of God' (Luke 1:35).

Mary's visit to her cousin

It is worth savouring the scene. Like any other young girl with exciting news, Mary cannot wait to tell her best friend. In this case, her friend is her older cousin. So off Mary goes, down to Judah to see Elizabeth who is pregnant with baby John the Baptist. John was sent by God to prepare the people for Jesus. The coincidence is not accidental: God is breaking his long silence of the years between the Testaments. He is coming to rescue his people. Salvation is on the way.

What happens when Mary arrives? There is quite a party. It seems that everybody is rejoicing, a real celebration. It is almost as though the balloons will go up. Mary is thrilled with Elizabeth's news. Elizabeth is thrilled with Mary's news. In fact Mary is so over the moon that she breaks into this song of praise: 'My soul magnifies the Lord, and my spirit rejoices in God my Saviour' (Luke 1:46-47). They are wonderful words. There is so much we can learn from them. They speak of an enlarged vision of God.

In a spiritual sense, we need that enlarged vision. What would it mean if our souls should magnify the Lord? For that to happen, we have to help ourselves to see him as he really is. For this is our need – to magnify our vision of him. Such a concern was the passion of the prophets. The means by which this may happen is by engaging with the word of God. 'Prophesy to these bones and say to them, "Dry bones, hear the word of the LORD!"' (Ezek. 37:4)

For us today it is still by the Scriptures that we enlarge our vision of God, as God's Word unfolds the developing drama of our redemption – the unfolding kingdom. The covenant and the kingdom speak of a mighty God, immeasurable in his holiness, strength and love. The larger our picture of God, the larger our understanding of his grace and power and purposes will be.

The manifesto of the kingdom

'My soul magnifies the Lord.' That phrase is not just the touchstone of true worship, it is also the manifesto of the kingdom. For God has to transform us inwardly and personally, if he is to remake our lives and the world he's placed us in. In his public ministry Jesus would tell the Pharisees, 'The kingdom of God is *within you*' (Luke 17:21).

The next phrase is the clue to Mary's joy. 'My spirit rejoices in God my Saviour.' The thought is simple, but profound. Mary knows God as her personal Saviour. This is the first statement of personal salvation in the New Testament. It is the trailblazer for all kingdom reality, where men and women come under the sovereign rule of God.

Without this knowledge of personal salvation from God, there cannot be any sense in worship, any strength to live the Christian life or any genuine hope for the future. Jesus went on record as saying that it is impossible to see or have any perception of the kingdom of God unless you are spiritually born again (John. 3:3).

To help us understand that knowledge, and to understand what Mary meant by 'God my Saviour' – here is how Mary expands on the character of God in these next three verses.

In verse 48 she speaks about *the grace* of God: 'He has regarded the low estate of his handmaiden.' 1 Peter 5:5 can be a commentary on that verse: 'God opposes the proud, but gives grace to the humble.' Mary had just that kind of humility, and so she received grace from God.

The grace of God is sometimes defined as the unmerited favour, love and mercy of God, and is the basis of our salvation. To receive that grace, our inward attitude towards him must be one of humility. For God opposes the proud, but gives grace to the humble.

In verse 49 Mary speaks of *the power* of God: 'He who is mighty has done great things for me.' Despite the changes which new age thinking has produced, many if not most westerners still hold to a rationalist outlook. Christians should therefore ask if we really believe in the power of God. Does God control all our destinies? Can he overrule human affairs 'according to the express wisdom of his own good purposes' (see Eph. 3:10-11). Is there a God who can do great things for us? For this is surely the God of the Scriptures. Such an affirmation is bound to be a challenge as we look to the future, however uncertain that future may be. But what a difference when that uncertainty is underwritten by the knowledge of the strength of the mighty power of God.

Mary then speaks of *the purity* of God: 'And holy is his name' (Luke 1:49). The God who is mighty in his power is also pure in his intentions. How unlike a human figure that is. Rarely in our world does supreme power go hand in hand with pure integrity. How often we see power and corruption going together in national and international affairs. President Clinton's impeachment trial is one of many instances in the twentieth century where the private behaviour of public figures brought their name and office into disrepute. The new century will certainly throw up many more examples.

But note the contrast of God. No-one has greater scope to his power, or depth to his integrity. He who controls the universe is absolutely pure in character and in action. 'Holy is his name.' That is why we can have hope for the future. Behind all human events, however dispiriting they may look sometimes, God is working out his purpose with complete righteousness.

How do we know that? We know that purpose is good because of what Mary says in verse 50, where she speaks of *the forgiveness* of God: 'And his mercy is on those who fear him from generation to generation.' God shows his mercy by his forgiveness, paid for by Jesus' death on the cross. Mercy by definition is offered freely – forgiveness from God is offered freely to anyone who responds to his offer of new life, through Jesus.

Topsy-turvy teaching

What is the purpose of all this? Mary explains again in verse 50: God is creating a people for himself. They will be gathered from throughout history, from Abraham's time to our own and beyond. In Mary's words, 'from generation to generation'. They will be a kingdom people, a people belonging to Christ the King.

God's plan of salvation has a goal. It is in the future. That future is so certain that for Mary it is as good as done. That is why verses 51 to 55 are all in the *past* tense, what is often called 'the prophetic perfect'. The Old Testament prophets would sometimes describe a future event as already accomplished. Likewise for Mary. When God says something, the outcome is so certain that the deed is already as good as done.

Mary's song is a prophetic statement about the future and the kingdom. She sees it all in a moment. The whole story – the whole panorama of what God will do – flashes before her eyes. Mary grasps it in a flash of inspiration as her mind is gripped by the Holy Spirit.

'He has shown strength with his arm, he has scattered the proud in the imagination of their hearts, he has put down the mighty from their thrones, and exalted those of low degree; he has filled the hungry with good things, and the rich he has sent empty away' (Luke 1:51-53).

It is a picture of the whole world turned upside down: proud plans shattered, tyrants toppled, the wretched rescued, the humble helped, the hungry fed. It is topsy-turvy teaching.

This – the Messiah's manifesto – is truly about Jesus, the baby in Mary's womb, who is to be the Saviour of this needy, uncertain, troubled world in which we live. The establishing of the kingdom all turns, in the end, on the death and resurrection of Jesus. That is the final turning-point of history, the focal point of salvation. It is the true pivot of the future of the world.

And yet to mention the future does bring a sense of uncertainty to many of us. We are only too well aware of the precariousness of the world in which we live. We can feel, and indeed we fear, the acceleration of the unfolding of history. We fear we are being thrown into a future that is more threatening, more dangerous, more frightening in every sense, than anything hitherto in our human experience.

Yet if we do feel like that, while being realistic about the issues which face us, we can be strengthened by taking serious account of these powerful and prophetic words of Mary concerning Jesus and the kingdom. They all hang on this covenant promise: 'He has helped his servant Israel, in remembrance of his mercy, as he spoke to our father, to Abraham and to his posterity for ever' (Luke 1:54-55).

That is our security: the covenant promise of God which he made to Abraham and his posterity – his spiritual descendants, of whom those who are children of Abraham by faith (see Gal.

3:7) are a part for ever. It is a promise that God will stand by his people. He is the God who saves. He does not accomplish salvation by halves. We belong to him for ever, and the future is in his hands. The coming, death and resurrection of Jesus have shown that conclusively.

Like the Jews of Jesus' time, we too are at a waiting-point in history. We await the return of Jesus to judge the living and the dead. The kingdom is inaugurated, but it is yet to be consummated. We feel that tension, sometimes acutely, between the now and the not yet. But, despite appearances, our future is secure in him.

As we wait and as we prepare ourselves for his coming, how strengthening it is to recover the broad strokes of Mary's panoramic estimation of the salvation of God. These prophetic words show the comprehensiveness of God's concern for the poor and the under-privileged, his abomination of pride, materialism and the misuse of power. If God is concerned about such issues, then we should be concerned about them too. Because we have a spiritual hope (meaning a hope of heaven), it does not mean we can opt out of the major issues facing our society.

The truth is, God is King of this, his world – and the King is coming. This is the message he has for us to communicate. This is the God who saves. He gets right to the heart of the problem, deep down into the inner motivation, personality and soul of man. God is establishing his kingdom. And when God comes into his fullest power in Jesus Christ, he will scatter the proud, bring down rulers and lift up the humble. He will fill the hungry with good things. And the rich – he will send empty away.

Summary Points

■ David's golden age was not the last word on God's purposes, for God planned all along to purify the hearts of his people.

■ The sacrificial system teaches the seriousness of sin, and God's provision of atonement.

■ What the sacrificial system looks towards is fulfilled in Jesus.

■ Only he can circumcise the heart.

■ Mary announces the Messiah's kingdom manifesto as the completed work of Christ in every aspect of salvation.

For Reflection

The truth about man and God is written in blood, so that its message should be unmistakeable (p. 52).

What would you say to someone who found the sacrifices of the Old Testament brutal and gory?

It would indeed be a strange God who could bring a people into such a privileged relationship with himself, command such whole-hearted and radical response of love, and yet finally fail to provide the ability, strength and power whereby that could be fulfilled (p. 55).

What does this mean for the Christian's struggle with sin and holiness? Refer to Romans 8:1-17 to work out your response.

The outside is only a reflection of what is going on within. Our untidy and rebellious inner lives need to be changed, radically and lastingly (p. 55).

How is this true of you, and what are your greatest areas of need in this way?

'Do not think I have come to abolish the Law or the Prophets...' (Matt. 5:17, p. 57)

So what is new about the New Covenant, and how does it relate to the covenant or covenants that preceded it?

Rarely in our world does supreme power go hand in hand with pure integrity (p. 62).

What does knowledge of the holiness of God mean for those involved in business and politics? Can you be involved by prayer or action in any way?

Thoughts of the future may bring a sense of uncertainty (p. 63).

What spiritual truths do the certainties of Mary's song teach and remind you?

The kingdom is inaugurated, but it is yet to be consummated (p. 64).

How do you feel the tensions of the now and not yet of the kingdom? What does this mean for our expectations in prayer, evangelism, and the ministry of healing?

And the rich he will send empty away (p.64).

What light do Paul's words to Timothy (1 Tim. 6:17-19) shed on this statement: 'Command those who are rich in this present world not to be arrogant nor to put their hope in wealth, which is so uncertain, but to put their hope in God, who richly provides us with everything for our enjoyment. Command them to do good, to be rich in good deeds, and to be generous and willing to share. In this way they will lay up treasure for themselves as a firm foundation for the coming age, so that they may take hold of the life that is truly life'?

Chapter 4

TEACHING THE KINGDOM (1)

For to us a child is born, to us a son is given, and the government will be on his shoulders. And he will be called Wonderful Counsellor, Mighty God, Everlasting Father, Prince of Peace. Of the increase of his government and peace there will be no end. He will reign on David's throne and over his kingdom, establishing it and upholding it with justice and righteousness from that time on and for ever (Isa. 9:6-7).

Expectation and hope

Eight centuries after Isaiah had prophesied the Messiah and his kingdom, the still-oppressed and suffering Jews longed passionately for their great delivering leader. Popular expectations cast him in the mould of a national hero – a new David to restore to them the Golden Age. But when and how would he come?

The combined powers of nostalgia, prophecy, bitterness and discontent provide a potent and explosive mixture in the life of any community. This is especially so in one as clearly aware of its own special calling – the subjugated people of Palestine in the opening years of the first century AD.

Against this background of expectation and hope, the impact of these striking words is hardly surprising: 'The time has come. The kingdom of God is near. Repent and believe the good news!' (Mark. 1:15). In such a manner, Jesus of Nazareth announced the beginning of his public ministry. If his declaration did not send a ripple of Messiah fever deep into Jewish hearts, then it is difficult to imagine what could. Waiting sharpens the senses. The Jews had waited for a thousand years.

They had looked for upturns in their fortunes. Such waiting sharpens expectations. Yet anyone who claimed 'the time has come' found himself on trial. Claims must be substantiated. Woe betide anyone who should choose to meddle with tender

yet explosive Jewish sensitivities. False Messiahs were shown
no mercy.

When anger bursts

Jesus' announcement caused many ripples. Luke records that
the news about Jesus spread quickly throughout the whole
Galilean countryside. It was a guaranteed talking point.
However, the reaction in Jesus' home synagogue at Nazareth
turned out to be more a rebellion than a ripple. Messiah
expectation was already rife when Jesus stood on a Sabbath
day and read from the scroll of Isaiah.

> The Spirit of the Lord is on me, because he has anointed me to preach
> good news to the poor. He has sent me to proclaim freedom for the
> prisoners and recovery of sight for the blind, to release the oppressed,
> to proclaim the year of the Lord's favour (Luke 4:18-19).

All eyes were fastened upon him. Standing before God's
ancient people ('Theirs is the adoption as sons; theirs the divine
glory, the covenants, the receiving of the law, the temple worship
and the promises,' Rom. 9:4) Jesus declared to them: 'Today
this scripture is fulfilled in your hearing!' (Luke 4:21). His
listeners were so angry, they tried to throw him over the cliff.
He was, after all, claiming to be the Anointed One – Israel's
long-awaited Messiah.

Mixed reactions

Throughout his public ministry Jesus met with two contrasting
reactions: ripples of joy or the outrage of rebellion. He inspired
either followers or opponents; there was rarely any middle
ground. But how much were the claims of Jesus fully
understood?

Jesus spent the greater part of his teaching ministry on the
subject of the kingdom of God. Then, as now, the kingdom was
badly misrepresented and misunderstood.

To understand the kingdom implies spirituality as well as

theology. Only those who have 'ears to hear' will truly hear. The kingdom of God is about the rule of God in the hearts of men and women of every period. If the heart is resistant then the mind cannot be properly informed.

Jesus said: 'The secret of the kingdom of God has been given to you. But to those on the outside everything is said in parables so that, "they may be ever seeing but never perceiving, and ever hearing but never understanding; otherwise they might turn and be forgiven!"' (Mark. 4:11-12). In itself the statement is puzzling – yet it is designed to be so. Jesus is pointing not to his method but to his motive. The parables are not made deliberately difficult to understand. But for those who do not wish to commit themselves to their inner message all they will 'hear' are stories – pure and simple. There is, however, a tougher message beneath the surface.

Communication or transformation?

God chose to initiate the process of revelation, to make himself known, through a culture which operates in a rather different way to that which is familiar to Western ways today.

We are used to instant communication, and not just at the speed of faxes and Emails. We expect that writings or sayings should be immediately *comprehensible*. We expect to watch world events as they happen. We heap honours upon our most able communicators. Words and pictures are for information. We want the facts – quickly and conveniently. If you can video it or speed read it – so much the better!

The Eastern mind works differently. For instance, in Eastern spirituality there are collections of strange sayings known as *Koans* which illustrate a different approach to communication. A typical saying like 'Listen to the sound of one hand clapping' requires a special process of thought. It refuses to convey an instant meaning. The failure is to write it off as nonsense. The Buddhist or Hindu idea is that its hearers are meant to struggle with its inner meaning. 'Listen to the *sound* ...', '*Listen* to the sound.' It seems strange to rational Western minds. But gradually, through the struggle, the meaning *behind* the words begins to emerge and become clear.

This comparison between East and West does lay down a challenge to our assumptions about the 'right' use of language and the way we approach the biblical texts. Scripture does not emanate from a high-tech, word-processed Western culture. God did not give his Word for the sake of instant communication. He is concerned for transformation. He gave the Scriptures, and ultimately Jesus himself, to transform living human beings into the likeness of the character of God. 'All scripture is inspired by God that the man of God may be complete, equipped for every good work' (2 Tim. 3:16-17).

In the light of that purpose, those who wish to know this transformation have to struggle with the meaning of Scripture. Instant knowledge, instant communication, will not transform us; only a deep desire to know and do the truth will do that. This is why Paul speaks of 'the mystery of God, namely, Christ, in whom are hidden all the treasures of wisdom and knowledge' (Col. 2:2-3). Jesus spoke of the kingdom as 'like treasure hidden in a field' (Matt. 13:44). If we are not prepared to struggle to find the treasure and let God transform us in the process, then our eyes will not see and our ears will not hear – even though we may have the impression that by seeing and hearing we are participating in the truth.

The kingdom is a secret revealed only to those who are prepared to become its subjects. Of course Scripture is always clear to those who want to know the truth. It has its own perspicuity. Jesus underlined this: 'If you hold to my teaching, you are really my disciples. Then you will know the truth, and the truth will set you free' (John. 8:31-32). Knowing the truth and the freedom it brings depends on your reaction and response to Jesus himself – the true king of the kingdom.

Stories with a punchline

Parables were his method. Transformation was his motive. The kingdom was his theme. Why did Jesus need stories to teach people about the kingdom? If the King has arrived, should it not be obvious to everyone? Should it not be clear that here is the one to whom God has given his royal authority, that God's kingdom has come on earth as it is in heaven? Why did Jesus use these stories with a punchline?

Once more, it is a case of first things first. Has the King come once and for all, or is there a sense in which his coming is preliminary? The truth is the King has come, but for the time being, incognito. The reason is, his people are not yet ready for him. There is major surgery to be performed before full health can be restored. Membership of the kingdom depends upon it. Isaiah's magisterial prophecy of a divine royal Messiah, the 'Wonderful Counsellor, Mighty God, Everlasting Father, Prince of Peace', must be linked, in overall context, with one who will be 'pierced for our transgressions' and by whose wounds we are healed, the one upon whom the Lord has 'laid ... the iniquity of us all' (Isa. 53:5-6). If the mind of Isaiah is understood correctly, there are to be two comings of God's Messiah. The servant precedes the king.

Not of this world

Jesus used visual aids, stories and straight teaching to correct wrong assumptions about the Messiah and his kingdom, and to redirect hearts and lives back to God. He said his kingdom was not of this world. What kind of Messiah can he then be?

Jesus' contemporaries were reluctant to accept that someone who drew the crowds as Jesus did, who preached and healed and exerted such sway over so many, did not in fact have a kingdom belonging to this world. For Jews of a nationalist frame of mind, Jesus the Messiah had tremendous potential for a new Israel, an earthly kingdom, a reign strongly redolent of the great times of David.

Their reluctance is understandable. They were reluctant to

accept that if Jesus staked his claim to the kingdom it would not mean revolution. They wanted an uprising and the chance to send the Romans packing. By contrast, Jesus' way was to be a way of peace. 'A peace which the world cannot give.'

All roads lead to ... Jerusalem

For centuries Jews had declared the psalmist's words: 'Pray for the peace of Jerusalem! May they prosper who love you!' They had contemplated the bitter lessons of the city's destruction in 586 BC. They had come, not simply to love the holy city, but to see it as the very centre of God's dealing with them as a covenant people, a people 'chosen by God and precious'. Beyond everything else, it was the temple and its ministrations which declared the privilege of belonging to a holy God. The temple was a monument to the reality of the covenant and the commandments of Sinai. The city lived for it – Jews died for it. The temple was the centre of the world. It was the meeting-place between earth and heaven. And for Jews the world over, all roads led not to Rome, but to Jerusalem.

Taken together, such nationalism and religious fervour contribute to a powerful set of messianic expectations. At this spiritual and historical turning-point in their national existence, Jesus had to make it clear what kind of Messiah and mission were before God's ancient people.

Demonstrating for peace

In the second part of the twentieth century, peace demonstrations focused widespread concern about the distrust and aggression between the world's superpowers and the possibility of thermo-nuclear warfare. By its public demonstrations, the Campaign for Nuclear Disarmament succeeded in drawing the attention of individuals and governments by its calls to demonstrate for peace. Yet peace demonstrations are not new. The most celebrated peace demonstration of all time is Jesus' triumphant entry into Jerusalem. This had nothing specific to do with warheads, but everything to do with the peace God wishes to forge with mankind. And so, in the clearest terms, Jesus took the opportunity to spell out both the nature of his Messiahship and the coming of his kingdom. Clear, that is, for those with eyes to see, who will struggle with the message.

Luke makes it clear that the events of the first Palm Sunday were a peace demonstration with a difference; for there can be no peace on earth without peace with God:

> The two disciples brought the colt to Jesus, and throwing their garments on the colt they set Jesus upon it. And as he rode along, they spread their garments on the road. As he was now drawing near, at the descent of the Mount of Olives, the whole multitude of the disciples began to rejoice and praise God with a loud voice for all the mighty works that they had seen, saying, 'Blessed is the King who comes in the name of the Lord! Peace in heaven and glory in the highest!' And some of the Pharisees in the multitude said to him, 'Teacher, rebuke your disciples.' He answered, 'I tell you, if these were silent, the very stones would cry out' (Luke 19:35-40).

Louder than words

The dynamic connection between the Old and New Testaments is particularly visible in this situation. As Luke records both word and action, the narrative is filled with important Old Testament references and allusions. The fulfilment of God's promises, expectations and patterns of teaching, flowing from the Old Testament, find their fullest expression in Jesus.

A special demonstration, of the kind found in the entry into Jerusalem, is something which was previously unique to the Old Testament prophets. It is found most often when there was resistance or apathy towards the spoken message that the prophet was commanded to bring from God.

In such situations prophets often reinforced what they said by a dramatic action. In a picture no one could fail to understand, the demonstration would act out what the prophets had to say from God; actions spoke louder than words. Demonstrations like this were acted parables. Jesus' own entry into Jerusalem is the only New Testament counterpart of such an acted parable. It is therefore to be viewed with special attention for its intended meaning.

Action man

There are many examples of acted parables from Old Testament times. In 1 Kings 11, Ahijah the prophet of Shiloh tears his brand new cloak into twelve pieces in front of King Jeroboam. The message? It is to show that the kingdom is to be torn out of the hands of Solomon as a direct result of his apostasy. Ten of those tribes were to be given to Jeroboam, to come under his jurisdiction from that point on.

In Jeremiah 27, the Lord instructs the prophet to construct a yoke. A yoke is a wooden neck-piece by which a pair of oxen would be held together. The meaning? It was to be a sign of the forthcoming enslavement of the people. It was designed to impress upon Zedekiah, the king of Judah, that Judah would serve the Babylonian king, Nebuchadnezzar. King Zedekiah had been deaf, resistant to the word of the Lord. He was more interested in the comfort, distortions and lies of the false prophets. Something dramatic was needed to impress upon him the seriousness of the situation and what the Lord wanted him to heed.

So in Jeremiah 27:12-15, wearing a yoke of wooden crossbars around his neck, Jeremiah approaches Zedekiah and says to him:

> 'Bow your neck under the yoke of the king of Babylon; serve him and his people, and you will live.... Do not listen to the words of the prophets who say to you, "You will not serve the king of Babylon," for they are prophesying lies to you. "I have not sent them," declares the LORD. "They are prophesying lies in my name."'

It was an acted parable. The classic method by which a prophet might bring a message from God at a time of spiritual resistance and crisis.

The city which kills prophets

The journey from Jericho to Jerusalem is about twenty miles. It was a more arduous journey in the days of Jesus than it is today. Yet for Jesus, this journey was a pilgrimage. Jerusalem was his goal. Jerusalem was the great citadel of God, the holy city, the place of action over many centuries since the Golden Age of David. The point, purpose and goal of Jesus' ministry would be fulfilled in Jerusalem, the city where they kill the prophets.

In travelling to Jerusalem, Jesus was conscious of the resistance and opposition to him. He had been warned by friendly members of the Pharisee party to escape Jerusalem (Luke 13:31). Herod Antipas was planning for Jesus to receive the same treatment as John the Baptist. Jesus was encouraged to leave Jerusalem, and he did so. But he replied poignantly and prophetically to those who had warned him:

> I must go on my way today and tomorrow and the day following; for it cannot be that a prophet should perish away from Jerusalem. O Jerusalem, Jerusalem, killing the prophets and stoning those who are sent to you! How often would I have gathered your children together as a hen gathers a brood under her wings, and you would not! Behold, your house is forsaken. And I tell you, you will not see me until you say, 'Blessed is he who comes in the name of the Lord!' (Luke 13:33-35).

In this way, Jesus left Jerusalem. But he planned to return in order to meet his death voluntarily. And just like the Old Testament prophets, Jesus planned a carefully constructed demonstration of what he had come to achieve. It was to be an acted parable. He would give a visual demonstration of what he wanted people to understand about his Messiahship and his kingdom, and of how he wanted them to respond, at least for those who had eyes to see. It was to be a peace demonstration – a peace demonstration with a difference.

Breaking the rules

Jesus was a wanted man. The wanted notices were up all over Jerusalem. Because Jesus was a political inconvenience, Herod was plotting to kill him. But to some, Jesus had been of even greater offence. Arrest orders were circulating throughout the city: 'The chief priests and Pharisees had given orders that if anyone found out where Jesus was, he should report it so that they might arrest him' (John. 11:57). As far as the Jewish authorities were concerned, Jesus was an outlaw. Jesus had not kept the rules. There was a whole catalogue of offences, not least of which was his blatant disregard of the Sabbath laws. Many sick people had been brought to Jesus on the Sabbath. They had been in need, in terrible pain and distress. Jesus had healed them. 'The Sabbath was made for man, not man for the Sabbath,' he had said (Mark. 2:27). Yet in the establishment, it caused outrage.

Controversy

By such words and actions Jesus had questioned the spiritual integrity of the Pharisees; but in the New Testament not all Pharisees get such withering treatment. It is unfortunate that the term 'Pharisaism' has become a synonym for bigotry in everyday speech. The Pharisees Jesus criticised were *bad* Pharisees. Not all were like them, and certainly not those who had laid foundations for their religious movement.

The fathers of Pharisaism were noted for a rich nobility of mind. The evidence, enshrined in the Mishnah, relating to the schools of Hillel, Gamaliel and Simeon, suggests a sincerity of spirituality which would surprise many of their latter-day detractors. The spiritual theology of this movement's origins is more complex than a first glance would suggest, and defies simplistic analysis.

To deal adequately with the life and times of Jesus and his critique of the Pharisees requires historical balance. It is undeniable that the majority of Pharisees who represented this stream of Judaism at the time of Jesus were clearly resistant to Jesus and his claims to Messiahship. What could be the reasons for this attitude? Was it simply that their religion had degenerated into concern for outward show only, with a corresponding diminution of inner commitment and love for God? It seems so. Jesus seems stirred to anger when he quoted their own scriptures to them. 'Isaiah was right when he prophesied about you hypocrites; as it is written: "These people honor me with their lips, but their hearts are far from me. They worship me in vain; their teachings are but rules taught by men"' (Mark 7:6-7). Yet if this critique of outward show without inward reality hits the mark, then clearly the Sadducees were just as bad.

When Jesus echoed the Lord's condemnation through Isaiah, his hearers were inevitably offended. As they come in Isaiah, these words flow from the mouth of God himself. Thus Jesus speaks as God, *and* in judgement – a massive assault upon the emptiness of the religious establishment.

However, Jesus' offence was compounded by other statements he made. Not only had he healed people on the Sabbath and dared to question the establishment's integrity and sincerity, but to top it all, Jesus claimed clearly that he could forgive sins (Mark. 2:1-12). Every Jewish schoolboy knew then, as today, that only God has the authority to forgive sins. The implication was obvious: Jesus bar Joseph from the town of Nazareth was claiming to be God's unique Son – the long-promised Messiah.

Eliminate him!

Of course there was much disagreement about the nature of the Messiah. Was he to be a divine figure, a political figure, or what? The Zealots knew who they wanted. The Pharisees had a shrewd idea who they favoured. One issue was clear to everyone: Jesus had broken the rules, so he must be eliminated.

Jesus told the Pharisees they would not see him again in Jerusalem until the people would say, 'Blessed is he who comes in the name of the Lord' (Luke 13:35). Personal rejection and widespread resistance to the kingdom of God were the constant accompanying themes of Jesus' ministry. This was the reality of sin, personal rebellion against God, writ large throughout his ministry. But at the entry to Jerusalem, Jesus insists that a particular message be made absolutely clear. What is it that Jesus wants the whole world to understand? What is the message concerning Jesus' mission which he demonstrated by the acted parable of riding into Jerusalem on the back of a donkey?

Two reactions
The message becomes clear in the disciples' immediate reaction as Jesus approaches Jerusalem astride the donkey's back. The disciples begin to rejoice and praise God for the extraordinary demonstrations of power and compassion they have seen enacted through Jesus: 'Blessed is the King who comes in the name of the Lord!' (Luke 19:38). This greeting which Jesus receives from the disciples is so loaded with implications that it receives an instant response from the Pharisees. Their reaction is rather different, and revealingly bitter: 'Teacher, rebuke your disciples' (v. 39).

The message has come home. What is it from Jesus' actions, which both the disciples and the Pharisees have seen, which elates the disciples so they cry, 'Blessed is the King who comes in the name of the Lord!', yet offends the Pharisees so they respond, 'Teacher, rebuke your disciples'?

The power of the word
In the time of Jesus, they may not have had modern printing methods, but the Jews were the people of a book – the Holy Scriptures, comprising the Law, the Prophets and the Writings. Jews were students of unprecedented diligence, because of divine command:

> These words which I command you this day shall be upon your heart; and you shall teach them diligently to your children, and shall talk of them when you sit in your house, and when you walk by the way, and when you lie down, and when you rise. And you shall bind them as a sign upon your hand, and they shall be as frontlets between your eyes. And you shall write them on the doorpost of your house and on your gates (Deut. 6:6-9).

The lives of God's people were and are to be saturated with his Word. Inward thought and outward experience, family life and responsibilities, waking and sleeping, the day's activity, the action of hands, the outlook of sight, the outward witness to the watching world – all is directed to be under the authority of Scripture.

Right up to the present day, in the morning service at home or in the synagogue, the Jewish worshipper symbolizes this concern as he puts on the phylacteries known as tephillin. These two small cube-shaped boxes contain portions from the Torah (the first five books of Moses). Worn on the arm and forehead, the tephillin remind him of his duty to God – a duty to subject heart, mind, soul and strength to the service of Yahweh, the Lord. In similar fashion, the Mezuzah is fixed to the right hand doorpost of Jewish homes. The scroll contained in the casing has the words of the Shema, Deuteronomy 6:4-9 and 11:13-21. Fixed to every doorpost (except the bathroom) in a Jewish house, it is a constant reminder of God's presence – and that the home is a place, as the law requires, where the living God is to be loved, worshipped and obeyed: 'Hear, O Israel: The LORD our God is one LORD; and you shall love the LORD your God with all your heart, and with all your soul, and with all your might' (Deut. 6:4).

The life of the Jews was determined by Scripture. Their education, behaviour, obligations and sense of history, were moulded by rigorous ongoing attention to the Word of God. As commanded, they knew it thoroughly and comprehensively. You did not misquote the Scriptures to a Pharisee and expect to get away with it!

The shape of things to come
As with other parts of Scripture, many of the psalms allow a glimpse of the future. Messianic psalms speak in hopeful expectation of God's coming One. Other psalms anticipate the great saving deeds of God which will signal history's climax and the full redemption of Israel, the people of God.

'Blessed is he who comes in the name of the LORD' (Ps. 118:26) is one of those famous and unambiguous phrases from the psalms which describes the coming of God himself to bring salvation to his people. Those present on the day Jesus rode into Jerusalem on the back of a donkey would know these words from Psalm 118 as a Messianic prophecy. This psalm speaks joyfully about the coming day of the Lord. 'This is the day the LORD has made; let us rejoice and be glad in it' (v.24).

'The day of the LORD....' The Jews spoke of it in hushed tones. For over eight hundred years the prophets and people had looked forward to the day when the Messiah would come to his people: 'The LORD alone will be exalted in that day. The LORD Almighty has a day in store' (Isa. 2:11-12).

Chapter and verse

When the disciples cry, 'Blessed is the King who comes in the name of the Lord,' it is not so much a *misquotation* as a *modification*. The introduction of the words 'the King', which the Pharisees noticed immediately, raises an important issue. It poses the question: what kind of Messianic expectation was in the disciples' minds? Or to put it in simpler terms: What kind of *king* was *Jesus*? On this, in preparation for his coming, the prophets had much to say.

Foretelling and forth-telling

The normal nature of the prophets' ministry was to *tell forth* the word of God. As God spoke through them, so they, from their human perspectives, struggled to apply the truth of God's written revelation in the law to the whole gamut of Israel's experience. Nonetheless, it has been estimated that over a quarter of the Scriptures were speaking of future events at the time they were written. 8,000 verses of predictive prophecy contain some 1,817 predictions made from 737 separate topics. This analysis covers some 28.5% of the Old Testament and 21.5% of the New Testament.

Such estimates are open to a broad range of interpretation. Furthermore, it is clearly inappropriate to be using Scripture as a crystal ball, by searching its pages for a blueprint of future events. But equally, it does violence to Scripture's own testimony to itself if we neglect the predictive element within the prophetic literature. Amos, who was a contemporary of Isaiah and Micah, and came from the hill country of Tekoa, was specific on this point: 'Surely the Sovereign LORD does nothing without revealing his plan to his servants the prophets' (Amos 3:7).

The focus of such plans is the coming of the Messiah. So it is no surprise that Jesus' whole life, his birth, the events surrounding his ministry and teaching, his death and resurrection, and his return to history and the culmination of time, are the subject of predictive prophecy in the Hebrew scriptures.

Royal peace initiative

In just this predictive way, the prophet Zechariah speaks in future terms. It is one of the classic prophetic statements concerning the coming of the Messiah:

> See, your king comes to you, righteous and having salvation, gentle and riding on a donkey, on a colt, the foal of a donkey. I will take away the chariots from Ephraim and the war-horses from Jerusalem, and the battle-bow will be broken. He will proclaim peace to the nations (Zech. 9:9-10).

The king who comes proclaiming peace will be riding a donkey. Modern minds hardly register the significance. Ancient minds sit up and ponder. The reason is the donkey itself. Donkeys were not used for beach rides in Palestine. Donkeys are given a far higher status in the East than they are in the West. In ancient times, only in war did kings ride upon horses. When they came in peace, a donkey was their chosen mount. A king riding upon a donkey was a king coming to bring peace.

When Jesus came as a king riding upon a donkey, it was indeed a peace demonstration. Two questions would have come to mind in those who observed Jesus, as the crowds waved their palms around him and cried their greetings of joy: If this is a

king who brings peace, then what kind of king is he? What
kinds of peace are in evidence?

Freedom fighters

Jewish nationalism had its own ideas. The Zealot party, which
according to the contemporary Jewish historian Josephus was
founded in AD 6 by Judas the Galilean in association with
Zadduk the Pharisee, regarded Roman occupation as nothing
less than intolerable. They saw themselves as successors to the
Maccabees (the leaders of the national party among the Jews
who suffered in the persecution under Antiochus Epiphanes,
who succeeded to the Syrian throne in 175 BC). Their longing
was to send the Romans packing – and that by force. They were
considered somewhat trigger happy, and were largely
responsible for the war with Rome which raged between AD
66-70 and ended in the disaster of the temple's destruction. In
AD 132 a final revolt under the leadership of Bar Kochba
resulted in the crushing of Judaism altogether, and Jerusalem,
the city of David, was completely refashioned by Rome as a
Gentile city.

At least one of Jesus' disciples had belonged to the Zealot
party. He was known as Simon the Zealot (Luke 6:15; Acts
1:13) or Simon the Cananaean, the Aramaic name (reproduced
in the Greek text of Matthew 10:4 and Mark 3:18). Some have
even argued for Judas Iscariot's membership. Other disciples'
names have also been linked in this way. On one occasion even
Paul was thought to be a Zealot (Acts 21:38). And the teacher
Gamaliel, the son of Hillel, may have thought that Jesus was
linked with the Zealot movement (Acts 5:36-37). However,
Jesus was not a Zealot, and whatever the disciples' backgrounds,
with the possible exception of Judas, they eventually severed
their links with this major political force of Jesus' time.

'My kingdom is not of this world,' said Jesus in John 18:36,
meaning Jesus came as a king, but not as a Zealot-inspired
political conqueror to establish a world-wide *political* kingdom
on earth. That is what the Zealots were desperate for him to do,

and as such he turned out to be a grave disappointment. Instead, he came not to bring political power but to establish spiritual peace.

The sin solution

What kind of peace was this to be? The whole human race is implicated in an outstanding failure of morality. Surely the Zealots were right to abhor the violent abuse of their land and people by their Roman conquerors; in the same way that today those who have demonstrated for peace in the twentieth century were right to vilify the wanton misuse of power by the Western nations, and the consequent threat to world stability and national and personal welfare. Yet the peace which Jesus brings goes many levels deeper. His peace penetrates to the very root of the malaise, where the problem originates in all its staggering and humanly irreversible proportions.

'Your iniquities have separated you from your God,' said Isaiah (Isa. 59:2). Because we are moral beings created by a supreme moral God, if we live in ways which violate the way and reason for our creation, we cut ourselves off from the knowledge of the One who is able to help us through the twisting maze of human life. We are held accountable because 'we suppress the truth by our wickedness' (Rom. 1:18). Man is in trouble with God. It is only peace with God that can make peace on earth any kind of a possibility.

Jesus is the peace-bringer. By riding into Jerusalem on a donkey, he declared openly both his Messiahship and the nature of his mission. It was an acted parable. Why was it important? It was critical for Jesus to spell out his Messiahship and to open up the opportunity for response. The issue of response to Jesus – to the King and to his kingdom – is the theme behind all of his teaching. It is the purpose of the gospel to provide a solution for sin and bring us into relationship with God.

The power of esteem

Our view or estimation of a person strongly affects the way we respond to them. In a school, an accomplished teacher who is fair in discipline and friendly in manner is more likely to win the esteem of students than a teacher who is bumbling, aggressive and inept.

In the world of music, the great French musician Nadia Boulanger, who died in 1979 at the age of ninety-two, provides a remarkable example of this principle in action. For well over fifty years Nadia Boulanger dominated the international music scene as the greatest teacher of composition and performance in the recent history of Western music. European and American composers and performers flocked to Paris and Fontainebleau to benefit from her direction. Many of the greatest names in the music of today owe their skilled technique and richness of outlook to Nadia Boulanger's inspiration and training.

Why should a humble, somewhat reticent teacher of music inspire such a remarkable following with such internationally acclaimed results? Why was she received by heads of states, decorated many times and often filmed? All her pupils are of the same opinion. They held her in the highest esteem. They worked to please her. Above and beyond every other factor, that was the deciding issue. It is a principle of enormous potential. Our estimation of a person can powerfully affect the way we respond to them and what we achieve in consequence.

It is the same with our view of God. How we see Jesus can radically affect the way we live for him, and what we achieve for his sake.

> Once, having been asked by the Pharisees when the kingdom of God would come, Jesus replied, 'The kingdom of God does not come with your careful observation, nor will people say, "Here it is," or "There it is," because the kingdom of God is within you' (Luke 17:20-21).

Here Jesus underlines the reaction of inner response to himself as the most important element in the coming of the kingdom of God. This is the reason why Luke links Jesus' entry into Jerusalem with his parable of three months' wages (sometimes known as the parable of the ten minas, or the parable of the pounds). It is to illustrate that a right understanding and estimation of who Jesus is has implications of the highest significance for the way we live for him. It is a question of the power of esteem.

The parable (Luke 19:11-27) immediately precedes Jesus' journey into Jerusalem, and is meant to highlight the issue of response. This response is later acted out in part by the reaction of the disciples and Pharisees along the road down to the Mount of Olives (Luke 19:37-39). But the issue of response goes deeper still, as the parable illustrates.

The reason for the parable

> As they heard these things, Jesus proceeded to tell them a parable, because he was near to Jerusalem, and because they supposed that the kingdom of God was to appear immediately (Luke 19:11).

Jesus excelled at presenting the telling incident; but he was not just a master storyteller, Jesus was a master point-maker. Every story Jesus told has a specific issue in mind. Every parable makes a point.

In past ages, it used to be popular to allegorize the parables of Jesus and find in them hidden meanings from every verse. Yet it does not seem that Jesus meant them to be understood in that way at all. The interpreter's task is to search to find the dominant idea he is wishing to put across.

The parable is linked ('As they heard these things' Luke 19:11) to the conversation Jesus has been having with the wealthy chief tax collector named Zacchaeus (see Luke 19:1-10).

Three reasons for the parable

The first reason is Zacchaeus has become a committed follower of Jesus, and the parable is partly in response to what has happened. What does it mean in personal terms to follow Jesus now that discipleship has begun?

The second reason is 'because he was near to Jerusalem'. Jerusalem spelt the climax of Jesus' mission. It also spelt his end. How would his followers react when all seemed desolate at the bleak scene of crucifixion?

The third reason is 'they supposed that the kingdom of God was going to appear immediately'. There is danger in misconceiving who Jesus is. He was not to be the Zealot hero, nor what his contemporaries conceived to be a new David. There was no easy way to bring in the kingdom. The patriots had misunderstood the identity of Jesus, and that raised important practical considerations for how their commitment to him would work out in their everyday lives.

The parable of three months' wages

While they were listening to this, he went on to tell them a parable, because he was near Jerusalem and the people thought that the kingdom of God was going to appear at once. He said: 'A man of noble birth went to a distant country to have himself appointed king and then to return. So he called ten of his servants and gave them ten minas. "Put this money to work," he said, "until I come back." But his subjects hated him and sent a delegation after him to say, "We don't want this man to be our king." He was made king, however, and returned home. Then he sent for the servants to whom he had given the money, in order to find out what they had gained with it. The first one came and said, "Sir, your mina has earned ten more."

'"Well done, my good servant!" his master replied. "Because you have been trustworthy in a very small matter, take charge of ten cities." The second came and said, "Sir, your mina has earned five more." His master answered, "You take charge of five cities." Then another servant came and said, "Sir, here is your mina; I have kept it laid away in a piece of cloth. I was afraid of you, because you are a hard man. You take out what you did not put in and reap what you did not sow." His master replied, "I will judge you by your own words, you wicked servant! You knew, did you, that I am a hard man, taking out what I did not put in, and reaping what I did not sow? Why then didn't you put my money on deposit, so that when I came back, I could have collected it with interest?" Then he said to those standing by, "Take his mina away from him and give it to the one who has ten minas." "Sir," they said, "he already has ten!" He replied, "I tell you that to everyone who has, more will be given, but as for the one who has nothing, even what he has will be taken away. But those enemies of mine who did not want me to be king over them – bring them here and kill them in front of me"' (Luke 19:11-27).

Jesus is going away – like the nobleman in this parable. Eventually, and in spite of opposition, he will be proclaimed King. But while he is away, and before he returns, how should his disciples, his servants in every age, show their commitment and allegiance to him in practical daily living?

The background story
Jesus used a hot news item as a kind of illustration of his point. It was a political story with which all his hearers would be very familiar. In our time it might have been about a prime minister or president; in the event it was to do with someone called Archelaus, one of the three sons of Herod the Great.

After his death, under his will, the three sons of Herod the Great had to travel to Rome to receive their inheritance, their kingdom. Archelaus was set to become king of Judea. Archelaus was almost universally disliked, and even hated. According to Josephus, on the first Passover after his succession in Judea, Archelaus massacred three thousand of his subjects. When he travelled to Rome to claim his title, the Judeans, sensing perhaps the direction of his future, sent a delegation to the emperor pleading that Archelaus should not become king.

When Jesus told this parable he was in Jericho (Luke 19:1). In that city, his hearers were in easy sight of the impressive palace built by Archelaus and the fine aqueduct he had commissioned. Archelaus and his reputation were in the forefront of people's minds in this area.

So this parable uses as its subject-matter a clearly

recognizable event from living memory. Jesus puts the action into general terms, then uses the story to make his own definite point.

The parable in action

In preparation for his journey, the nobleman calls his ten servants before him, giving each the equivalent of three months' wages (a mina) each. The nobleman tells his servants to invest their money wisely until his return. But they are not keen on his new status which is about to be ratified: 'We do not want this man to reign over us' (Luke 19:14). It is the same opposition Archelaus found in his visit to Rome. But the nobleman returns, duly crowned; and he calls in the ten servants for an audit. The king wants a thorough look at the accounts to see how well the servants have used what was given to them. We are only told about three servants; the major contrast is between the last servant and the rest.

The presentation of accounts

The first came. He had traded with the money and made a high return on his master's investment: 'Lord, your mina has made ten more.' This met with approval and promotion: 'Well done, my good servant!' his master replied. 'Because you have been trustworthy in a very small matter, take charge of ten cities.'

The second servant presented himself. He too had used the money wisely: The second came and said, 'Sir, your mina has earned five more.' His master answered, 'You take charge of five cities.'

The two servants' efforts had seen a 1000% and a 500% increase in value respectively. Neither claims personal credit for the investment value. Each, self-effacingly, ascribes the increase to the initial value of the capital the nobleman had left him. 'Lord, your mina has made....' Consequently the reward they receive is not rest, but further opportunities for wider service; authority over ten and five cities respectively.

Use it or lose it

The third servant is different altogether. He simply hands the cash back. It has been safely hidden away in his top drawer in a napkin. There was no attempt to respond to the request to invest the money. The justification is a pathetic whimper of an excuse: 'I was afraid of you, because you are a hard man. You take out what you did not put in and reap what you did not sow.'

The nobleman uses the servant's own words as the basis of his condemnation. If the servant genuinely believed those accusations about the king, then he should at least have put the money in the bank to earn some interest on deposit, rather than doing nothing. The money is therefore taken away and given to those who can make use of it: 'I tell you that to everyone who has, more will be given, but as for the one who has nothing, even what he has will be taken away.'

The concluding slaughter, the destruction of the king's enemies, is a fierce conclusion. But Archelaus, upon whom the story is based, was a fierce man. The reference may well be to that notorious Passover massacre. Those who set themselves in opposition to the king must take the consequences.

Who's who?

Is Jesus meaning his hearers to identify him with the nobleman in the story? It is an important question, but made easier by remembering that the parable is not an allegory, so every detail does not need to be tied together.

Let's go back to the reason Jesus told the parable. Like the nobleman, Jesus is going away – in this case to Jerusalem, first to die, eventually to be proclaimed King, and finally to return at his second coming. How, then, should Jesus' subjects, those who are committed to him, live in the interim between his going away and his return?

Jesus is not the king in the story. He is not a despot. But *like* the king in the story, Jesus' subjects also have responsibilities towards him; Jesus will be away long enough for his servants to make full proof of their responsibilities and commitment towards him; there is time for those who oppose him to reveal their real enmity towards him.

It boils down to these questions: are Jesus' followers, the King's subjects, prepared to be faithful servants as they await the King's return? Are they prepared to be productive in the service of the kingdom? Or are they to take the title of subject, but in reality be only concerned with self and individual well-being? The kingdom needs kingdom workers. Passivity in the service of Christ is a contradiction in terms. It is what we do with the gifts the King has given us which matters most in the final reckoning. Every person has a part to play. This is the joy of belonging to the kingdom. Every Christian is a servant of Christ. But sad to tell, as the parable makes clear, servants can be irresponsible, lazy and unproductive.

We observed that our estimation of a person radically affects the way we respond to them. What makes the difference in response to the King is our estimation of his character, identity and purpose – the esteem in which we hold him. The third servant's excuse for inactivity was that the king was a hard man, and cruel opportunist. Jesus is no such King. This King did not shrink from giving everything to his people. Isaiah's servant picture finds authentic outworking in Jesus' daily living. He was, and is, the King who served. The humility of his entrance into Jerusalem upon a donkey, his compassion towards those whose lives were decimated by suffering, and the sight of his body torn apart by Roman crucifixion show that this is no ordinary King. Jesus is a Messiah who invites allegiance and industry in the service of the kingdom. He is a King who brings peace with God.

The highest good

As in the parable, servants of God today have to recognize the accounting which will take place when Jesus returns. As far as our gift is concerned, if we do not use it we will lose it: 'I tell you, that to everyone who has will more be given; but from him who has not, even what he has will be taken away.' In teaching about the kingdom, and correcting distorted, wayward and frenzied ideas about the Messiah, Jesus made clear, for those with eyes to see and ears to hear, that the kingdom of God depends on the response of individuals to Jesus the King. Transformed lives in productive service are the only authentic basis for membership. For such are the membership rights and responsibilities of a kingdom where the rule, wisdom and will of God become the *summum bonum*, the highest good.

Summary Points

■ Jesus' public ministry sent ripples of Messiah fever pulsating through Palestine.

■ His journey into Jerusalem was an acted parable, a peace demonstration, revealing the nature of his Messiahship.

■ Jesus was a disappointment to the Zealots and an affront to the rigid piety of the Pharisees. Only his disciples recognised his mission.

■ Correcting wrong thinking about the Messiah and his kingdom, Jesus made clear that it is response to the king in devoted service which counts for all eternity.

For Reflection

The kingdom is a secret revealed only to those who are prepared to become its subjects (p.70).
    What insight does this give you in how you should pray for unconverted friends, neighbours and members of your family?

The life of the Jews was determined by Scripture (p.79).
    To what extent and in what ways should our lives today be shaped by Scripture?

Over a quarter of the Scriptures were speaking of future events at the time they were written (p.80f).

If you were pointing out to a non-Christian just a few key predictions about Jesus, to which passages would you turn, and how would you explain these Scriptures and how they have been fulfilled? (Try Isaiah 53 as an example, but try and think of others.)

Your iniquities have separated you from your God (Isa. 59:2, p.83).

How would you explain the meaning and importance of this to a child, an agnostic, a young Christian, and to yourself?

How we see Jesus can radically affect the way we live for him, and what we achieve for his sake (p.84).

How do you see Jesus, and what effect does your view of him have on you?

Do you need to revise how you see Jesus in the light of what you have learnt so far?

Which servant are you in the parable of the three months' wages?

Is to live under the rule of the King, with a transformed life, your highest goal?

Chapter 5

TEACHING THE KINGDOM (2)

*'The time is fulfilled, and the kingdom of God is at hand;
repent and believe in the gospel'* (Mark 1:15).

The kingdom of God depends on the response of individuals to
Jesus the King. The goal of the truth which sets men free is
transformation. The communication process is the means and
not the end of the Word of God. But how does the kingdom
grow?

The purity of the race
If membership of the kingdom depends upon response and not
birthright, a radical departure from the doctrine of racial
incorporation and solidarity of Old and Inter-Testamental
consciousness emerges in Jesus' teaching. For his Jewish
disciples, such teaching must have come as strange news indeed.

During all the years of hardship, had not the Jews survived
because of their efforts to preserve the purity of their race? Had
not Moses underlined God's command not to intermarry when
the people settled in the promised land (Deut. 7:1-4)? Had not
Ezra pleaded with God, in a prayer of heart-rending penitence,
when the blatant unfaithfulness of the exiles and their leaders
was revealed by that very sin of intermarriage (Ezra 9)? His
actions spoke as fearfully of God's impending wrath as did his
trembling words. He tore his tunic and his cloak, pulled the
hair from his head and beard, and sat down appalled in a
demonstration of despair. This, after all, was a most dreadful
sin for a unique people to commit: 'They have mingled the holy
race with the peoples around them' (Ezra 9:2).

The covenant implied uniqueness: a people set apart for God.
Did not the covenant sign of circumcision remind the Jews that

they were a special people, that the Lord had made his covenant with them. 'For you are a people holy to the LORD your God. The LORD your God has chosen you out of all the peoples on the face of the earth to be his people, his treasured possession' (Deut 7:6). Who could deny it? Born a Jew, always a Jew. The big questions must be: does Jesus' teaching mean all this had gone to the wind? Could he rewrite history? Or was this all along the intention of the covenant made with Abraham?

These understandably fixed ideas about the boundaries of belief and discipleship were issues Jesus had to face immediately he began his public ministry. The spreading flame of the kingdom's power and dominion depended on *the removal* of boundaries and barriers – to the sharing of the good news to the ends of the earth.

Such reluctance to break beyond the barriers of the known has its counterpart in the church today. When Christians feel a sense of discouragement that family, colleagues, neighbours and friends seem impervious to the Christian message, it can drive them into stasis. Discouragement may lead to an abandonment of the evangelistic task. Many in the church today are demoralized, apathetic, and seem not to care about God or his kingdom. Yet with the parallel growth of Islam and secularism and the proliferation of the cults, for the first time in recent Western history we live in a multicultural, multifaith environment. Competing voices and claims babble their wares all around us.

In a world like this, some question the effectiveness of the spreading of the good news of the kingdom. How much use is it? Is it worth the effort? Why agonize over hard, uninterested hearts – those countless, faceless masses all around us? Will the effort ever be effective? Those so demoralized may wish to consign the message of Jesus to a cultural and religious relativism. They come to see Christianity as a new Judaism, as God's new covenant for one race only. 'Let the others stick to their own gods,' they say. 'Who are we to tell them what to think?'

Jesus had to confront such responses concerning the spread of the kingdom message. His words, though aimed at a different spiritual worldview, are equally relevant to the mission of the kingdom today, at theological and practical levels. The issues resolve into these two questions: How *effective* is the message, and how *widely* should it be made known?

How did Jesus respond to the attitude he had identified? In what way did he attempt to redirect the expectations of those whose worldview was anything but ready to accept the world-wide nature of the kingdom of God? It is these issues which form the subject matter behind the parable of the sower.

The background to the parable

What was Jesus' underlying concern, in choosing to tell this story about a sower?

The front-page cover pictures of magazines like *Time*, *The Economist* or *Newsweek* provide striking pointers to their inside stories. The newspaper industry is noted for effective front-cover illustrations of the issues they plan to examine on the inside pages.

In dealing with Jesus' parables, it helps to realize they also are pointers. Our task is to look for the inside story. In order to interpret the picture Jesus is drawing, we have to look at what lies behind the parables.

Mark makes the inside story particularly clear: 'Now after John was arrested, Jesus came into Galilee, preaching the gospel of God, and saying, "The time is fulfilled, and the kingdom of God is at hand; repent and believe in the gospel"' (Mark 1:14-15).

This is Jesus' first statement in Mark's Gospel: 'The kingdom of God is at hand.' It is Jesus' underlying and major concern – the kingdom of God. But what does that actually mean? The headline 'The kingdom of God is at hand', as we have noted earlier, can mean different things to different people.

Communication gap

There is often a gap between what we think we are communicating and what actually comes over. The existence of a set of words meaning one thing to one group of people and something else to another was of concern to Jesus. He knew there was a communication breakdown on a very important issue – the kingdom of God.

The situation is not that different today, though circumstances and definitions have changed. Many of the Jews of Jesus' time had come to see the kingdom and its Messiah in narrow political terms. It was understandable, since invaders and occupying forces had treated God's chosen people in an appalling and degrading way ever since the exile in 586 BC.

Jewish history from the exile onwards gives cause to reflect that atrocities such as the holocaust are no one-off event in the troubled annals of Jewish experience. Historically, the Jews have been abused, murderously ill-treated and slaughtered by one despotic nation after another. This must be understood if the strong currents of feeling which lie underneath the surface of kingdom understanding at the time of Jesus are to be properly appreciated.

In Jesus' time, the Romans are now in occupation. There is a puppet king called Herod, an ineffective governor named Pilate and an ongoing cruel exploitation and oppression of Jewish life and livelihood. The story has been the same ever since Pompey marched into Jerusalem some ninety years previously in 63 BC. Times are hard, and every Jew knows it.

Against that background, if someone arrives and says the kingdom of God has come, it is quite a claim. The Jews are aching for a Messiah. They are longing for a deliverer, to boot out the Romans and put Israel back on the map. Make no mistake, they want that kingdom.

Bridging the gap

Jesus says the kingdom of God is at hand. It is good news. But this is good news of a different level to the political expectations of the popular Jewish press. The kingdom of God involves deeper changes than just booting out the Romans. It involves repentance and belief. More than anything, to be effective, for there to be any growth, the good news of the kingdom involves the sowing of seed, and that seed taking root.

There are certain things which must be communicated clearly in order that no one confuses the message and misses its point. Transformation is the end. But the lines of communication have to be open for the kingdom message to be heard. The kingdom of God is the master theme in all of Jesus' teaching. The growth of the kingdom must not be thwarted by wrong understandings, wrong expectations or wrong assumptions. The boundaries must be flung wide open. This is why Jesus tells the parable.

The story and its purpose

> And in his teaching, Jesus said to them: 'Listen! A sower went out to sow. And as he sowed, some seed fell along the path, and the birds came and devoured it. Other seed fell on rocky ground, where it had not much soil, and immediately it sprang up, since it had no depth of soil; and when the sun rose it was scorched, and since it had no root it withered away. Other seed fell among thorns and the thorns grew up and choked it, and it yielded no grain. And other seeds fell into good soil and brought forth grain, growing up and increasing and yielding thirtyfold and sixtyfold and a hundredfold.' And he said, 'He who has ears to hear, let him hear' (Mark. 4:3-9).

No one need be an agricultural expert to realize that something about the sower in the story appears a little strange. He sows indiscriminately. What sower would normally waste 75% of his precious seed on totally useless soil? That is the situation here. An odd piece of sowing!

We are meant to take the story at its face value. In the

Palestine of those days, farming methods were not particularly efficient. In particular, sowing was done before ploughing, not the other way round. So there was not much of a chance to assess what kind of ground was being dealt with before the sowing began. But this still does not account for a farmer apparently wasting three quarters of his seed.

Surprise, surprise

The point is elementary. This is the only field the farmer had. It was not promising land. It had rocks and thorns and was organized in strips with its paths running alongside. It was all the farmer had to work with. You could wish that he had much better material, but this kind of subsistence farming using broadcast sowing was the only method open to him.

So it is not a case of a sower not knowing his job, wasting his seed. It is an illustration of the sower's *persistence*. He is working with very poor land. Others might not have bothered. He does – and sticks with it.

Here is the surprise. The sower really does know what he is doing! Who would have believed it? After ongoing, persistent action, the field yields a tremendous harvest. We are meant to sit up and take note. It is meant to surprise us. Who would have believed it? A sower, working with an almost barren piece of land, far from giving up like most others would, persists in his task. And to everyone's surprise, the field ends up yielding a hundredfold crop of grain. Jesus will have more to say on this.

Jesus' comment

Jesus spoke in private to the disciples, concerning this and the other parables: 'To you has been given the secret of the kingdom of God, but for those outside everything is in parables; so that they may indeed see but not perceive, and may indeed hear but not understand; lest they should turn again, and be forgiven' (Mark. 4:11-12).

In Jesus' time, as in the world today, the rule of God, his kingdom, was not obvious to the unaided eye. The average, contemporary, fair-minded non-Christian person can have no real clue, outside the indications of Scripture, that God is establishing his kingdom. The secret of the kingdom is revealed only to those who are willing to become its subjects. With the eyes of faith, the kingdom can then increasingly be seen, and the way is opened for the actions of faith as the kingdom is established.

God wants to create a people to be agents of influence for his kingdom. The fact is, Jesus' earliest disciples had to face – as we have to face today – the reality of resistance to God's rule. Many who will hear will prefer not to have the rule of God present in their lives. That is realism. But it does not mean failure.

For various reasons, from a human point of view, Jesus' disciples might have been predisposed to write off certain people. Maybe they thought that Gentiles were beyond salvation because they did not belong to the covenant people. Or alternatively, when they met with the discouragement of spiritual resistance, as they would, they may have concluded that there was no way of breaking through the opposition which their message generated.

Jesus had to show them that in the most surprising ways God can break through all manner of barriers and reach the most resistant of people. Given even the most unpropitious ground with which to work, God the Sower persists in his work. The kingdom is growing and, despite appearances, there will be a harvest. Looked at purely from the point of view of the ground to be sown, who would have believed such a harvest was possible?

A master class for the disciples

> The sower sows the word. And these are the ones along the path, where the word is sown; when they hear, Satan immediately comes and takes away the word which is sown in them. And these in like manner are the ones sown upon rocky

ground, who, when they hear the word, immediately receive it
with joy; and they have no root in themselves, but endure for a
while; then, when tribulation or persecution arises on account
of the word, immediately they fall away. And others are the
ones sown among thorns; they are those who hear the word,
but the cares of the world, and the delight in riches, and the
desire for other things, enter in and choke the word, and it
proves unfruitful. But those that were sown on the good soil
are the ones who hear the word and accept it and bear fruit,
thirtyfold and sixtyfold and a hundredfold (Mark. 4:14-20).

It is common to refer to Jesus' words here as an *interpretation*
of the parable. Although this seems right, it is slightly
misleading. Jesus is really taking the teaching *further*. It is a
kind of master class for the disciples' benefit. He is drawing
out pastoral applications rather than offering an interpretation.
It is spoken only to the disciples, not the crowds, so that they
will have a deeper insight into the issues involved in
communicating the good news about Jesus and the kingdom
across the boundaries to the wider world in which they will live
and serve the gospel.

The seed and the ground

'The sower sows the word.' From this application it becomes
clear that the message to be received is a message to be
understood. It has content. It is the word.

Jesus came into Galilee preaching the gospel of God and
saying, 'The time is fulfilled, and the kingdom of God is at
hand; repent, and believe in the gospel.' This is the content of
the message. Of course Jesus' followers must earn the right to
speak. The church must be a sign of the kingdom to the world.
Disciples must learn to communicate in the widest sense the
concerns and affairs of the kingdom: care for the poor, the needy,
the underprivileged, the suffering; love for God and each other.
Such care and love are a powerful witness to Jesus himself.
They communicate both King and kingdom.

However, unless individual responsibility is taken to communicate the word, to actually *speak* to an otherwise preoccupied and uninterested world, how will the kingdom grow? In the end, the message has to be communicated verbally. Otherwise no one will understand. As in Jesus' day, so in ours, what happens is only too obvious: people keep quiet. The watching world concludes that kingdom people are either nice or religious. Such silence blurs their vision – they fail to see that the kingdom belongs to the King, the King who beckons.

In New Testament terms there is no such thing as an effective *silent* witness or the liberal concept of the Christian presence – a kingdom without a King desiring to rule. Being kind to people is highly praiseworthy, but it does not turn them into Christians, into kingdom people ruled over by the King.

The sower sows the word. However sensitive we should be in certain circumstances, however quiet we may need to be before we have earned our right to be heard, eventually we have to speak it. To speak the word is the only means of producing the harvest. There are, of course, times when silence is required, in families and some other situations. But even then, it is as a prelude to speaking appropriately when God opens up the opportunity. There will always be different types of response. Jesus pointed out the importance of not foreclosing the issue by second guessing what that response might be.

Four responses
When we examine 'the ground' we see how Jesus illustrates the different kinds of human soil: the range of response to be experienced when the word is sown.

The path
Here is Jesus' first note of realism. His disciples in every age have to be prepared for there to be no response at all to the kingdom's message. It is as though he says, 'Be aware of the spiritual struggle of evangelism for there is an opposition to this work beyond the human.' Jesus knew the reality of satanic

opposition firsthand from his own wilderness experience. He did not underestimate the dynamic power of evil manifest in a personal devil. There is a spiritual struggle. 'Satan immediately comes and takes away the word which is sown in them.'

The rocky ground

Here Jesus speaks of those who will not make it to the goal. There is always a certain amount of fall-out in all gospel work. There are those in whom the message of Christ will only ever be received in a shallow way. They may look like Christians for a while, saying and doing the right things, but the proof of their discipleship is whether they endure. It is as though Jesus says, 'When they fall away, because the good times are past and the action has toughened up, it is sad; but do not be surprised, you were warned.' This is why later on, the apostles were to place such importance on becoming established in the Christian life. It is why Paul refers to 'the commission God gave me to present to you the word of God in its fullness...so that we may present everyone perfect in Christ' (Col. 1:25, 28). It is indeed playing with fire to settle with being a part-time or half-hearted subject of the kingdom and so prove to be rocky ground. Jesus said, 'He who endures to the end will be saved' (Matt. 10:22).

The thorns

The potential strangle-hold of materialism is real in practically every culture, even the poorest. Jesus says the cares of the world, the delight in riches and the desire for other things can enter in and choke the word, and it can prove unfruitful. Nothing has changed in this regard from the disciples' time. Don't we still need to be warned that we can be spiritually choked to death if we allow the wrong kinds of material concerns and aspirations to get the better of us?

The good soil

Here, at last, are the ones who hear the word, accept it and bear fruit – thirtyfold and sixtyfold and a hundredfold. And now the real point of the parable becomes clear. There are different types of ground, but only one message. And truthfully, like the sower sowing on unploughed land, the kind of ground being dealt with cannot be known until the word has been sown and it has been given time to take root and grow.

Hidden action

We live in an instant culture, and our contemporary world is highly results-conscious. Jesus has a different and timeless outlook. He emphasized the importance of quiet and steady growth. The action may be hidden, but it does not mean nothing is being accomplished.

> The kingdom of God is as if a man should scatter seed upon the ground, and should sleep and rise night and day, and the seed should sprout and grow, he knows not how. The earth produces of itself, first the blade, then the ear, then the full grain in the ear. But when the grain is ripe, at once he puts in the sickle, because the harvest has come (Mark 4:26-29).

Sometimes the process of germination and growth takes quite a time. The results may seem far from instant. But it is a mistake to think that after the seed has been sown, nothing is happening. It is just that we cannot see beneath the surface. This is why in sowing the word, we have to sow widely. Since we cannot know what kind of ground we are dealing with, selective sowing must be out. And we are warned not to give up simply because we do not see instant results. Every conversion is preceded by God's inner work of preparing that ground. It is what the old writers called 'prevenient', or preparatory, grace: 'No one can come to me unless the Father who sent me draws him' (John 6:44).

People only prove their ultimate spiritual nature by their personal and long-term response to Jesus Christ. And so Jesus was preparing the disciples for apparent discouragement. There will be many different responses; some will be for him, some against him. Equally they were being shown that what may look like an extremely unpropitious opportunity is eventually going to issue in a harvest. Jesus tells his disciples in his and every generation, 'Do not let yourself become discouraged or depressed by what appears on the surface to be an unpromising situation. At the harvest, you will be in for a surprise!'

So whatever different kinds of ground there may be, there is only one field. Until it is all ploughed up, no one knows what kind of ground is being dealt with. There is also only one seed which will make any kind of impact on ground like this. The conclusion is straightforward, the seed must be sown, and sown as widely as possible, without worrying too much about the kind of ground it will fall upon.

Sowing today

Christians concerned for the gospel of the kingdom are meant to be challenged by this parable. With all the difficulties of human response, it is all too easy to write off whole groups of people or individuals because we reckon they are poor ground. But the message of the sower redraws the perspectives. We cannot tell what kind of soil anyone is until the seed has been both sown and given a chance to take root and grow. This means positively – we should exclude no one. Yes, be prepared for opposition. Yes, be prepared for failure. But on no account give up. Instead, catch the vision of the harvest. It does not matter if our work is three-quarters wasted. Some will take root.

It is indeed a question of vision – of letting the mind and heart develop a vision of the possible under the promise of God. Our confidence is well-founded in this, since it is God, not us, who converts people. It is the message, not the messenger, that matters. The seed is the word.

A sower went out to sow, and as he did so, he widened the dimensions of the realm of God, so a kingdom may grow, extending beyond all human barriers of race, class and creed. Today, especially in the increasingly resistant western world, and in other parts too, our vision needs to widen, even where humanly speaking we estimate hardly any response. How wrong it is possible for us to have been about the response we are likely to see at the harvest, when we will see the results of our sowing.

Sometimes a follower of Christ may be born following a simple gospel presentation. At other times, it may take years, even a lifetime of prayer and witness, before someone acknowledges Jesus as Saviour and Lord. However it may be, Jesus says we are to be encouraged. Like the sower, we are to stick to the task and be persistent. One day we will see the great surprise – the day the harvest comes and 'the kingdom of the world' becomes 'the kingdom of our Lord and of his Christ' (Rev. 11:15). What a truly great day that will be!

Summary Points

■ The idea that God could move outside of Judaism was hard for some, and has its counterpart in the church today.

■ Jesus countered this by teaching on the effectiveness of the kingdom message and how widely it must be sown.

For Reflection

Jesus' underlying and major concern (p.95).

Why is Mark 1:14-15 to be understood in this way, compared with his statements on love for God and neighbour, and his teachings on holiness? Did the kingdom matter more to Jesus than his other teachings?

God can break through all manner of barriers and reach the most resistant of people (p.99).

What does the parable of the sower say to us today about evangelism?

How are you challenged by this parable?

What could it mean for the way you pray?

What could God be saying to your church about reaching people for Christ?

There are times when silence is required, in families and some other situations. But even then, it is as a prelude to speaking appropriately when God opens up the opportunity (p.101).

Compare 1 Peter 3:15 with its context in 1 Peter 1:1-2 to see what you can learn about this.

Jesus illustrates the different kinds of human soil (p.101).

What have you learnt about human responses to the message of the kingdom, in others and in yourself?

Compare your thoughts with 2 Peter 1:10-11 and read it in its context. 'Therefore, my brothers, be all the more eager to make your calling and election sure. For if you do these things, you will never fall, and you will receive a rich welcome into the eternal kingdom of our Lord and Savior Jesus Christ.'

The seed must be sown, and sown as widely as possible, without worrying too much about the kind of ground it will fall upon (p.104).

What implications does this have for your church's work with young people, the elderly, the disadvantaged, refugees and immigrants, and those of other faiths?

Chapter 6

TEACHING THE KINGDOM (3)

*'My own little children,' Jesus said, 'it is from your
Father's good pleasure to give you the kingdom'* (Luke 12:32).

Many times throughout their history God's people had to be
reminded that their special status in the covenant rested not on
merit but on grace. Moses had spoken warmly of the privilege
of belonging: 'What other nation is so great as to have their
gods near them the way the LORD our God is near whenever we
pray to him?' (Deut. 4:7). For generations such a standing before
God was the treasured inheritance of every son and daughter of
Abraham.

Yet privilege became mingled with disobedience and
distortion. Several centuries later, the Lord instructed the prophet
Jeremiah to declare to his people: 'This is the nation that has
not obeyed the LORD its God or responded to correction. Truth
has perished; it has vanished from their lips' (Jer. 7:28).

The truth distorters

In teaching the kingdom, Jesus came as a *restorer* of truth. So
much of what had been revealed in former times had become
overlaid with the varnish of hardened hearts and distorted
doctrine. In the period between the Testaments, layers of
tradition were added to the teaching of the Torah. Such were
the distortions of truth and moral action propounded by
influential members of the Pharisee party that Jesus found
himself constrained to spell out the issue clearly and bluntly.
The Pharisees were 'a plant not planted by his heavenly Father'.
They were blind guides, distorters of truth. The logic was
inescapable: 'If a blind man leads a blind man, both will fall
into a pit' (Matt. 15:13-14).

Such a critique accounts for the dialogue that Jesus continued with the Pharisees throughout his public ministry. Similarities in the sayings of Jesus to the celebrated Pharisaic rabbi Hillel confirm that Jesus was careful to speak at the level of the Pharisees' understanding. Jesus often took a saying of Hillel which would be well known to the Pharisees, and turned its meaning subtly, so re-establishing the fundamental nature of kingdom truth.

Beyond the strangely distorted ways of tradition, Jesus also had to contend with the calloused nature of the human heart. 'The heart is deceitful above all things' (Jer. 17:9). The privilege of belonging had done nothing to change man's inner weakness. There was still the self-deception, still the shallow optimism of self-justifying works, still the sluggishness of obedience, still the natural inability to perceive the truth of God.

It was not just the Pharisees and Sadducees who required correction. The whole human race is implicated in a tragic failure of morality. But it is a serious issue when God's people grow insensitive to their unworthiness before a holy God. Covenant truth can become obscured in covenant privilege.

There is not much sense in building the kingdom if there is no conviction of the human changes required within. There will be no urgency if man's alienation from God is not realistically perceived; no passion for the gospel if the lostness of mankind and God's coming judgment are not clearly recognized. The loss of such a worldview demotes the staggeringly sacrificial love of the Father in sending his Son to die in the place of fallen humanity to a pallid gesture of example-setting. The message of the stupendous love of God, which has been unfolding in Hebraic history from the time of Noah, through Abraham, Moses, David and the prophets, is finding its culmination in Jesus. If his people are not clear on this grace from God, the truth, as a first priority, must be straightened out.

The kingdom grows by sowing. But it is to mind and will, understanding and response, that Jesus aims the content of the seed. For in whatever ways the truth may become distorted, those ways originate in the rebelliousness of the human heart itself.

The long search

The Pharisees of Jesus' time had not exactly forgotten the truth of man's fallen condition. They had simply come to a settled conclusion on the matter. Their exaggerated pride in belonging to the God of Israel had caused them to adopt a hard and narrow outlook, not only to non-Jews, but also to those who did not share their rigorous and meticulous approach to ritual purity of life. Saddest of all, they were guilty of obscuring the passionate concern of God to search and find those lost in their worldly alienation and guilt. 'God is the God of *Israel*,' they reasoned. 'How could he be interested in the Gentiles?'

This failure to appreciate God's deep and passionate concern to seek that which is lost has swung to the opposite extreme in our own day. The British television series, *The Long Search*, a major BBC documentary in thirteen parts, which took some four years to make, is a typical illustration. During the period of its first showing, week by week the television magazine, the *Radio Times*, received from the Long Search office 'the billing' – the title of the programmes, comprising a few details and a short paragraph of description designed to entice the audience. Only the most careful readers would have noticed certain tell-tale modifications in the wording over that period of three months. But the changes were significant.

For the first eight films, the announcement began: 'The Long Search is a thirteen-part world-wide film series on man's religious quest.' The next three went 'The Long Search – a thirteen-part world-wide series on man's quest for meaning.' The last two announcements, with a hint of bewilderment, read: 'The Long Search – a thirteen-part world-wide series.' It seems the long search had ended up nowhere!

Modern man thinks he can search out God in whatever way he chooses and at his own convenience. However, four years of responsible documentary film-making told a different story. Man cannot pierce through the heavens and perceive the truth of God unaided.

The long search of man is a mission doomed to failure, for the distortions of the human heart are his barrier. It comes, then, as an eye-opener to Pharisee and rationalist alike to discover that God is the one engaged in the long search. God's search for man, who is lost and whom he loves with passion and concern, is an active and effective search; in a real sense, it is a mission with a clear determination that what is lost shall be found.

Lost and found

When something is important, you try to make it easy to understand. When people wrap up their best thoughts in impenetrable jargon, they give the impression their message cannot be crucial. Jesus was concerned to make his teaching on this aspect of the kingdom as accessible as possible. He chose three pictures from the world of everyday experience to underline one basic truth about God: he is passionately concerned about his lost children and searches for them. It was a truth which had become so distorted with the jargon of Pharisaism that God's love and joy had been relegated to the impenetrable and inaccessible. This was so much the case that strict Pharisees would say, 'There is joy in heaven over one sinner who is obliterated before God.'

To correct and restore the nature of this truth about God, Jesus told three related parables. They are about a sheep, a coin and a son – all of which were lost, but then were found. Luke links the three together in one chapter to emphasize that they are one in their message and cumulative in the conviction they bring.

The Lost sheep

What man of you, having a hundred sheep, if he has lost one of them, does not leave the ninety-nine in the wilderness, and go after the one which is lost, until he finds it? And when he has found it, he lays it on his shoulders, rejoicing. And when he comes home, he calls together his friends and his neighbours, saying to them, 'Rejoice with me, for I have found my sheep which was lost.' Just so, I tell you, there will be more joy in heaven over one sinner who repents than over ninety-nine righteous persons who need no repentance (Luke 15:3-7).

The popular writers of Jesus' time were sure God cared for the Pharisees; they were just as sure he didn't care for anyone else. Popular philosophy today is not sure there is a God at all, but if there is, he, she or it certainly wouldn't be able to care – for that, surely, would be far too human.

In the Judean countryside pasture is scarce. To this day there are dangers from high cliffs and the bleak devastation of the desert. When a sheep gets lost the shepherd drops everything. The sheep matters to him. It is not just that his livelihood depends on it. In fact, one sheep more or less is not going to make a great deal of difference; though many of the flocks then belonged not to individuals, but to whole villages. Granted, sheep can appear foolish creatures, easily frightened and not that good at looking after themselves. But every shepherd will tell you the same – you do come to care for them. If a sheep gets lost, off you go, dropping everything, until you come back victorious, the sheep over your shoulders.

In those days, shepherds would go out in teams of two or three. When, as would often happen, two would arrive back at the village, leaving the one on the mountainside because a sheep was lost, the whole village would go out to greet him as a community, to share in the thanksgiving when he returned with the lost sheep that had been found.

Luke mentions the reason why Jesus told this parable. The tax collectors and sinners had been gathering all around Jesus, and the Pharisees and the scribes had not made any secret of their feelings: 'This man receives sinners and eats with them' (Luke 15:2).

It is a mistake, of course, to caricature the Pharisees and

suggest they thought it was outrageous that Jesus should have any contact at all with those whom they found distasteful. In their strange way, they did believe in repentance, that sinners could make representations of penitence and regret for sin. The issue which really upset the Pharisees is that Jesus seemed to make repentance an excuse for a party. How dare he get so enthusiastic about it! Sackcloth and ashes are one thing; supper parties are another. As far as they were concerned, God would be brought into disrepute. Religion would degenerate into meetings for praise! From their sober viewpoint there was no need to get so enthusiastic about repentance.

The only reason to become enthusiastic, according to Jesus, is that God cares. If an ordinary shepherd cares that much about an ordinary sheep, how much more, then, does God care about human beings – about any single one human being who is lost? Will God not do all in his power to seek and find that which is lost? And when he is found, is God not full of joy? Jesus' reason was clear: 'I tell you, there will be more joy in heaven over one sinner who repents than over ninety-nine righteous persons who need no repentance' (Luke 15:7).

Jesus is keen to underline the fact, for such an important issue must not be obscured. Three different stories are used to drive the point home, lest there be any confusion on the subject. So the same comment is made in the second parable (Luke 15:8-10) when the woman finds her lost coin: 'I tell you, there is joy before the angels of God over one sinner who repents' (v. 10).

The forgiving father

Luke records a similar emphasis in the third parable (Luke 15:11-32) but also adds a further dimension. The joy of discovery is still there. But whereas the sheep was by its nature *stupid*, and the coin merely *lost*, the prodigal son was *guilty*. Yet the parable is not so much about the son in the story, as the forgiving father – the father who, at only the slightest hint of his son's willingness to return, is prepared to reach out towards him and forgive his son unconditionally.

To illustrate the point further, Jesus told them this story: 'A man had two sons. The younger son told his father, "I want my share of your estate now, instead of waiting until you die." So his father agreed to divide his wealth between his sons. A few days later this younger son packed all his belongings and took a trip to a distant land, and there he wasted all his money on wild living. About the time his money ran out, a great famine swept over the land, and he began to starve. He persuaded a local farmer to hire him to feed his pigs. The boy became so hungry that even the pods he was feeding the pigs looked good to him. But no one gave him anything.

'When he finally came to his senses, he said to himself, "At home even the hired men have food enough to spare, and here I am, dying of hunger! I will go home to my father and say, 'Father, I have sinned against both heaven and you, and I am no longer worthy of being called your son. Please take me on as a hired man.' "

'So he returned home to his father. And while he was still a long distance away, his father saw him coming. Filled with love and compassion, he ran to his son, embraced him, and kissed him. His son said to him, "Father, I have sinned against both heaven and you, and I am no longer worthy of being called your son."

'But his father said to the servants, "Quick! Bring the finest robe in the house and put it on him. Get a ring for his finger, and sandals for his feet. And kill the calf we have been fattening in the pen. We must celebrate with a feast, for this son of mine was dead and has now returned to life. He was lost, but now he is found." So the party began.

'Meanwhile, the older son was in the fields working. When he returned home, he heard music and dancing in the house, and he asked one of the servants what was going on. "Your brother is back," he was told, "and your father has killed the calf we were fattening and has prepared a great feast. We are celebrating because of his safe return."

'The older brother was angry and wouldn't go in. His father came out and begged him, but he replied, "All these years I've worked hard for you and never once refused to do a single thing you told me to. And in all that time you never gave me even one young goat for a feast with my friends. Yet when this son of yours comes back after squandering your money on prostitutes, you celebrate by killing the finest calf we have."

'His father said to him, "Look, dear son, you and I are very close, and everything I have is yours. We had to celebrate this happy day. For your brother was dead and has come back to life! He was lost, but now he is found!" ' (Luke 15:11-32 [New Living Translation])

Jesus' parable is intended to reveal a marvel: that God is a supremely loving, forgiving Father, prepared, where there is repentance, to forgive the guilty and adopt them into his family. The Pharisees, who might have identified themselves with the elder brother in the story, would have to realize they had no exclusive right to God's interest. God welcomes those who repent, irrespective of fault or failing. He longs to be known as 'our Father'. The forgiveness comes free, though the prodigal must show a willingness to return, even though he can bring nothing to justify his Father's acceptance.

Quote, misquote

The Pharisees were convinced they had an automatic right to God's care and interest. In teaching the kingdom today, followers of Jesus will often face a similar attitude. Jesus' teaching on the fatherhood of God was new and revolutionary, but it speaks of a depth of privilege, unrecognized by the Pharisees, and still hardly perceived today by those outside the kingdom. It is usually put something like: 'Surely God is the Father of all?' or 'Aren't we all children of God anyway?' It is a case of 'quote, misquote'. To think of the fatherhood of God in this way relegates the care of God and the privilege of belonging to his family to a shallow level of relationship, sapping them of their force as gospel truth.

The statement 'God is the Father of all' is a fallacy, based on a theological confusion between God the Creator and God the Saviour. Yes, God is the Creator of all. And in that creation sense, he is the originator of all things. He is the Father in the general sense of Creator. He loves all that he has made. But the biblical emphasis is that the world as a whole is in rebellion against God. (As it is written: "There is no one righteous, not even one," Romans 3:10 quoting Psalm 14:1.) The world no longer knows God in his kingly authority over creation and individual lives. Since the Fall of man, no one has any right to call God 'Father', except through the saving intervention of Jesus Christ.

It is God the Saviour, in Jesus Christ, who has put the relationship right. And it is only those who respond to God through Jesus who can properly be called children of God – children of the Father of the kingdom. The Bible is clear: God is the Creator of all, but he is the Father only of those who put their trust in Jesus Christ.

The truth about being a child of God

This is far more than a doctrine. It is meant to be experienced. That God is our Father and we are his children is a relationship which thrilled Christians of New Testament times. They bubbled over with enthusiasm because they knew what a barrier had been removed between the Creator and themselves. John's first letter illustrates the excitement of this relationship: 'Consider the incredible love that the Father has shown us in allowing us to be called "children of God" – and that is not just what we are called, but what we are' (1 John 3:1, Phillips).

There is no sense here of taking the relationship for granted. Being children of the Father is regarded as a supreme privilege: it is what we are by grace, not by right of creation. Naturally, we are alienated from God the Creator. It is only by salvation, through what God has given us, that this supreme privilege can be ours. It comes through the intervening work of Jesus Christ. Now we can be – and be known as – God's children. This kingdom reality resonates throughout the pages of the New Testament. The apostle Paul in particular makes the Christian's privilege of the fatherhood of God explicit, notably in Romans 8:14-17.

(1) Citizens of the kingdom have a new access to God as Father

'All who are led by the Spirit of God are sons of God' (v.14).

One of the simplest definitions of Christianity is that it is a relationship with God. And it is true. When someone becomes a Christian there is a new sense of relating to God personally, of being led by the Spirit. The big change is that God is no longer distant or unreal. There is a strong sense of a living relationship. We are no longer separated from God by our sin. We are forgiven people. We are members of his family. We are sons and daughters of the living God. It is the essence of the covenant.

This is a rich and many-sided relationship. And consequently the New Testament uses a variety of pictures to illustrate this new and fulfilled way in which we relate to God through Jesus.

Christians are described as branches in a vine in John 15, as stones in a building in 1 Peter 2, as limbs of a body in 1 Corinthians 12, as soldiers in an army in 2 Timothy 2. They are all relational metaphors. They are pictures of belonging *together*, being part of the whole, and having a purpose as part of that wider identity.

But whereas these are pictures designed to illuminate and fill out our understanding, the term 'sons of God' is the factual truth behind the metaphors. It is because we are sons of God in reality that we can now relate to God in these rich and varied ways. And it all depends on having access to God as Father.

Paul elaborates on the richness of this privilege. We have access to God as his children. God the Holy Spirit guides us in our lives. That in itself, as Paul explains earlier in Romans 5:2, is a direct result of what Jesus has achieved by his death and his resurrection: 'Through him we have obtained access to this grace in which we stand.' Paul explains Jesus' role in making a way open, in making access to God possible.

The idea of standing in grace refers to a new and permanent position. It implies a security about our relationship to God.

Once we were estranged. We stood as objects of judgment before God. But, because of Jesus Christ's intervention on our behalf, God's attitude to us has now changed. We stand in grace, not judgement. It means security. Circumstances will never change. We have access to the Father as his sons and daughters for ever. That access is secure because it has been obtained through Jesus himself. That is Paul's argument all the way through Romans up to the end of chapter 8.

Why is Jesus' part so significant in all this? Jesus has the exclusive right to make that access available. Kingdom rights are bestowed by the King himself. Only Jesus makes access possible, because only Jesus deals finally and completely with our sin.

That is what makes Christianity unique in all the world's religions. It offers forgiveness. A forgiveness paid for, in history, and completely, by God's own Son. This is the point from which the misconceptions about God's fatherhood usually spring. Some people fail to take into account that sin, our moral failures as human beings, prevents us from relating to a holy God.

Yet sin has to be paid for. Its effects are too drastic on the spiritual level, as well as on the human and social levels, to be overlooked. It is only through Jesus Christ, who alone has the qualifications needed, that the relationship can be restored, and we can call God, 'Father'. That is why Christian privilege No. 1 has to be a new access to God as Father. It provides a new way of relating to him, and a new experience of his strength and guidance.

(2) Citizens of the kingdom experience a new assurance of acceptance by God as Father

'You did not receive the spirit of slavery to fall back into fear, but you have received the spirit of sonship' (Rom. 8:15).

We all have fears of various kinds. Fear is a powerful psychological and spiritual factor. Fear affects our confidence, our direction, our motives, our ambitions, our relationships and many other issues. It may take different forms: we may be afraid of other people – of what they may think or say about us; we may be afraid of what might happen in the future; afraid of sickness; afraid of pain; afraid of death or dying. There is no shame in having fears. Everybody has them. It is how we handle our fears which counts.

The New Testament emphasis is that applied confidence in the loving, caring fatherhood of God is the proper way to begin to handle these fears which can so easily depress us and render us ineffective in our lives.

'He loves me – he loves me not.' The most undermining and destructive fear for the Christian is a deep down feeling that we are somehow unacceptable to God, and that we have no real right to be called his children. This comes back to lack of assurance of salvation.

Without that assurance, we will inevitably lack confidence as Christians. Certainly, we become unable to apply that confidence to the pressure our anxieties exert upon us. The external fears of our lives begin to take control. We become spiritually timid. God's promises mean little in practice. Dryness rather than vitality and power characterizes the little prayer we are able to muster. And in our heart of hearts, it is possible to forget all about standing in grace. We begin to think of God not as a loving, forgiving Father, but as an angry, accusing Judge.

Have we any right to be called God's children? The answer is 'Yes and no'. 'Yes', because of the promises of the gospel, but 'No', if we are looking to our own qualifications or religious efforts to achieve such a status.

In this respect, something subtle can happen. The temptation is to look to ourselves rather than to Christ. Human beings have not changed. It has been the case for countless hundreds of years. The psychological pressure to make ourselves acceptable to God is enormous. As history illustrates, it does not work.

Luther and the spiritual blues

In the beautiful city of Rome there is a strange building which stands opposite the Cathedral Church of St. John Lateran. It is a rather unusual structure which houses the Scala Santa, the holy stairway. These are twenty-eight marble steps which were brought to Rome from Jerusalem by one of the earliest popes, and then erected into a shrine for the faithful.

The Scala Santa is the original authentic main stairway from Pontius Pilate's house. They are the steps which Jesus himself is said to have walked upon before he was taken to be crucified. So today they are an enormous attraction for pilgrims of various kinds, and they have been for centuries.

You can watch the pilgrims going up those steps on their knees, saying the rosary as they go. It has not changed since the days the young Martin Luther made his own celebrated pilgrimage to Rome. His story illustrates this issue of spiritual assurance, and the damage which can be done if this teaching is distorted.

The medieval church was a strange affair, not so different in some respects from the self-justifying world of the Pharisees of Jesus' time. Salvation had become a matter of trying as hard as you can, by all kinds of strange religious efforts, to keep yourself out of their theological invention, purgatory. The medieval church had devised all kinds of ingenious devices designed to clock up credit for the final reckoning.

In 1511, Martin Luther was still an Augustinian monk. He had struggled for years to find acceptance with God. God was so holy, and Luther so sinful, where could poor Martin find rest for his troubled soul? His spiritual history of this period portrays vividly what horrifying misery he went through.

With the opportunity to visit Rome for the first time, Luther took full advantage of all these old holy places to try to settle his spirit and find his elusive peace with God. The Scala Santa, the holy stairway, was the first attraction.

With some anticipation, Luther made his pilgrimage. Like the other pilgrims, he began to climb Pilate's stairs in the footsteps of Jesus. Slowly and painstakingly he ascended on his hands and knees, following the rules as he went: the rosary in his hands, repeating the Lord's Prayer and kissing each step for good measure. He hoped, by such a work of piety and merit to deliver a soul from purgatory, and to find peace for his own heart.

This kind of desperate spirituality was real for people in those days, however ludicrous it may sound now. In understanding this spiritual struggle, it is important to try to envisage the torment faced by the young Luther.

Eventually, the star attraction of the pilgrimage came to completion. The stairs were climbed, the 'Our Fathers' repeated; the steps kissed, the rosary completed. Luther had reached the summit of this medieval spiritual mountain. 'How can a man find peace with God?', was the question which had brought him to Rome. It had taken him to the top of the pilgrim's highest goal, the Scala Santa.

Luther recounts that at the very moment of the last step of Pilate's staircase, a personal miracle happened. Words from Paul's letter to the Romans came bursting into his mind and soul. He says it was like a shaft of sunlight, illuminating that which previously had been dark and impenetrable. On the very top step – there on his knees, his head bowed down, the rosary clenched in his hand – these words from Paul's letter to the Romans penetrated his consciousness: 'The just shall live by faith' (Rom. 1:17). They meant that forgiveness is free; it does not need to be earned, rather it is Jesus' gift from the cross.

Luther says he was bowled over. It appears he careered down those steps, knocking over other pilgrims higgledy-piggledy as he went. And as he careered towards the bottom step, he proclaimed the words responsible for his conversion at the top of his voice: 'The just shall live by faith.'

It is said, perhaps with a hint of exaggeration, that at this moment the reformation was born. Certainly, seeds were sown and Luther's life began to be changed. The church has never been the same since that Reformation of belief which Luther eventually inaugurated. It goes back to that moment of encounter with God, the day when the scriptures were opened to his heart, the day when Martin Luther found peace with God through the forgiveness of Jesus Christ.

Though we cannot tell how precisely accurate this story is, from this point on, there was a sea change in Martin Luther's understanding of the nature, will and ways of God. No longer did Luther think of God as an angry judge who had to be appeased by monumental human effort. He now recognized the God of the scriptures as his loving, forgiving and merciful heavenly Father, because of faith in the sacrifice of Jesus Christ at Calvary. This certainly in time became the bedrock of the Reformation.

Our acceptance by God today has not changed, it is on the same basis. 'Therefore, there is now no condemnation for those who are in Christ Jesus, but through Christ Jesus the law of the Spirit of life set me free from the law of sin and death' (Rom. 8:1-2).

The mumps and measles of the soul
Some Christians, like Martin Luther all those years ago, still live with a sense of constant condemnation. How should we respond to others or even ourselves when in that unhappy situation?

Sometimes this sense of condemnation has more to do with psychological feelings than spiritual fact. Our feelings can be an unreliable guide to reality and Christian living. It is as well to be warned. Our aim should be to believe in the promises of God, rather than to be thrown to and fro by the ups and downs of our emotions. Our feelings do need to be disciplined by truth. Otherwise truth will be undermined by our feelings.

Most people's feelings are like a sine curve. They have their peaks and their troughs, ups and downs which may not necessarily correspond to the reality of things at all.

Presupposing there is no clinical depression, but a moody, gloomy frame of mind, what can the person who wakes up early

in the morning, feeling glum and unworthy, do to establish a
greater sense of spiritual confidence? Those who suffer a nasty
attack of the spiritual blues are well advised to meditate on the
transforming statements of the Scriptures concerning God's
forgiveness and fatherhood. 'The blood of Jesus cleanses me
from all sin' (1 John 1:7). 'To all who received Jesus, to those
who believed in his name, he gave the right to become children
of God' (John 1:12). The response *can* be: 'It is true. I am
accepted. I am a child of God. I didn't have to contribute
anything. Every single failure and cause of shame has been dealt
with. He has done it all.' This is the kingdom reality. God would
not be King at all if he were powerless to grant such freedom to
his subjects.

A spiritual health warning

One of the subtlest tricks of the devil, when he finds himself
unable to get at kingdom people via wine, women and song, is
that he becomes religious! He loves to throw all our sins and
failings at us and make us feel guilty. In the book of Revelation
the devil is described as 'the accuser of the brethren' (Rev.
12:10). We should expect him to live up to his name. He will
accuse us by parading all our weaknesses and failings before
us, as though they had never been forgiven by Jesus.
Psychologically and spiritually we are poised very finely. Guilt
is a major human problem, and Christians easily become
overwhelmed by it.

Of course, the Holy Spirit uses our consciences to remind us
when we are going off track. But when guilt gets out of
proportion, especially when sin has already been repented of
and confessed, then we should be warned not to believe those
annoying little messages in our head when we are feeling low.
They become bad habits of mind which we need to deal with
before they get the better of us. James' letter suggests some
wise preventative measures. Quoting Proverbs 3:34, 'God
opposes the proud, but gives grace to the humble,' James
comments, 'Submit yourselves therefore to God. Resist the devil

and he will flee from you. Draw near to God and he will draw near to you' (Jas. 4:6-8).

If we have a low view of ourselves, we can easily be persuaded that we are not good enough to be used in any way by God. But if we know we are children of God, not only are our sins and failings and failures forgiven, not only are we accepted, but God our Father wants, indeed delights, to use us in his service.

Remember then, Paul's words: 'You did not receive the spirit of slavery to fall back into fear, but you have received the spirit of sonship' (Rom. 8:15).

(3) Citizens of the kingdom enjoy a new intimacy with God as Father

This is why we may enter boldly into the presence of our heavenly Father: the Holy Spirit inspires a deep sense of the intimacy of this new relationship. As Paul says: 'When we cry, "Abba! Father!" it is the Spirit himself bearing witness with our spirit that we are children of God' (Rom. 8:15b-16).

The little word *Abba* is the distinctive name Jesus used to address his heavenly Father. It is used by Hebrew children to this day, and it means 'Daddy' or 'Dear Father'.

Most little children when they begin to speak make a similar sound: Abba, Dadda, or Daddy. It is a child's expression of recognition, warmth and trust. When we begin to recognize God as our heavenly Father, when the truth of our relationship to him seeps all the way down to our hearts, then the Spirit begins to inspire that deep sense of recognition, trust and love that is natural to a child of God. In a spiritual sense, we do cry 'Abba! Father!' as inwardly and personally we recognize the love and stability of knowing God as Father. It is this new intimacy with God which lends a sense of warmth and closeness to the sometimes overwhelming grandeur of the kingdom privilege.

(4) A new inheritance from God the Father

Paul reserves the most staggering of his affirmations about sonship till the very last: 'We are children of God, and if children, then heirs, heirs of God and fellow heirs with Christ, provided we suffer with him in order that we may also be glorified with him' (Rom. 8:16-17).

It is presented as a simple step of logic – a clear consequence of belonging. It is the language of inheritance. If we are children, then we are heirs. This speaks with tremendous power of a future hope which touches and transforms our experience of life in God, and our day-by-day fellowship with Christ in this present order.

'My own little children,' Jesus said, 'it is from your Father's good pleasure to give you the kingdom' (Luke 12:32). It is our inheritance because, as Paul says, we have been adopted; by grace we have been made sons and daughters of the living God. But as we shall examine further, along with this experience of glory, for the present also belongs the experience of suffering. It is indeed a condition as Paul makes clear: 'provided we suffer with him in order that we may be glorified with him.'

If the King did not escape suffering in this world, then neither can we. If, as the letter to the Hebrews makes plain, the King was made perfect by what he suffered, he will also prepare for the eternal kingdom through suffering those whom he has incorporated into his realm. 'For it was fitting that he, for whom and by whom all things exist, in bringing many sons to glory, should make the pioneer of their salvation perfect through suffering. For he who sanctifies and those who are sanctified have all one origin' (Heb. 2:10).

Suffering and glory taken together are key themes of sonship and the kingdom. They bring together the tantalizing inner tension of the 'now and the not yet'. Those who inherit the kingdom as sons bear a family likeness to their fellow heir, Jesus. They too will be glorified; but in some sense, great or small, they too will suffer.

Thus the issue about whether God is the Father of all becomes clear. The Fatherhood of God is a privilege belonging only to the follower of Jesus Christ. It means a new access, a new assurance, a new intimacy, and a new inheritance, knowing God, the Creator from whom we were once estranged, as Father; and knowing the blessings of his kingdom, which alone are his right and joy to bestow.

> For all who are led by the Spirit of God are sons of God. For you did not receive the spirit of slavery to fall back into fear, but you have received the spirit of sonship. When we cry, 'Abba! Father!' it is the Spirit himself bearing witness with our spirit that we are children of God, and if children then heirs, heirs of God and fellow heirs with Christ, provided we suffer with him in order that we may also be glorified with him (Rom. 8:14-17).

Summary Points

■ The truth of the gospel was distorted in Jesus' day as it is in ours.

■ Part of Jesus' mission was as a teacher, a restorer of truth.

■ Modern man cannot search for God and find him.

■ Jesus tells three related parables in Luke 15, to emphasise God's search for mankind.

■ Our acceptance by God today has not changed. Like Luther we find peace with God through the forgiveness of Jesus Christ.

For Reflection

'The heart is deceitful above all things' (Jer. 17:9, p.108).

Take a quiet moment to examine your heart before God. Use the words of Psalm 139 as a meditation. 'See if there is any offensive way in me, and lead me in the way everlasting' (Ps. 139:24).

'God is the God of Israel,' they reasoned. 'How could he be interested in the Gentiles?' (p.109).

Can you think of modern counterparts to this attitude? Is there any way in which you ever write people off in this way, however subtly?

Modern man thinks he can search out God in whatever way he chooses (p.109).

What would you say to someone who thought this way? What scriptures would you turn to for illustration? How would you pray for someone in this situation? Who do you know who thinks this way that you could pray for right now?

God welcomes those who repent, irrespective of fault or failing (p.114).

How would you retell the prodigal son story to a child, a teenager, and a businessman or woman, making the same points as Jesus does?

One of the simplest definitions of Christianity is that it is a relationship with God (p.116).

If you are studying in a group, share your experiences of what makes your relationship with God special. Then choose the names of some contrasted individuals, real or fictional, and decide how you would explain the gospel to them, and how they can enter this special relationship.

Luther now recognized the God of the Scriptures ... as his heavenly father (p.121).

Has Luther's experience of grace any parallels in your walk with God?

Most people's feelings are like a sine curve ... they have their ups and downs (p.121).

How do your feelings affect your spiritual confidence. How has what you have learned affected your attitude to this?

Chapter 7

COMMUNICATING THE KINGDOM

*'Of this gospel I was appointed a herald
and an apostle and a teacher'* (2 Tim. 1:11).

As it communicates the gospel of the kingdom the New Testament embraces a variety of patterns. They are complementary models, and the principles they embody assist in shaping mission today. Such models are not formulae. There is no foolproof recipe for success! Only God can give the increase.

The New Testament models encourage us to see where our role begins and ends. Our human responsibility is to communicate accurately and effectively. Above all, this means clarity about the message. Words *alone* are not sufficient, though as the sower parable insists, clear and faithful words matter greatly.

Beyond the clear communication of the message, the Bible says little about techniques. This reminds us that *we* do not convert anyone – it is God who changes people's hearts. As in the domestic art of baking a cake, he supplies ingredients *and* the effective outcome. He will effect the changes and bring his subjects into his kingdom, if we will be faithful heralds of his message.

Those who emphasize the sovereign will of God in evangelism have sometimes underplayed the role of God's subjects in heralding the King's good news. The fact that the apostle Paul uses the language of persuasion and appeal is ignored in favour of the great power of God to save – to call, convict, and deliver from sin. Yet however great our reliance on the sovereignty of God (and it should be great!), God rejoices in our part – he trusts us with an essential ingredient in bringing people to a living faith in Jesus Christ. This principle emerges from Peter's preaching on the day of Pentecost – the first example of public preaching in the life of the early church. It has been recorded in detail in Acts 2:14-36.

Peter – preaching about God
Peter's sermon on the day of Pentecost is one of the central models for mission of the New Testament. These are models of principle not pattern. They provide a standard by which our approach to communicating the kingdom today can be measured.

There are five elements which make up the ingredients and the method of the Pentecost sermon. The principles can be summarized as the visible, the prophetic, the personal, the historic, and the factual. We will analyse each in turn.

The visible

> Peter, standing with the eleven, lifted up his voice and addressed them, 'Men of Judea and all who dwell in Jerusalem, let this be known to you, and give ear to my words. For these men are not drunk as you suppose, since it is only the third hour of the day' (Acts 2:14-15).

In this way Peter begins his address to the crowd. Luke emphasizes that Peter was preaching out of the visible context of changed lives. The visible was a particular feature of the day of Pentecost.

It was an extraordinary day. Everybody heard the gospel in their own tongue. The Holy Spirit had given the disciples a supernatural ability to speak in other languages. These are the same disciples who only a few weeks before had been shattered by the crucifixion, and had huddled together in an attic for fear of the Jews. Humanly they had been rendered completely ineffective. And now they are remade at Pentecost. The Spirit of Jesus has changed their lives.

So the scornful accusation of alcoholic intoxication – 'But

others mocking said, "They are filled with new wine"' (Acts 2:13) – is not so much to do with their Spirit-given ability to speak in tongues; it is more to do with their Spirit-given joy. This is why the onlookers thought the disciples were tipsy. The disciples were different people. What had happened to the gloom? They were full of joy, their dejection wiped away. In a word, they were transformed.

Just as it is obvious that Peter's preaching rose from changed lives, so our world needs changed lives in those who follow Jesus today. Communicating the message of the kingdom will be of little use unless God is allowed to transform his messengers. For this the Holy Spirit's role of sanctification is central. Our words matter, but they are borne along by our living witness. We have to communicate the kingdom out of the visible context of our changed lives. Only then is the gospel taken seriously.

This transformation, which everybody could see, gave Peter his platform. 'Look at these examples of the change which God has wrought. These are just ordinary people, touched by the Lord,' he said. 'They are not drunk as you suppose. It is the work of God alone.' What do we learn as a principle from this? The world will listen to us today, when we can show that both the truth and the Spirit of God have made a tremendous difference to our lives too.

So when we say the method matters, that does not mean the fine details of organized evangelism. There should be a debate as to whether Alpha, Christianity Explained, Emmaus, Credo, friendship evangelism, rallies, door-knocking, evangelistic supper parties or the latest ideas are the most effective, desirable means of evangelism. Different cultures and areas will always have different needs. All these approaches are a matter of negotiation, provided the gospel content is finally made clear. But the method we see at work at Pentecost is different. The New Testament is not always *prescriptive*. In evangelism, it does not say, 'This is what you must *do*, do it this way, do it that way.' But it is perfectly clear what you must *be*. It is straightforward. Being precedes speaking. We must be changed people.

We have already seen that the idea that we should be transformed if we are going to be the people of a King runs throughout the Scriptures. This is so the message will have integrity. That Peter spoke from the visible context of changed lives is a challenge for us to put down deeper roots for our own witness and discipleship – the integrity of the message depends upon the visible.

The prophetic

In Acts 2:17-21, 25-28, Peter quotes from Joel's prophecy and from Psalm 16, one of David's psalms. Both are passages of prophecy. But this is no piece of arbitrary Bible study. Peter is referring to the grand plan of God.

What does the word *prophetic* mean? Prophecy means the declaration of God, concerning what he has done, what he is doing and what he will do. The prophetic has a past, a present and a future. Prophecy is alive, real and active, because it is about God and what he does.

Peter is referring to the prophetic nature of this message, in its past, present and future aspects. In the past God had spoken through the prophet Joel, whom he now quotes:

> 'In the last days it shall be,' God declares, 'that I will pour out my Spirit on all flesh, and your sons and your daughters shall prophesy, and your young men shall see visions, and your old men shall dream dreams; yea, and on my menservants and my maidservants in those days I will pour out my Spirit; and they shall prophesy' (Acts 2:17-18).

In effect Peter says, 'God spoke that in the past, but it is happening now. God has poured out his Spirit. No longer do you have to be a king, high priest or prophet to have a living knowledge of the Most High God. He has come to all of us, young and old, male and female, the ordinary and sophisticated. You can see the evidence in our lives. This evidence was promised in the Scriptures. What God declared would happen in the past is being fulfilled in the present.'

That covers the past and the present, but there is also a future dimension.

> And I will show wonders in the heavens above and signs on the earth beneath, blood, and fire, and vapour of smoke; the sun shall be turned into darkness and the moon into blood, before the day of the Lord comes, the great and manifest day. And it shall be that whoever calls on the name of the Lord shall be saved (Acts 2:19-21).

The day of the Lord is the favourite term of the Old Testament prophets for the day of judgment. It is an event as yet still in the future.

In quoting this prophecy of Joel, Peter is clearly aware of the past, the present and the future of God's dealings with us. The good news of the kingdom is for now – anyone who calls on the name of the Lord shall be saved. It is set against that future day of the Lord, the day of judgment, when everyone will have to give an account of their lives.

Past, present and future intermingle. Gospel and kingdom intermingle. Their hope and promise is present in the Old Testament, poised to unfold as God directs all human history to its culmination in Christ. In Joel's prophecy such hope is made explicit. It was not fulfilled till the coming of Jesus Christ. Today we must be sure in our own communication not to lose this prophetic sense of the message. God is active. His purposes are unfolding through history.

Where, then, should the emphasis in gospel communication be placed? Some today concentrate not on God and his purposes, but on man and his needs. Jesus will make you feel better, help you live longer, work harder. Jesus will make you happy, make you successful. Jesus will heal you, feed you, or whatever. Some such claims have truth, but they are spin-offs. They are not the message itself. We have to recover the panoramic view of what

God is doing in salvation: the unfolding of his purposes in history – past, present, and future. The message has to be directed to where any individual or group of individuals find themselves. But at the same time, the content of the message is prophetic. It is not primarily about man and his needs, though the gospel would not be good news if it did not ultimately fulfil all the needs of humankind. The essence of the message, however, is about God and therefore prophetic in its nature.

The personal

Jesus of Nazareth is the person of the message. When it is said that the message is prophetic, that it has a past, a present and a future, we are not speaking about an abstract philosophy. The message focuses in upon a person, Jesus of Nazareth. It is instructive to see how Peter presents Jesus here as the person of this message.

> Men of Israel, hear these words: Jesus of Nazareth, a man attested to you by God with mighty works and wonders and signs which God did through him in your midst, as you yourselves know – this Jesus, delivered up according to the definite plan and foreknowledge of God, you crucified and killed by the hands of lawless men (Acts 2:22-23).

As Peter says, 'God has made him both Lord and Christ, this Jesus whom you crucified' (v.36). But significantly, when he presents the message about Jesus to his hearers in verse 22, he is speaking of the man from that town in Galilee in the high valley in the southernmost hills of the Lebanon range – Jesus *of Nazareth*. Everybody knew his home town. Everybody knew of his three year public role. Everybody knew his claims, and what had happened to him.

It is a simple point: people today in general do *not* know these things about Jesus. If the names Florence Nightingale, John F. Kennedy or Albert Einstein are mentioned, most people are able to say fairly easily what these figures are famous for. But it may not be quite so easy to report with accuracy what they said or the details of their lives.

This is certainly true of the average person's knowledge of Jesus today. We cannot assume knowledge about him. Equally, many people do have quite wild misconceptions of what Jesus did say and do. So we should be clear that Peter presented Jesus *the man*. There is no doubting his divinity, but his humanity was as complete as any other human being, except that he never gave in to the power of sin. Like the Gospel writers we present the attractive picture of Jesus, God made man, rather than abstract pictures of divinity. The heretical second century Docetists fell into this trap. Their mistakes should warn us.

To communicate the brilliantly rich humanity of Jesus requires a continual absorption in all that he said and did; a regular study of the Gospels, getting to the root and heart of Jesus' teaching. Then when we communicate this message we will focus in upon the man in such a way as to present the message as it really is, about Jesus, 'who, being in very nature God, did not consider equality with God something to be grasped, but made himself nothing, taking the very nature of a servant, being made in human likeness. And being found in appearance as a man, he humbled himself and became obedient to death – even death on a cross!' (Phil. 2:6-8).

Unless we are captivated by the *person* of the message, kingdom communication will be dry as dust. Instead it should be a combination of admiration, love, fascination, awe, gratitude and friendship. It comes from being absorbed in all the things Jesus said and did and what he has done *and is* for us.

Those who are captivated by him without doubt communicate the good news of his love with tremendous faith and enthusiasm. But an un-nourished faith can slip back into a dry, dull philosophy. It is then that it becomes lifeless. By contrast, Peter was talking about a person, not a system of ideas. For the person of this message transforms lives!

The historical

'This Jesus God raised, up, and of that we all are witnesses!'
(Acts 2:32).

There is an indispensable historical element to the message.
When we talk to friends and contacts about the good news of
Jesus, we are bound to encounter a variety of questions and
responses, many of which will be reasonable. Some may be
obstructive. The majority of reactions are honest questions
requiring honest answers.

Like in any aspect of life – there are some questions to which
we do not know the answers. It is always best to admit that. But
what we do know transcends what we do not. What emerges in
this sermon of Peter's, and also from Paul's preaching elsewhere
in Acts, is the supreme importance of the historical nature of
their message.

They were asking people to come to terms with the evidence
for the most unusual fact of history ever recorded: that a man
who had claimed to be God's own unique Son, who was put to
death by crucifixion for the crime of blasphemy, had come back
to life again through a mighty act of God by resurrection.

That is the historical nature of the message. Philosophers
like Wittgenstein, Russell and Ayer argued for years about the
language of religion. If the historical nature of the message is
true, it does not matter what they or anyone says; we have to
come to terms with facts of history.

This is why, along with Peter, Paul and the others, we must
always bring our contemporaries back to consider the historical
nature of the message. It saves many cul de sacs. For everyone
who looks at the claims of the gospel must come to terms with
the evidence and claims for Jesus' resurrection. This is evidence
which simply cannot be ignored. Peter makes the same point in
his sermon. It is the same issue today.

The factual

> 'Let all the house of Israel therefore know assuredly that God
> has made him both Lord and Christ, this Jesus whom you
> crucified' (Acts 2:36).

These are the facts, he is both Lord and Christ. All evangelism
springs from this truth, that Jesus Christ is Lord and God's
Messiah – the source from which our confidence springs. As
Peter says, we need to know this assuredly, because from
beginning to end the message we are talking of is a message
conveying the sovereign rule of God in this world, past, present
and future.

God has placed Jesus Christ into the ruling position in this
and all universes. He has made him Lord. From that position of
complete supremacy Jesus now offers forgiveness, new life,
and the strength and power of the Holy Spirit to those who turn
in repentance and faith to him. It is all about the kingdom of
God.

So no one now will defeat the purposes of Jesus Christ. Not
the people we care for, who sometimes seem to have such
powerful objections to our faith in Christ; not the outright
opponents of Christ and Christianity; not the massive powers
of evil and destruction in the world today. Nothing will beat the
purposes of the living God.

God has placed Jesus Christ into the supreme position. He is
poised to return to this world. The day of the Lord will come.
And when Christ returns he will bring in the fullness of his
kingdom with him. It will be an end to war, an end to suffering,
an end to pain and death, and an end to rebellion against God.

These are the facts. As facts, they should affect our world-
view, our confidence and our desire to share what is really best
described as good news. He is Lord and Christ. Those two facts
are meant to spur us forward into action.

Evangelism matters. It matters that our lives and our message
reflect this model which God has given us. Ours is to be a

transforming gospel, proceeding from transformed lives.

The visible, the prophetic, the personal, the historical and the factual comprise both the ingredients and the method, but they are not a recipe for instant success. However, the five elements are integral parts of the truth which it is our responsibility to communicate faithfully and effectively.

Luke – communicating the truth

Luke, the evangelist, took special care to examine the truth claims of the gospel. This is particularly obvious from the prologue to his Gospel.

> Inasmuch as many have undertaken to compile a narrative of the things which have been accomplished among us, just as they were delivered to us by those who from the beginning were eyewitnesses and ministers of the word, it seemed good to me also, having followed all things closely for some time past, to write an orderly account for you, most excellent Theophilus, that you may know the truth concerning the thing of which you have been informed (Luke 1:1-4).

Behind the scenes

Luke is the author of the Gospel which bears his name and the Acts of the Apostles: they are like a two volume set, and both are dedicated to Theophilus.

Luke was a follower of Jesus Christ, and was converted some time soon after Pentecost. He was a Greek-speaker though, in fact, racially nobody knows whether he was Jew or Gentile. Luke was a doctor, in the limited sense of medical knowledge of the first century. He was the friend and companion of the apostle Paul, who describes him as 'the beloved physician' in Colossians 4:14.

Luke is an impressive figure. He was educated, cultured, and a skilled historian. As a companion of Paul, he had worked in the forefront of the evangelistic strategy of the early church. Luke was also a communicator. His concern for effective communication is clear from the prologue to his Gospel. He says he has assembled and presented all the facts about Jesus Christ. 'That you may know the truth concerning the things of which you have been informed' (v.4). Luke had a passion for communicating the truth.

What can we learn from Luke the communicator – the author of Luke's gospel and the Acts of the Apostles – that will help us construct our model for mission today?

(1) The authority of Luke's message

Many other narratives about aspects of Jesus' life and teaching had been written before Luke began to research and compile his Gospel: 'Many have undertaken to compile a narrative of the things which have been accomplished among us' (v.1). The word 'accomplished' refers, as what comes later makes clear, to the birth, life, teaching, death and resurrection of Jesus, his subsequent ascension, and the pouring out of the Spirit upon his disciples.

One way to date Luke's account is from the absence of any reference to the Romans' destruction of Jerusalem, which took place in AD 70. We can reasonably assume Luke's Gospel predates that event. The sacking of Jerusalem was such a horrifying, significant event that, had it already taken place, it would have received a mention in Luke's Gospel – and in any other New Testament writing for that matter – had these documents been written after AD 70. The conclusion is that Luke's Gospel is an early document, dating from the late 60s of the first century, and compiled during the lifetime of many of the foundation figures of the early church.

It is no surprise that many others had compiled narratives about Jesus. This means more than Matthew, Mark and John: there may have been hundreds of early documents or fragments about Jesus. It was natural this should happen. Any famous figure tends to have much written about him, and it will take all kinds of forms. The issue is – what basis of authority and authenticity lies behind such documents?

Major figures attract major attention. Luke's reason for adding to the library of information was not that the other accounts were wrong. As with Matthew, Mark and John, Luke produced what in some ways is akin to an *authorized* biography. Under the divinely-guided hand of inspiration, he was aiming to set the record straight. The authority for his Gospel, as Luke says in verse 2 of his prologue, is vested in 'those who from the first were eyewitnesses and ministers of the word'.

Luke investigated the original sources: the eyewitnesses, which included Mary, the mother of Jesus. His was not fifth, or sixth, or seventh-hand information. It came from those who were with Jesus during his lifetime, the disciples themselves, and those closest to Jesus.

Like Luke, if we are going to have anything to say about the kingdom to the world in which we live, we must be clear about the authority of our message. We must be clear about the facts. We must measure everything we say about God and his purposes for the world against the authentic and authoritative teaching of Jesus and the apostolic writers. This we find in the Gospels and the other pages of the New Testament. The writers of the New Testament were either with Jesus themselves or in first-hand touch with those who were. Where else are we to get our truth?

Luke also points to the objectivity of his message. His first concern in presenting the truth to Theophilus was that there was a proper authoritative basis concerning, as he puts it, 'the things of which you have been informed'. It is objective: he has not made it up.

This concern for integrity and fidelity to the facts and the teaching of Jesus is impressive when we consider that this almost scientific approach was unknown in the first century, except inside the small, emergent Christian community. This is our authority too. We have nothing to say to our world, or to any of our friends or family, about Jesus Christ unless its authority reflects the teaching we have received from those who were with Jesus himself. We have no liberty to change their teaching. If we depart from it, we should not be surprised that people's lives are not liberated, because God only blesses the truth. Like Luke, we must become students who immerse ourselves in the message of truth and grace.

(2) The accuracy of Luke's reporting

'It seemed good to me also, having followed all things closely for some time past, to write an orderly account for you' (Luke 1:3).

For a considerable period of time, it appears that Luke dedicated himself to assembling an accurate picture of the teaching and the news about Jesus. Every single Christian today has the same responsibility of assembling as accurate a picture as possible of the teaching and news about Jesus; then, when there is opportunity to do so, we can present it to people in our own way.

'Always be prepared to make a defence to any one who calls you to account for the hope that is in you' (1 Pet. 3:15).

Peter's words present a command addressed to all Christians: we are exhorted to be prepared to explain our faith to anyone who gives us the opportunity to say something on the issue.

There are a whole range of public issues which give Christians opportunities to say something incisive for the kingdom. But what do we say to people who repeat back some of the stranger things they have heard about Christ and Christianity from the media? When they show they cannot grasp the resurrection or the divine claims of Jesus, will we feel threatened and cross inside and blurt out bland orthodoxy? Or will we prepare ourselves with the facts and arguments at our fingertips so we can explain, graciously and persuasively?

An accurate presentation of the facts – what happened, what was taught, and what we can be sure of – is irreplaceable if we are to communicate effectively about Christ today. People have to be shown what the gospel means and have a right to have their questions answered. In so far as each of us is able, we must follow the model which we see in Luke himself: to assemble the facts to make the picture clear.

(3) The accessibility of Luke's language

'It seemed good to me ... to write an orderly account for you' (Luke 1:3).

When Luke says he aimed to write an orderly account for Theophilus, we gain some insight into his concerns for communication. The Greek word *kathexes*, translated 'orderly', probably does not mean strict chronological order. It implies that Luke wanted to present his message as a connected whole so that the complete and undistorted picture about Jesus could be seen.

The accessibility of his language means that Luke is clear about the message. He presents it as a coherent, connected, orderly whole. Luke's language serves that end. His use of Greek is a model of clarity and effectiveness. He is the great stylist of the New Testament. He is a communicator and there are several lessons here for our attempts at communication.

First, effective communication is not an ability the few pluck out of the sky. Like so many other areas, successful communication is 1% inspiration and 99% perspiration!

A boxing champion begins with a punching bag. A concert pianist starts by practising scales. The composer Brahms tore up every thing he had written before the age of forty; he considered only at this age was his apprenticeship as a composer completed. He was a rigorous self critic to perfect his communication skills.

Effective communication, like any other skill, does have to be practised: the more effortless and effective it seems, the more sure you can be that it will have taken hard work to achieve.

Are Christians effective at communication? The presentation

of orthodox statements about doctrine is not adequate. Doctrine is important, but there is more to it. The way some Christian leaders come over through the media is sad evidence that all is not well. It highlights a weakness. With some exceptions, Christians are not good at communication to our wider society. We have a terrific product, but we package it abysmally. It is no use just having the doctrine right. If we package up the truth in the clichés of our chosen brand of orthodoxy, how do we expect the world around us to be intrigued, let alone gripped, by what we are saying?

The Holy Spirit can, and fortunately does, overrule in our communication. Though he so often gets through where we fail, that must not be our get-out clause. God is concerned for communication, and he expects us to be also. We have to remember how staggering a fact it is to say, 'The Word became flesh.' The incarnation of Jesus as God is the biggest exercise in effective communication history has ever seen. Effective communication is as important as right doctrine, prevailing prayer, holiness of life, and all the other imperatives of Christian living. Evangelism depends on it. It is an inescapable priority.

The other point to learn from Luke's communication is to pray for the Lord to develop the effectiveness of our own communication. This should not just focus on the words we will use, but how we come over as total personalities. Remember, 'What we are speaks just as powerfully as what we say!'

Christians who are professional communicators in broadcasting and the media, programme makers, researchers, presenters and writers, are right in the front line. They have to be communicators of the first order. They need our prayers; they are in strategic situations and sometimes they are really up against genuine difficulties and opposition.

Another strategic area for prayer is for the emergence of new Christian communicators of the stature of C. S. Lewis who did so much in his time to find ways of explaining God's ways in contemporary language. In our generation, on both sides of the Atlantic, there is a dearth of able Christian communicators who deeply understand both the Bible and our contemporary culture and can build bridges between them.

All these matters are genuine kingdom concerns, and close to the heart of God. Millions will listen to the gospel of the kingdom if we have apostolic authority in our message; if we present as a connected whole an accurate picture of Jesus and his teaching; and if our language and persona are accessible to a non-Christian world.

(4) The approach of Luke's ministry

> 'That you may know the truth concerning the things of which you have been informed' (Luke 1:4).

What was the approach, the purpose, the goal of Luke's ministry? It was to help another person to 'know the truth'. That is why this is a model for mission. It shows us our responsibility to help others appropriate the truth for themselves. It is not about knowing the truth intellectually on its own; it is about making the liberating truth of the gospel your own by taking hold of it. As Jesus said, 'You will know the truth, and the truth will make you free' (John 8:32).

If we aim to present the good news, this is its essence: people from whatever background, facing whatever crisis or circumstance, can know freedom. It is a freedom from the penalty of sin. It is freedom from the power of death. It is a freedom which comes from knowing and taking hold of the truth about Jesus Christ which transforms lives. It is a freedom to know and love God, and to be adopted into his family for the rest of eternity. All this flows from the lonely cross of Calvary.

Does that conviction burn in you? The Word of God, the word of truth, changes people from deep down inside. This is God's way of doing it. The work of evangelism consists in lining up our own efforts and approach in conformity with God's way of working as he has objectively declared it in his Word.

This is what it means to communicate the kingdom, to have models for mission. Both Peter, who spoke about God at

Pentecost, and Luke, who communicated the truth in a new written form, were major Christian communicators of their own time. They were men whose passion for truth was equalled only by their concern to communicate it. God intends their work to provide principles for today, to be our models for the kingdom. This is how we can become effective communicators of truth, people who speak to a needy world about the eternal purposes of God the King.

Ingredients and method form part of the same package. The provision of kingdom truth which changes people's lives requires all followers of Jesus Christ today to work out their salvation with fear and trembling. And to continue doing so until the whole world hears and understands the transforming truth, power and purpose of God's Master Plan for the kingdom of God, and welcomes its crucified, risen, ascended, and coming King.

Summary Points

■ The New Testament gives vital principles for mission today. Peter's sermon at Pentecost gives five such principles: the visible, the prophetic, the personal, the historic and the factual.

■ Luke's concern for factual truth about Jesus reminds us to be clear on the facts we have received.

■ Luke's practice of communication challenges Christians to be more effective in the media as well as in public and private teaching and conversation.

For Reflection

God has placed Jesus Christ into the supreme position. He is poised to return to this world (p.137).

What difference does Peter's affirmation that God has made Jesus 'both Lord and Christ' make to your view of the world?

What difference will it make to your confidence to take seriously the supremacy, the authority and the lordship of Christ?

And what difference will it make to your concern for evangelism?

What difference will it make as you share this message about Jesus Christ – a message about what God has done, is doing and will do through him?

How will it affect your perception of every opportunity you have before you, under the supreme lordship and direction of Christ, the Master of the universe?

Like Luke, we should be working on the accessibility of our language. We will never improve if we do not work at it (pp.142-43).

The next time you have a discussion with a Christian friend, if it concerns a Christian issue, spend some time at the end talking about how you would explain that same issue to someone who is not a Christian.

Then, as you read the Bible day by day, spend some time working out what kind of language you would use to explain the passage to someone who has no Christian understanding at all.

If you read a daily newspaper, find one story each day to which you can make a Christian response. Then write out your view seeing if you can learn to communicate as clearly and effectively as the original newspaper story did, but in non-Christian language.

Chapter 8

KINGDOM PEOPLE

'You are a chosen race, a royal priesthood, a holy nation, God's own people, that you may declare the wonderful deeds of him who called you out of the darkness into his marvellous light' (1 Pet. 2:9).

The kingdom of God is a community concept. The New Testament makes clear that those who are brought into the realm of salvation enter in as fellow members of God's family. The people of God are kingdom people because they derive their identity from Christ the King. He is guiding his people to the consummation of history, when he will return in divine power as King and Judge, and as the bestower of eternal blessing for those who have given their full allegiance to him.

While God's people await the coming of their King, they are not to remain passive. They are a people with a purpose. Corporately, as well as individually, they are to 'declare the wonderful deeds of him who called you out of darkness into his marvellous light'. In short, God's people are to be a sign of the kingdom. Just as Isaiah graphically prophesied the impact of the Messiah ('the people who walked in darkness have seen a great light'), so the people of God today are called to take on that same role of messianic witness in openly declaring the saving deeds of the one who rescues from the realm of darkness and transfers to the kingdom of light.

Church and kingdom
With a calling to identify with the role of the promised Messiah, what relationship do today's followers of Christ have to the kingdom of God? Is the church synonymous with the kingdom? What is the relationship between them?

The two biblical truths, church and kingdom, are part of the

147

same whole; but they also exist as separate realities. Jesus makes
this clear by saying in the same breath, 'On this rock I will
build my church,' while going on to speak of 'the keys of the
kingdom' (Matt. 16:18-19). In the same way, at the beginning
of Acts, in the context of a question about the kingdom, Luke
speaks of the international ministry of the Holy Spirit spreading
out from Jerusalem to 'Judea and Samaria and to the end of the
earth' (Acts 1:6-8). Then, in the next chapter, he refers to the
fellowship (Greek, *koinonia*) of believers, recording that day
by day the Lord added new converts to the church (Acts 2:43-
47).

Where, then, lies the distinction, and where the inter-
relationship, between the church and the kingdom?

The kingdom sums up all aspects of God's rule in the past,
present and future dimensions of life. The church is the company
of the redeemed; it comprises those who have drawn near to
God, have made entry into his family and are ruled over by the
King. However, while being sanctified by the indwelling Spirit,
they are still to be perfected. When Christ returns, when the
last trumpet sounds, they shall all be changed. But until then,
the church has to embrace the full reality of the kingdom which
is God's rule and realm forever. God is at work among us. In
our own integrity and devotion – our commitment to each other,
our quality of life and, above all, our service to Christ – we
must be a sign to the world of the rich reality of God's saving
grace, power and love.

So in this, everyone has a part to play. Indeed each person's
part is essential. If we as the church are to represent the kingdom
of God to a world in darkness, then we have no choice but to
pull together. Pulling together means having a clear vision of
our reason for being. For without a biblical vision of what truly
constitutes the people of God, the church becomes separated
from the concerns of the kingdom. There can then be only one
result: the kingdom mission to powerfully and attractively
commend the King becomes ingloriously thwarted.

In consequence, a question Christians continually have to

face involves the nature of what the church is and what it is meant to be.

It is clear from Paul's organic picture of the body in 1 Corinthians 12 that the church is designed to be an every-member ministry, where everyone contributes something of value by exercising their God-given gifts to the ministry of Christ's body as a whole. Paul underlines this in 1 Corinthians 12:27: 'You are the body of Christ and individually members of it.' He then goes on to describe different aspects of that body life in terms of mutual service and care, and the corporate life of the church.

From a casual reading of the New Testament, the dominant image of the body of Christ in the first century is of a church where everyone pulls together. Or is it? Was that the true situation? Did not Paul spend a great deal of effort in the Corinthian correspondence, as elsewhere, in *corrective* teaching? Was not the danger that lurked menacingly behind his words that followers of Christ, unchecked, can become passive? Then, as now, the church ran the risk of becoming a vehicle of passengers – a happy band, not of pilgrims but spectators. Happy, that is, to let others do it all – to the detriment of the church's overall impact on the contemporary world and society in which Christ had placed his people for the sake of the kingdom.

We can read the Pauline correspondence through rose-coloured spectacles. All was not well in Corinth. All is not well today. We still repeat the old mistakes of the first-century Christians who, though they knew Christ, did not always live up to his calling.

Like kingdom and church, service and commitment belong together. The church cannot be a sign of the kingdom if the very essence of the church's organic identity as the body of Christ is ignored in practice. To separate what God has joined together spells trouble for the people of God. This concern accounts for the special emphasis Paul gives to this issue in several places, notably towards the end of the letter to the Romans: 'I appeal to you therefore, brethren, by the mercies of

God, to present your bodies as a living sacrifice, holy and acceptable to God, which is your spiritual worship' (Rom. 12:1).

As befits his background and education, Paul uses words with extreme care, so that every word and phrase counts in what he wishes to say. It is instructive, therefore, to analyse both the way Paul presents his argument, the tone of what he is saying, and the argument itself – the subject matter of what he wishes to communicate.

There are three separate aspects to note about the manner of Paul's presentation of his concerns. They are all present in the phrase, 'I appeal to you therefore, brethren, by the mercies of God....'

The weight of Paul's words

'I appeal to you,' says Paul.

The musician, Bob Geldof, is a household name on both sides of the Atlantic. As well as being a leading figure in the music business, back in the eighties he became celebrated for his work in fund raising for famine relief. The international, world-wide Live Aid broadcast of 1985 raised a tremendous amount of money for Ethiopia, as did several subsequent appeals for other stricken areas of the world.

One of the most striking aspects about Bob Geldof is his passionate intensity and conviction. There was a moment during that famous Live Aid broadcast, when suddenly and without warning, in front of many millions of viewers, Bob Geldof crashed his fist down on to the table. With convincing passion, he addressed the watching world directly, 'We want your money. Give us your money right now!' It was an appeal of telling conviction, concern and determination. In view of the terrible scenes of death, poverty, disease and deprivation which television viewers had been witnessing for some weeks, it was as disquieting as it was moving.

When Paul says, 'I appeal to you,' he is just as passionate in his concern. His expression in Greek is strong and weighty. It is the word *parakaleo*. It means 'I beseech you' or 'I beg you'. The same Greek word is used in Mark 1:40, when the leper beseeched Jesus to heal him: 'The leper came and knelt in front of Jesus and begged to be healed' (Living Bible). *Parakaleo* is a strong and weighty expression. Paul was making a passionate appeal.

The addressees of Paul's words

'I appeal to you therefore, brethren....' The *you* is plural. In translation it would be easy to miss the corporate nature of Paul's appeal. Paul is addressing the brethren, meaning the whole church, not just isolated individuals.

This then is an appeal to all the churches, not simply to an individual to tighten up his performance; it is a passionate, committed appeal to the whole church to pull its efforts for Christ into shape. Paul chooses his words carefully. Each member of a church has a part to play. He does not want any part of the body to be in doubt. The word *brethren* is an instance of this.

'Brethren' may sound a little old fashioned today (except that it has an inclusive feel to it) but it does mean something specific. It means that real Christians are brothers and sisters in Christ. It means we are members of a family in which we have been given a deep bond of belonging.

If that is true, then there is a question: Will we take seriously the implications of such a bond? Does the church – the real church, the family of believers – really matter to us? Or are we spiritual isolationists, interested only in *individual* Christianity and willing only to be spectators?

Paul's appeal is plural because for him the church as the body and as family really does matter. Furthermore, he is clear that each individual is responsible for the health of the whole. We cannot escape that equation. Sad to tell, the powerless churches are the ones in which people duck out of their corporate responsibility. The churches which really hum with life and effectiveness are where every member is properly involved and used in God's service.

The theology of Paul's words

'I appeal to you therefore, brethren, by the mercies of God....'

In any household with young children, breakfast time can be a combination of high comedy and a struggle to get the breakfast consumed, rather than having it projected missile-like all over the kitchen. It has certainly been the case with our family when our three girls were at this stage.

Halfway through breakfast one memorable morning, Rebecca, then two years old, suddenly decided she did not want any more of her Rice Krispies. She preferred the look of her father's toast and marmalade.

After failing miserably to persuade her to eat up, I tried an appeal. Instead of saying, as I normally did, 'Go on, Rebecca, eat it up ...', I thought I would appeal to her better nature. So for the first time I tried, 'Come on Rebecca – do it for Daddy.'

There was a moment's silence. The cereal was contemplated thoughtfully. Then, in Rebecca's best baby-speak, out came the words, 'For Daddy.' Like magic, in went the Rice Krispies. The appeal worked. I was amazed!

When we make an appeal, we're asking for a response. A response can be to someone or to something; whichever it is, we are asking that pure self-interest be set aside, and that the interest of the object of the appeal should take precedence.

Within the limits of our fallenness as creatures, we all learn from a very early age that pure self-interest can be set aside, and a response can be made to another or higher interest. The higher interest in this case being 'Do it for Daddy.'

It may be a homely illustration, but it can illustrate the basis and theology of Paul's plea. He appeals to a higher interest, he appeals 'by the mercies of God'.

What in practice is he asking for? What he wants is the

involvement of every member of the church. This is not to be on the basis of pleasing yourself, nor to please the Rector, Minister, or Elder; it should be to please God alone. As such, it is to be a *theological* or *spiritual* response – to the mercies of God.

'The mercies of God' is a revealing phrase. Why does Paul choose this particular expression? First, it is a summary response to all Paul has outlined in this letter.

Those who serve God with dedication deeply value their salvation through Christ. Yet it is equally obvious that those who have little concern for dedicated service have scant understanding of the value or cost of what Jesus has done for them.

For Christian service to have any lasting value, it has to be a response to the gracious, unmerited work of mercy exercised by God in salvation. If not it can hardly be termed service, it is something else. We can call it good works, charity – whatever we like – but it is not service.

'I appeal to you therefore, brethren, by the mercies of God.'

In that short sentence we see the manner of Paul's appeal and the weight of the words. We also see to whom those words are addressed, as well as the theology underlying them. With our increased perception of Paul's approach, we can now enter in more fully to the content of his appeal.

Paul's priorities

Get the attitude right

'I appeal to you ... to present your bodies ....'

This phrase means 'offer yourselves'. We have to get the attitude right if we want to involve people properly in the church.

It is no good cajoling people into service or entering into service ourselves as though we are doing someone a favour. We have to be willing to serve, and willing to offer ourselves.

We must be willing without wanting to add wrong kinds of preconditions.

I was impressed by someone I met coming in our front door one day; he had turned up to lend a hand when we were moving house. What he did was very ordinary, but it was his simple willingness that impressed me. As soon as he came in, he took off his jacket and just said, 'Here I am. What can I do?' That is the attitude for Christian service – being willing, available – offering yourself and being prepared to serve.

Sometimes we may not automatically feel we have that attitude. But if we let feelings come in second, we can work on the attitudes, even though we may not be overwhelmed with enthusiasm for a project. As human beings, we are always going to be battling with self-centredness – this is one of the reasons God has given us Christian service. It is a means of grace. It can help us overcome our natural inclination to please ourselves.

Attitudes can be worked on, but at some time decisions have to be made. Whatever excuses we may wish to make, we may have to decide to do the costly thing and offer ourselves to serve God.

Get the standard right

'I appeal to you therefore, brethren, by the mercies of God, to present your bodies as a living sacrifice.'

If Christian service is not sacrificial, it is not worth very much. This is why Paul chooses these words so carefully. He asks us to offer ourselves as *a living sacrifice.*

This means the standard must be right. Sacrifice is called for. If we are to serve God, we will have to make sacrifices of some kind or other. It is best to enter with eyes wide open. In the end, such sacrifice brings deep liberty. But to start with, you have to be clear about the standard of sacrifice.

Get the values right

> 'I appeal to you ... to present your bodies as a living sacrifice,
> holy and acceptable to God.'

Christian service always has a moral dimension – as well as a
practical one. Part of sacrificial service is sacrificial living. In
an important sense, it is a quest for holiness in order for our
lives to be properly consecrated to God.

These values matter in the spiritual realm. Holiness is
something to take seriously; but perspectives matter too. None
of us has to be a super-saint. What really matters is a willingness
to live to please God. As Paul says, this is what God finds
acceptable – the willingness counts.

There is no one who is not good enough to serve. If anyone
feels an under-achiever spiritually, we should not let that hold
us back from Christian service. It is not what we have achieved
so far which matters, but how dedicated we are prepared to be
for the future.

Get the heart right

> 'All this is your spiritual worship.'

Has it ever struck you that Christian service is in essence a
form of worship? We tend to limit the use of the word *worship*
exclusively to what we do in church on Sunday. But in the New
Testament, the idea of worship is broader by far.

What is spiritual worship? According to Paul it is an attitude
of the heart towards God. An attitude of worship is to want to
please him. In saying that, we have come full circle; we are
back to the idea of response to the mercies of God. Real worship
is a response of gratitude; and that response can take many forms.

If we want to worship God, we will serve him. We serve
him not only in our jobs, our studies, our homes, or our
communities, we will also serve him in some way in the church.

All Christians, from whatever background, need to get their thinking about worship straight. For it is no good singing hymns and choruses, engaging in liturgy, reading the Bible, praying, and thinking that in doing these things we are *worshipping God*. We have to serve God both inside and outside the church. That, according to Paul, is our true and spiritual worship.

In the end, this kind of worship proceeds from our hearts. It is a subtle but important balance, and makes the essential difference. We have to put the object of Christian service into perspective. It must be clear. *We are not serving the church, we are serving the Lord.* That balance matters, for unless we serve him with love, the service will be of doubtful spiritual value. By contrast, if we are concerned to worship God out of sheer devotion to him, what a real difference that will make!

The church is meant to be an every-member ministry, but lazy Christians have the effect of stifling the work of the Holy Spirit. Consequently the church becomes ineffective. The ministry of any church – and remember the church is designed to be an effective sign of the kingdom – will not become truly effective unless each of us plays our part, singly and together. That is why Paul appeals so passionately. The stakes are high. This is why we must not shirk the application. Will I get involved? Will I serve Christ from my heart? Will I help the church to pull together? It does matter, for the impact of the church, for the gospel and the kingdom depends on it.

Paul makes a passionate appeal for committed involvement. He desires that church and kingdom should be one in purpose. He wants every member to play their part: 'I appeal to you therefore, brethren, by the mercies of God, to present your bodies as a living sacrifice, holy and acceptable to God, which is your spiritual worship.'

Facing opposition

'Blessed are those who are persecuted for righteousness' sake, for theirs is the kingdom of heaven' (Matt. 5:10).

Jesus linked the experience of service with the fact of opposition. In a curious way, when opposition is encountered, it is a sure sign of true membership of the kingdom. If the King himself did not escape persecution, then neither will his subjects. That is a constant New Testament theme. Yet we Christians often become half-hearted in our service; we are often tempted to give up altogether. Why is that? Mainly because we have received inadequate preparation for the opposition which kingdom people inevitably meet if we set out to serve Christ in the world.

Paul's first letter to the Thessalonians offers insight into what it means to suffer opposition for the sake of the kingdom. In the first part of 1 Thessalonians 2, Paul's response to some of the issues of opposition clarifies what is to be the proper reaction of kingdom people to such apparent hurdles.

First, however, we need to sketch in some of the background to this situation; that will illuminate the particular forcefulness of Paul's radical approach.

At the time of writing, Thessalonica was the capital city of Macedonia, which in turn was a Roman province. Today, it is part of northern Greece, and Thessaloniki, as it is now known, is still a flourishing and important city. It is the government and administrative centre for that northern part of Greece and second only in importance to Athens itself.

1 Thessalonians was written around or just after AD 50. This was at about the time when Paul, along with Silas and Timothy, travelled on their second missionary journey. The church at Thessalonica was founded by them during that journey and precise background details are recorded by Luke in the first part of Acts chapter 17.

Paul experienced unusually forceful opposition at this time. In particular, there was tremendous antagonism from the Jews. The synagogue community did not like the new teaching of Paul and his friends. The vocal element within this Jewish group was intolerant of Paul's teaching in all its aspects – including what he said about the Messiah, about Jesus' sacrifice on the cross, and about his resurrection. They made trouble for Paul. Acts describes it vividly. 'The Jews were jealous; so they rounded up some bad characters from the marketplace, formed a mob and started a riot in the city' (Acts 17:5).

The Jews were so jealous of Paul and his preaching that they rounded up the local thugs, formed a mob and started a riot. On top of that, the Jewish opposition heaped the blame for the riot on Paul and the Christians, claiming dishonestly that Paul was proclaiming Jesus as a new king over Caesar.

Paul's mission to Thessalonica stimulated significant antagonism. The Jewish opposition was physically violent, intolerant and abusive. The Jews had stirred up mob violence in a big city, and the situation had bubbled up to boiling point. As a consequence, Paul and his companions did not stay long in Thessalonica. But the foundations they laid did take root, and the church began to grow very effectively in numbers and in quality. So what happened to that initial opposition?

The physical violence of opposition came to an end, but the intolerance and abuse did not. The new tactic of the opposition was to conduct a whispering campaign. This was a campaign against Paul himself, undermining his integrity and denying his message. It was designed to unsettle the allegiance of those who had given their lives to Jesus Christ through hearing Paul's message.

Public figures – from footballers and cricketers to pop stars and politicians often attract this kind of attack, and Christians are in no way immune. The mud-slinging at Thessalonica was clearly directed at the apostle Paul. It was as though the Macedonian press were filling their gossip columns with stories about him. Whatever form it took, it was a carefully orchestrated smear campaign. The whispers had grown into a roar of bitter character assassination. The aim? That was simple: they wanted to undermine Paul's message; they wanted to show up Paul's teaching as bogus – to prove him a fraud and a liar.

Our knowledge of the venomous attack that Paul faced in Thessalonica illuminates with force the truth behind Jesus' warning concerning opposition. No one is immune, all must be prepared. Paul's reaction to the vilification and attack he received can assist us today.

Motives and methods

1 Thessalonians 2:1-12 contains Paul's response to these accusations. He sets out his rebuttal of the whispering campaign which had been conducted against him. The reason Paul commits himself to print is because the campaign had unsettled the faith and witness of the Thessalonian Christians, and he wants to reassure them of his motives and his methods. They needed to be assured of the *validity* of the message they received and believed.

Paul's main concern is how to combat opposition. He mentions three responses to opposition and five elements of example setting when facing opposition. How then will all this apply to us?

We may not necessarily be public figures, but all devoted Christians will face some kind of opposition. The world around us has a different set of values. Our world has always disliked the purity and truth Christians stand for. Jesus made it clear from the outset kingdom people will always face opposition.

How should the kingdom people of God react when facing such conflict?

(1) Paul's courage in God

> For you yourselves know, brethren, that our visit to you was not in vain; but though we had already suffered and been shamefully treated at Philippi, as you know, we had courage in our God to declare to you the gospel of God in the face of great opposition (1 Thess. 2:1-2).

How do you react when the pressure mounts? Are you the kind of person who battles on? Or are you the person who wilts in the heat? We are all different: constitutionally, some of us do seem to sink under pressure while others of us seem to be natural survivors.

For Paul, it does not matter how we are constituted, whether we are naturally a winner or a loser; it is the difference made by being in Christ which matters. The issue is to have courage in God. The language Paul uses in the Greek text is illuminating. The word Paul uses for having courage in God is the Greek expression *parresiazomai*. It means a kind of boldness – based upon precedent and on lessons learnt from the past. Furthermore, it opens up an aspect of faith in an illuminating way.

When our eldest daughter, Rebecca, caught chickenpox at the age of two and a half, I had only recently recovered from it myself. She had observed my recovery with interest, and took it on herself to learn an important lesson from my experience. As parents we had not prompted her. During the time of her illness, when we or anyone asked Rebecca about her chickenpox and how she was feeling, she had one standard, confident reply: 'My spots will get better.' That is all she said. And she said it every single day for two weeks, whenever anybody asked her. She was right. They did get better!

Sometimes children are better at learning the basic lessons of life than adults. They learn quickly, and they remember. Spots get better. Rebecca's confidence was based upon the simple lesson she had learnt from seeing my own spots disappear. It gave her courage. If Daddy's great big spots could get better, then so could Becky's little ones.

Learning our lessons is the only really dependable basis for courage and boldness. We have to take hold of the lessons we have learnt in the past and apply them to the present. This applies especially in the spiritual realm.

Why did Paul have this courage and boldness in God? He had seen God prove his power so many times before. He had learnt the lessons of the past, and he applied those lessons to this present situation. This is why he could direct the Thessalonians back to the past, to think again about the outcome of his mission in Thessalonica.

Have they learnt the lesson? Paul says, 'Our visit to you was not in vain.' He directs their gaze backwards. There is the church, now steaming ahead. The mission was no failure. God did it. God does not fail. Because of the lessons he learnt in the past, his courage in God gave him boldness to declare the gospel in the face of opposition.

There is no strength for us in the present, unless we learn the spiritual lessons which God has taught us from our past. That is why Israel had its festivals. That is why we Christians have Christmas and Easter, baptism and the Lord's Supper. They help us to learn the lessons of the past. They are great reminders of the ways in which God has revealed his utter dependability to us. But there are other lessons, personal lessons, we also need to learn.

It is of such value to look back in a personal way and review what God has done for us. This was the constant practice of the psalmist. The backward gaze strengthens us to trust in someone who does not change – someone who can be trusted in all circumstances, even when the going becomes difficult.

Your lessons

What kind of lessons from the past do you need to learn about God? Are there lessons God has taught you, but which you have not really heeded? Is your memory getting short?

It does not matter what kind of person any of us may be naturally. Some sink under pressure; some are naturally fighters. What we really need to be is a *learner*. We need to learn objectively from what Jesus has done on the cross and through the resurrection, and we need to learn personally from what he has done in our own lives and the lives of others. Then we can have that kind of boldness, that courage in God, which will carry us through when the going becomes uphill and we are in the midst of opposition. If you have never faced opposition, be patient, it will come in some form or other. That is why we need to learn the lessons now. It is the basis of Paul's courage in God.

(2) Paul's confidence in his calling

> 'For our appeal does not spring from error or uncleanness, nor is it made with guile; but just as we have been approved by God to be entrusted with the gospel, so we speak' (1 Thess. 2:3-4).

Political debates, as we see them reported through the media, are not always worthy affairs. Different positions on issues are often out-matched by the strenuous efforts employed to undermine each other's arguments. In fact it is the classic method of confrontational politics – to undermine not only the arguments, but the character of the opponent.

Leaders of all parties are skilled at this. Demolish the man or woman first and the chances are you will bring their message into disrepute because you are undermining motives, competence or both. That, at least, is the theory.

Paul faced this kind of opposition. He came under fire, not only for his message, but as a person. The antagonized and outraged members of the synagogue tried to write him off.

His response? 'We speak as men approved by God' (1 Thess. 2:4). Paul had confidence in his calling.

Confidence in our calling makes all the difference. We should not be surprised that people see things differently to us. But when we face opposition, what is important is to remember our calling. Why? Because we belong to God for ever. We must remember that he has called us to the specific situation we are in at the moment. If Paul could face intolerable abuse and vilification at Thessalonica, yet still recognize his calling to be valid in that very place, so can we – wherever we are.

This means, wherever we are situated – no matter what the opposition – we are in the right place to do things for God: in an office where there is a manager who plays unfair; in a family where one member's behaviour – husband, wife, parent, brother or sister – has become a burden to us; in a flat where one of the people we share with is difficult – wherever we are, we are in the right place to do things for God, and to see these pressures as potential opportunities.

We can have confidence in our calling. Opposition, discomfort and difficult times all provide opportunities in which God can act, just as he acted through Paul in Thessalonica. His experience is an object-lesson for us. Look at what was achieved there in the face of opposition. When the going becomes a struggle there are the opportunities for God to act. It is *human* to feel the pressure; but it is *immature* to run away.

Paul's concern was to honour God, not man. 'So we speak, not to please men, but to please God who tests our hearts' (1 Thess. 2:4b).

One of the ways we set limits to our effectiveness as Christians is when we become too concerned about our reputations, when we worry too much about how we come over to others and how they see us. Our self-image becomes paramount, so we concentrate on the way our self-image governs what we let other people see of us. Much of our behaviour is constrained by how we like other people to see us and we work very hard at controlling their image of us.

Do you have a gap between how you see yourself – your self-image – and the way you want others to see you – the image you try to project to other people? This embraces a subtle fact about our human nature which we have to come to terms with if we want to be effective servants of Christ in this world.

We do not have to have skeletons in the cupboard, which we are trying to hide – though some do have those still-undealt-with issues lurking away in the background. But everyone has something to keep away from public view, something they do not like or which they find unacceptable about themselves. Unfortunately, that kind of attitude ends up eroding our effectiveness.

One problem is to do with the energy this concealment uses up. We can spend so much effort worrying about the way we come over to others, that we can make ourselves ineffective spiritually. Sometimes it is a failure to let the gospel go deep into our lives, a failure to see how deeply God loves us, how completely he accepts us, and how thoroughly he forgives us.

He will deal with our skeletons if we let him. And when we let him transform us, how powerfully that can work in our witness to others.

God wants us to be *transparent* people. There should be no difference between the outside and the inside. We should behave no differently in private than in public. Transparency is a wonderful Christian quality and a powerful Christian witness. Again it is all part of the church living up to its calling, and being a sign of the kingdom. How will people believe our message that Jesus Christ transforms lives, unless we ourselves are transformed? And that transformation has to become transparently visible for the kingdom to break through the sometimes cynical criticisms levelled against the church by the outside world concerning its integrity and vitality.

Of course, no one becomes an angel overnight. But I can think of Christian people who, because they have let the work of Christ go deep into their lives, appear to wear no mask at all. I think of three elderly sisters in their eighties. They are Christians of astonishing spiritual maturity, delightful people, prayerful, life affirming, passionate about Jesus and the gospel. These are lives where there is no gap between the private and the public. Nothing is hidden. The skeletons have been thrown out of the cupboard. These three wonderful ladies illustrate the importance of a life saturated in the truth of the gospel, in the Word of God, in prayer, and in the changing work of the Spirit. They would say they are not wonderful at all: it is simply by grace they have been saved.

This kind of transparency of character is not beyond any one of us. These dear Christian friends will be the first to recognise their failings. But such transparency flows from the desire to honour God, and not to be over-concerned for our personal reputation.

Do you know how all these inner conflicts and turmoil of ours can be dealt with? It is when we give up pandering to them. Do not let your self-image be the back-seat driver of your life: 'Do this. Do that. Go this way. Go that....' When we start putting God first and honouring him, we will overcome the stranglehold which our self image so powerfully exerts upon our life. Then there's the chance to become truly effective for God.

In Thessalonica, in a situation of potentially deep discouragement, Paul broke through – and his responses should spur us on too. We need, today, that same courage in God – and we need to be prepared to learn from the past. We need, today, that same confidence in our calling. We need, today, that same concern to honour God.

So often it is the uncomfortable situations which are opportunities for God to act. When we learn about courage, confidence and concern to honour God, then there will be consequences – consequences to do with the effectiveness of our ministry to others.

So, having outlined the three elements that go to make up a Christian response to opposition, Paul sets out five consequences concerning his example when facing opposition – consequences which involve the effectiveness of our ministry to others.

Paul's manner. 'We were gentle among you, like a nurse taking care of her children' (1 Thess. 2:7). Note the gentleness of manner, and the love it implies.

Paul's openness. 'Being affectionately desirous of you, we were ready to share with you not only the gospel of God but also our own selves, because you had become very dear to us' (1 Thess. 2:8). Note the openness of life. Paul was prepared to share himself as part of his ministry.

Paul's commitment. 'For you remember our labour and toil, brethren, we worked night and day ...' (1 Thess. 2:9). What can we learn from that quality of persistence and commitment? Is there something in you requiring more of an effort, a deeper dedication for God?

Paul's purity. 'You are witnesses, and God also, how holy, righteous and blameless was our behaviour to you believers' (1 Thess. 2:10). There is that transparency again. Who does not need to work on this? Purity and transparency are such important elements in our witness and communication to others.

Paul's goal. 'We exhorted each one of you and encouraged you and charged you, to lead a life worthy of God, who calls you into his own kingdom and glory' (1 Thess. 2:12). There is the vision – of lives lived to the glory of God and for the sake of the establishment of his kingdom. It is in fact the goal against which to measure any vision we have for living out the Christian life.

Learning the lessons

Opposition is the practical consequence of living a life dedicated to the kingdom of God. How do we face opposition?

By exercising courage in God.
By having confidence in God's calling.
By being concerned to honour God, and not men.

This is the way to respond when you are living in the face of opposition.

Opposition in some form or other is all around us. Opposition will either knock us out of the ring or will succeed in sharpening the effectiveness of our life and service. Christians today face tremendous pressures. It is when we are up against it that our standards are most likely to slip. That is the point of smear campaigns, character assassinations, and the quieter undermining of our confidence by stupid jokes, comments and insinuations.

Unfair treatment and opposition can take many forms. Paul spoke about the opposition he faced in Thessalonica because he wanted the Christians there to learn the same lessons he had learnt. And they are the same lessons we also must learn today.

We can and should have courage in God. It affects our boldness. We must learn the lessons of the past and, in particular, the personal lessons which God has taught us.

We can and should have confidence in our calling. We belong to God. Where we are is where God has led us to be. Until he moves us on, this is the place of opportunity and not somewhere else.

We can and should be concerned to honour God and not men. It is of first importance that we redirect the concerns of our lives spiritually towards God. How many of us waste valuable spiritual energy pandering to the commands and desires of our own self-image? Do you need to do some work on inner purity, self-acceptance and putting God first at the levels of your life where it really matters?

How can I best glorify and honour God in all that I do? If we make God our goal, then many of our inner struggles will simply slip into place. When we have set ourselves to glorify God, we can aim, like Paul, at these qualities: gentleness in our manner, openness in our lifestyle, commitment to God's work, and purity in our motives.

This is what Paul learnt in times of very tough opposition. It is for the tough times in whatever form they may take that we are in training in order to fulfil our calling as kingdom people.

The kingdom of God needs people who are courageous, confident and transparent in the service of God. We need not be discouraged, for none of us is born like this; but every one of us can change by the grace of God. That is the transforming work of Christ through the Spirit within us. It is the gospel. But our response and co-operation are required. We will change when we have, along with Paul, this goal above all: 'To lead a life worthy of God, who calls you into his own kingdom and glory' (1 Thess. 2:12).

Summary Points

■ The kingdom sums up all aspects of God's rule in the past, present and future dimensions of life. The church is the company of the redeemed; it comprises those who have drawn near to God, have made entry into this family and are ruled over by the King.

■ Paul appeals for a response to the mercies of God.

■ He asks for a right theology, standard, values and heart.

■ Like Paul we will face opposition if we respond to God in this way.

■ We are asked to embrace a similar courage, confidence and transparency, honouring God and not men.

■ We are to learn from Paul's manner, openness, commitment, purity and goal.

For Reflection

Corporately, as well as individually, God's people are to 'declare the wonderful deeds of him who called you out of darkness into his marvellous light.' In short, God's people are to be a sign of the kingdom (p.147).

In what ways are God's people to be a sign of the kingdom? Illustrate your answer by reference to 1 Peter 2:9.

The church is designed to be an every member ministry (p.149).
How far is this true of your church?
How could this ministry be shared more widely?
Should you be playing more of a part?
Should you be playing less of a part, so others can participate?

Are we spiritual isolationists, interested only in individual Christianity and willing only to be spectators? (p.151).

How true is this of you or your Christian friends?

How do you need to pray for those of whom this is true?

Why not pray for them now?

When opposition is encountered it is a sure sign of true membership of the kingdom. If the King himself did not escape persecution, then neither will his subjects (p.157).

Is someone you know suffering for their faith, at home, in school, at work?

What can you do to help or encourage them?

What do you know of Christians who suffer for their faith in other countries?

Try to obtain information from mission magazines, and monitoring organisations, so you can pray and support in some way.

There is no strength for us in the present, unless we learn the spiritual lessons which God has taught us from our past (p.161).

How can you review the big lessons God has taught you?

What lessons do you need to re-learn?

Can you share with other Christians lessons God has taught them in a practical way from his Word?

God wants us to be transparent people. There should be no difference between the outside and the inside (p.164).

What should this mean for you?

Chapter 9

KINGDOM RESPONSIBILITIES

'*You cannot serve both God and money*' (Luke 16:13).

When Jesus said it is impossible to serve both God and money, he explained it is like a servant who attempts to serve two masters. 'Either he will hate the one and love the other, or he will be devoted to the one and despise the other' (Luke 16:13). Jesus made these observations while speaking of the new era where the kingdom of God has moved from the realm of promise to the dawn of its fulfilment.

'The Law and the Prophets were proclaimed until John. Since that time, the good news of the kingdom of God is being preached, and everyone is forcing his way into it' (Luke 16:16). Jesus' words have a threefold meaning. He speaks of a new movement from God, initiated by John's announcement of the kingdom, which is growing in momentum as the kingdom is preached. He is aware of the political enthusiasms of Jewish activists and their desire for the overthrow of Roman rule, and the establishment of a kingdom of God *on earth*. And he is also aware that entering God's kingdom takes courage, faith and endurance, because of growing levels of opposition towards him and his followers.

Revolution and repentance

Mention the kingdom of God in the turbulent times in which Jesus lived, and the political temperature immediately rose. Revolution rather than repentance was the reflex thought among the passionately nationalistic first century Jews – living, as they did, under the cruel, oppressive ways of Caesar and Rome. The Zealots wished to force the issue. To bring in the rule of God, they leaned towards violent revolution. Jesus was as radical, but to a depth greater than any freedom fighter. It was only when Jesus spent those forty days teaching the disciples about the kingdom of God (Acts 1:3) that the full extent of the Jesus revolution became clear for them.

Throughout his public ministry, Jesus' teaching was radical and revolutionary, but in a quite different way. Jesus made a requirement of repentance. As Luke makes clear, Jesus said when the kingdom of God is preached, the good news requires a response every bit as determined and radical as that urged by the now notorious Zealot freedom fighters who sought to achieve their results by sheer force of arms.

Repentance, not political revolution, is the proper response to the kingdom. God requires a reworking of our life allegiances. When we take up privileges as kingdom people, we also take on responsibilities. Whatever was our attitude *before* becoming incorporated into God's eternal plan for the kingly rule of Christ, *now we are God's people* we must share the concerns of the King for the world. 'He has showed you, O man, what is good. And what does the LORD require of you? To act justly and to love mercy and to walk humbly with your God' (Mic. 6:8).

Whose property?

Allegiance involves security. Today the Western world knows only too well the pressure of materialism: it comes at us from advertising, TV and business. We are pressurized to find our security in material wealth at the expense of the spiritual dimensions and responsibilities of our lives. It is a tension shared not only with modern times. Jesus saw this issue as one which would eventually determine our true allegiance: 'You cannot serve both God and money.' Whose property are we? To whom do we belong? Where lies our true devotion? Luke points out that when Jesus said this, the Pharisees (who were lovers of money) scoffed at him, as would many also today.

In the affluent first world economies, as a goal for personal security, material wealth exerts a powerful hold. Yet we cannot escape the message of the prophets – privilege implies responsibility. This is clearly so in the grand plan of Jesus' kingdom teaching. Jesus taught the Pharisees by way of a parable – about an anonymous rich man and a poor man named Lazarus – thus indicating the crucial nature of kingdom responsibilities. This is a parable where the relationship between allegiance and security, and the exercise of responsibility is made plain for all who have ears to hear.

The parable of the rich man and Lazarus

> There was a rich man, who was clothed in purple and fine linen and who feasted sumptuously every day. And at his gate lay a poor man named Lazarus, full of sores, who desired to be fed with what fell from the rich man's table; moreover the dogs came and licked his sores (Luke 16:19-21).

(1) Two characters
We are told four main details about the rich man, three directly, and one later, by implication. The direct information concerns his financial standing, his taste for fashion and his gourmet-like enthusiasm for elaborate food. He was rich. He dressed himself in purple and fine linen. He feasted sumptuously every day.

We can imagine the kind of person. Perhaps the rich man owns substantial amounts of property in Beverly Hills or the West End of London. He buys his shirts from Jermyn Street or Fifth Avenue, his ties from Harrods or Bloomingdales, and his tailor visits him personally from Savile Row. He is a gourmet too. When he flies in by private jet to London, he takes breakfast at the Savoy Grill, has lunch at Simpsons in the Strand, tea at Claridges, and dinner at the Dorchester.

The second character is a poor man named Lazarus. He is described as lying outside the gate of the rich man's house. He is sick and covered in sores. All he can do is lie there, hoping for scraps thrown out with the garbage – whatever should fall 'from the rich man's table'. It is a terrible plight. He is undernourished, weak and sick. The poor man is powerless to help himself. His dignity degraded, even the stray dogs slobber over him and lick his sores. He has not the strength to stop them. That is the extent of Lazarus' misery and decline.

Paved with gold?
Today, many a large Western city has the same sad pictures of shattered humanity. When as a family we first moved to the West End of London, to live next door to the BT Telecom Tower, a few moments' walk from Oxford Street and Regent Street – two of the greatest shopping areas in the world – it came as a complete eye-opener for me.

I walked up Regent Street about midnight one bitterly cold January evening. At that point I had not realized the extent of poverty there is in London. In one shop entrance there was such an ugly contrast. The shop itself was brightly lit, selling shoes at a starting price of £250 a pair! By stark contrast in the doorway, huddled together in cardboard boxes, were three unshaven old men, wearing torn clothes and doing their best to sleep out there in the cold. I felt sick. I felt ashamed that I could think of nothing practical I could do to help them. There are people like Lazarus effectively just round the corner from where most of us live.

Two characters, the rich man and Lazarus. The one has all he wants. The other has nothing. What was that fourth detail about the rich man? It is implied when Jesus says Lazarus lay outside the gate. The word used for gate means portico – like the entrance to a palace or a city. This implies the rich man's house was huge. Lazarus was placed by the main entrance. The rich man could not have missed him. From what the story implies, he did nothing. Lazarus lay there day after day – no action was taken.

That scene provides a clue to the meaning of this parable. It is not a condemnation of wealth or riches as such. The scriptures provide *warnings* to the rich – 'Better a poor man whose walk is blameless than a rich man whose ways are perverse' (Prov.

28:6). The scriptures also provide *counsel* to the rich. 'Command those who are rich in this present world not to be arrogant nor to put their hope in wealth, which is so uncertain, but to put their hope in God, who richly provides us with everything for our enjoyment. Command them to do good, to be rich in good deeds, and to be generous and willing to share' (1 Tim. 6:17-18).

The scriptures do not condemn riches outright. God's Word is more concerned as to how we *use* the wealth we have been entrusted with. This is an issue of kingdom responsibilities, which we will explore in more detail. For the while, Jesus places before us two characters, a rich man and a poor man.

(2) Two destinations

> The poor man died and was carried by the angels to Abraham's bosom. The rich man also died and was buried; and in Hades, being in torment, he lifted up his eyes, and saw Abraham far off and Lazarus in his bosom (Luke 16:22-23).

Everyone is going somewhere. Each life has a destination. We not only have to come to terms with our own mortality, but also to realize our lives have a destination beyond death. Jesus is unambiguous. The right question to ask is not, '*Is* there life after death?' But, 'What *kind of life* is there after death?'

So, what are the options? Jesus' unambiguous answer in this parable is that there are two kinds of life after death – heaven and hell. The decision and actions of the present, and our personal response to Jesus, determine which destination we will arrive at in the future. What characterizes our lives deep down? What is our true security? Where is our true allegiance? What determines our future in God's hands? There are two possible destinations.

Destination one

> The poor man died and was carried by the angels to Abraham's bosom.

Yes, it's sad he died, but for this poor man, his death marks a reversal in fortunes. The angels carry him to Abraham's bosom. The language here, about angels and the patriarch's bosom, may sound unfamiliar to us. The angels speak of the caring activity of God. The Lord lovingly brings this poor man to the place of rest, refreshment and joy. It is a typical Jewish way of speaking about heaven. The metaphor about Abraham's bosom may indicate close fellowship with Abraham at the Messianic Banquet (cf. John 13:23: 'the disciple whom Jesus loved, was reclining next to him'; Revelation 19:9: 'Blessed are those who are invited to the wedding supper of the Lamb'; Revelation 19:17: 'Come, gather together for the great supper of God').

The poor man's fortunes were reversed. But as the story progresses it becomes clear that the rich man was taken to a place where he truly belonged.

Destination two

> The rich man also died and was buried; and in Hades, being in torment, he lifted up his eyes, and saw Abraham far off and Lazarus in his bosom (Luke 16:22-23).

The rich man went from riches to rags. He was in a place of torment. The rich man was separated from God.

Hades means the place of the dead. As the parable develops, it is clearly implied that this is a permanent separation of the rich man from God. It is a tragedy of the rich man's own making. There are clearly two destinations.

An important question raised by this and scriptures on a similar theme is, how can a loving God send anyone to hell? It is raised because such a situation sounds like a contradiction in terms.

The Bible's response is that a loving God does not actually send anyone to hell. If anyone ends up in hell it has everything to do with their own decision. The biblical understanding of hell is one of eternal separation from the presence and person of God, and it is, therefore, a place of absolute torment and an awesome prospect.

If we shut God out of our lives now, making the decision that we do not want anything to do with him and his ways; if we refuse the offer from Jesus of a brand new life to know and serve God as the real basis of what we are meant to be as human beings; if we say 'no' to God now – why should we expect anything to change when we die?

Doomsday

Nine hundred years ago, William the Conqueror, King of England and Duke of Normandy, sent out commissioners to survey the country he had taken by force some twenty years before. Information about the people of England and their landholdings was collected and collated in volumes amounting to some two million words. It was a record of immense value and authority throughout the period of the Middle Ages. Within ninety years of its compilation it had acquired the nickname 'Doomsday', meaning the record was fixed. It was a true and faithful picture of the facts; and like the book of life itself, from which its popular name was derived, there was no appeal against it.

'And I saw the dead, great and small, standing before God, and books were opened. Also another book was opened, which is the book of life. And the dead were judged by what was written in the books, by what they had done' (Rev. 20:12). There will be a day of judgement, a day when the full reality of our lives will be completely revealed and thoroughly cross-examined – to see precisely where we have stood in relationship to God and the responsibilities of his kingdom.

If God is shut out now, he will be shut out then. God underwrites and underscores our decision. He allows us to take the decision to be for him or against him, though he does long that we should not ruin ourselves. 'For I take no pleasure in the death of anyone, declares the Sovereign LORD. Repent and live!' (Ezek. 18:32).

This is why the Lord sent Jesus to die as a substitute, to enable the kingdom, the rule of God, to become a living reality. The measure of God's concern for us is Jesus' sacrifice on the cross to offer us the possibility of heaven. It is one of the prime reasons Jesus himself tells this parable.

Jesus offers forgiveness and a new start to those who are prepared to follow him and his teaching. But we all have to beware of complacency. Such complacency badly rebounded on the rich man.

(3) Two conversations

There are two conversations, or rather two parts to the conversation. The first part of the conversation is between the rich man and Abraham. As the rich man speaks, he reveals his unchanged character: 'He called out, "Father Abraham, have mercy upon me, and send Lazarus to dip the end of his finger in water and cool my tongue; for I am in anguish in this flame"' (Luke 16:24).

The unchanged character of the rich man is obvious: 'Send Lazarus. You tell Lazarus to get up off his backside and do something useful for a change. I am parched to death down here. You remember, Lazarus used to sun himself all day in front of my house. My house! You tell him he's got a debt or two to repay me. You send him along. Send Lazarus.'

The rich man reveals his unchanged character. As Abraham replies, he reveals God's unchanged decision: 'Son, remember that you in your lifetime received your good things, and Lazarus in like manner evil things; but now he is comforted here, and you are in anguish. And besides all this, between us and you a great chasm has been fixed, in order that those who would pass from here to you may not be able, and none may cross from there to us' (Luke 16:25-26).

God's decision is unchanged. The rich man squandered his

opportunities. In his lifetime he received good things, but there is not a shred of evidence of anything but self-centredness in his character. Though the opportunity to help someone was laid at his very gate, he did not lift a finger to help.

The rich man's character has not changed. That is why God's decision is unchanged. Unless we take seriously the Lord's call to repentance, we remain locked in selfishness. We are not necessarily as selfish as this rich man – this is an extreme example to make the point. But we are selfish enough to insist on our own way, keeping God and his claims at a distance, rejecting his final say in our affairs.

If we are like that, we will hate heaven. Heaven is a place where God comes first, others second, and self last. It would be like asking a teetotaller to spend the rest of his life in a brewery. It would be the very reversal of all we stood for.

To change the picture, to get into heaven with our hearts unchanged by God would be like the day you had brand new carpets fitted at home. There they were, plain pink, unpatterned. Just what you've always wanted. But it's a filthy rainy day. The children, grandchildren, your nieces or nephews are playing in the garden. The grass is sodden, sticky, sludgy mud. The carpet man left only a few minutes before. There you are, admiring the deep pile pink, when suddenly in run four muddy booted children. With sudden, acutely mounting anxiety, you exclaim at the top of your voice, 'Change your shoes!' But it's too late. Little dinky boot marks, etched in mud all over your beautiful carpet. It's ruined.

That's what it would be like if God let us into heaven without changing us first. We would ruin it. Our muddy boot marks would be all over the place. Soon heaven would be indistinguishable from hell. That's what would happen if evil and sin is allowed in unchecked. 'If we are going to live in heaven, we have to be naturalized or else we die,' said the novelist, and contemporary of C. S. Lewis, Charles Williams. That is why there has to be a judgement. A sorting out. A separation of the sheep and the goats.

Jesus says that in the life beyond there is a great chasm fixed between those who receive Jesus' gift of new life, through repentance and faith, and those who insist on going their own way. The time of opportunity is now: there is no going back, for then fortunes will be reversed. For some the reversal will be from riches to rags. It is topsy-turvy teaching, turning the accepted values of life on their head.

The parable has a chilling end which carries a clear warning. Some people can put off their decision in these things one day too many.

The rich man's character and decision remained unchanged. The second conversation revolves around the rich man's appeal for an easier way, an assured future.

The rich man asks that Lazarus should be sent along to warn his family, his five brothers, of the miseries in store if they do not mend their ways ... 'Come on, Abraham. Can't you make it easier for them? Get old Lazarus to get out there and tell them.' To which Abraham replies, 'They have Moses and the prophets; let them hear them.' They have the Bible's message. God has sent prophets from Moses onwards. He has sent his Son Jesus Christ. These are the ones they should listen to for they have the complete message of God. There is nothing for Lazarus to add. 'Now look here, Abraham, if someone were to rise from the dead, surely then they will get their lives sorted out.'

So here comes the irony. 'If they do not hear Moses and the prophets, neither will they be convinced if someone should rise from the dead. If they are not prepared to take account of the Bible's message, then they are hardly going to be impressed by the resurrection, are they?'

'You make it so hard, Abraham.'

'What's hard is your heart.'

Which is hard, the way of God or the heart of man? The parable of the rich man and Lazarus reveals two characters with two very different destinations. Their fortunes are reversed, as these two conversations show. The implication of this story is not that we can earn our way into heaven by our good deeds – it is far from saying that. The rich man was clearly nothing more than a nominal believer. He referred to Abraham as Father, showing his Jewish background, but that is all there was.

There was nothing in his life to show either that he had listened responsively to the Bible's message of new life for those who humble themselves before God or that he had taken into account the prophet's teaching about the manner of life appropriate to the people of God.

Who is the rich man today?

Undoubtedly, in our affluent society, the rich man is you and I. In the West most of us are rich in a variety of ways: rich in opportunity, education, ability, and financially. This is certainly so when judged by the standards of some people on the edge of life in our cities and towns, and most definitely by comparison with the poor nations of the world.

As we have seen, Jesus' parable is not condemnation of wealth, but it does raise, among other things, the question of what we should do with our wealth. It revolves around what is the basis of our personal security.

Four questions

The message of God

Have you taken, and are you taking, practical account of God's message? James tells us to be 'doers of the word, and not hearers only' (Jas. 1:22). We can deceive ourselves into thinking we are acting rightly while ignoring what God is saying through his Word. Is God still waiting for you to respond to his message?

The grand plan of the kingdom cuts to the heart of our human responsibilities. Through the prophets God has spoken unequivocally about his abhorrence of injustice, poverty and the structural sin which gives rise to it. As the eighth-century prophet Amos makes clear, our responsibilities extend beyond the borders of home, society and nation. We are to reach out to anywhere where there is injustice, and act with the passion of God.

Responsibility to God

Are you taking the opportunities to exercise social responsibility to God's glory? Moses and the prophets are full of God's concern for the poor, the sick, the underprivileged. Is there something on your own doorstep that you can do to help someone in need, perhaps by visiting the sick or elderly, or by doing something concrete in the way of practical help? The exercise of social responsibility in the name of Christ is, according to this parable, to the glory of God. To neglect this is to betray the kingdom.

Money

Are you spending your money in the interests of God? Are you giving to his work? Relatively speaking, most of us are rich. We have enough to be able to give something to the poor, as well as to the ongoing work of God for his kingdom. The biblical starting point for Christian giving is the tithe, 10% of our pre-tax income. There is no fixed rule, as our response is a matter of generosity from the abundance God has given us, remembering and believing that the Lord supplies all our needs.

To the rich Corinthians, the apostle Paul held up the Macedonian Christians. 'Out of the most severe trial, their overflowing joy and their extreme poverty welled up in rich generosity. For I testify that they gave as much as they were able, and even beyond their ability. Entirely on their own....' (2 Cor. 8:2-3). This is the New Testament standard: to give as much as you are able even beyond your ability. It is a response to the generosity of Jesus Christ. 'For you know the grace of our Lord Jesus Christ, that though he was rich, yet for your sakes he became poor, so that you through his poverty might become rich' (2 Cor. 8:9).

Giving helps our deep down security to get properly anchored, and it serves the interests of God. So which is more radical – revolution or repentance? To change the economic system by force, or to redirect the wealth of nations by a revolution of love, concern and action towards the poor? Surely the latter is the truly radical.

Talents

Are you using your talents, your gifts, in the service of God? We are all rich in various abilities. As we have already learnt, God means each of us to have some form of ministry. Do you view your life as given in the service of Christ? Kingdom people have kingdom concerns to which to respond. We are the body of Christ. He has no other arms but our arms, and no other hands than ours.

This completes our survey of the two characters, two destinations and two conversations. They highlight important and vital issues for today. For a while, there were clear opportunities for this privileged character in Jesus' parable. It seems from those conversations that the rich man had every chance to take account of God's message and to exercise his divinely-charged social responsibility. He could have spent his money in the interests of God and used his talents in the service of God. Instead, the rich man put off that opportunity.

Opportunity will not last for ever. There came a moment for the rich man when opportunity came to an end, and it was all too late.

Living for the kingdom

The message is unambiguous. We must not shirk our opportunities. There comes a point in the life of every dedicated follower of Jesus when the pressures of existence, temptations to compromise, and questions of how to live rightly for God become issues requiring definite guidelines for kingdom life. Jesus not only clarified the basic issues of security and allegiance to God; he also highlighted the exercise of kingdom responsibilities.

Right living depends on a right relationship

'If you love me, you will keep my commandments' (John 14:15).

Jesus reiterates that remark twice more but in different ways in John 14: 'He who has my commandments and keeps them, he it is who loves me' (v.21); and 'If a man loves me, he will keep my word' (v.23).

Right living depends on a right relationship to Jesus himself – and above all is characterized by love.

Every father or mother knows that they do not respond to children out of duty, they respond with devotion, even sacrifice. Because of their love they want to please their children, be involved in their concerns and interests, sharing in their life together.

This is Jesus' point – if we love him we will respond to him, share our lives with him, and take regular account of his interests and concerns for us. In a word, we will keep his commandments.

What does loving Jesus mean?

When you read and understand Jesus' teaching in the Gospels, see him as a man and perceive what he stands for, then your reaction is likely to be one of growing admiration and esteem. When you take the further step of recognizing that when Jesus died, he died for you – that he went through agony for you – then you become increasingly grateful for what he has done for you and what he means to you. Such admiration and gratitude grow eventually into love for Jesus.

Jesus' highest concern is for the way we live as his followers. If we have not entered into this relationship with Jesus, we will not be concerned to respond in love to him. His strength and power will be denied us. This is the first direction. Right living depends on a right relationship with Jesus.

A right relationship implies an obedient lifestyle

'If you love me, you will keep my commandments' (John 14:15).

Jesus is saying, 'If you admire me, are genuinely grateful to me, if in fact you love me, then why do you not do what I want you to do?'

Obedience is a less popular word these days, perhaps because it is associated with uncaring authority – or if not uncaring, then ill-informed authority. I heard of a piano teacher who, every time her pupil played a wrong note, took a ruler and rapped the pupil over the knuckles – poor educational practice, but not unknown.

None of us likes the kind of authority which raps us over the knuckles, and we do not care to be obedient to it. Jesus and his authority is quite different. His is the *ultimate* authority in the universe, yet he rules by love, and by deep understanding of our needs.

The fact is, we still rebel against his authority. Why is that? The Bible's answer is that being fallen creatures, we would rather please ourselves. We would rather follow our natural inclinations than please anyone else, including God. Unless two things happen: (a) Jesus himself comes into our life, and (b) conversion is matched by our willingness to follow and obey him.

Here are two contrasting illustrations. The first concerns a girl who asked to come to see a Christian counsellor. She wanted to discuss feelings of guilt from which she was suffering. She was a pleasant, intelligent Christian girl who had been to university, and had a responsible job. After some discussion of the background to these feelings, it emerged she was having a physical relationship with her boyfriend.

The Christian counsellor sensitively pointed out there might be a connection between the two; between behaviour which she knew as a Christian was inappropriate, and her guilt feelings. She agreed. Yet her agenda was simply to remove the guilt feelings not to change her behaviour. In the end she admitted she wanted to please herself. There was little else the counsellor could do for her.

The second illustration involves a different situation and outcome. This middle-aged man was distressed about the tensions in his marriage. He seemed constantly to explode with anger against his wife and children. In the end he was very much helped by Jesus' words: 'If you love me, you will keep my commandments.'

This man worked on his anger and was prepared to change. He disciplined himself in the things he said, and the way he said them. In the meetings with the counsellor he spoke several times of his desire to obey Jesus' commandments and put them into practice. It was such a help to him to discover that obedience is the way to liberty. Today his marriage is restored and the family are going from strength to strength as Christians.

All Christians have to learn to obey. It is helpful to realize there is something within us impeding our progress, asserting often our self-will and independency. The way of liberty is to take seriously and obey the teaching of Jesus. It does not come easily, but it is necessary. This is why it is so important to be exposed day by day to the teaching of Scripture.

Do you read and take to heart part of the Bible every day? You cannot keep Jesus' commandments if you do not know them. You make yourself unnecessarily weak for the Christian life if you neglect Scripture. It is a provision of God for us. A right relationship implies obedience of lifestyle.

Obedience releases the power of God – through the Holy Spirit
It is not surprising to learn that verse 16 of John 14 follows verse 15! But that order is highly significant. Taken together those two verses introduce a strengthening perspective, for God's power comes to us in the context of our obedience: 'If you love me, you will keep my commandments. And I will pray the Father, and he will give you another Counsellor, to be with you for ever' (John 14:15-16).

Have you ever felt a sense of failure and powerlessness? Have you asked God for power to change, yet found yourself back at square one with your same old failures? Have you found yourself without strength to do anything about it? Then here is help from Jesus for you.

God's power comes to us in the context of willing hearts and obedient ways. To those who love him, and obey his commandments, Jesus promises the help of the Holy Spirit. Notice the order of events. When we obey, then we will know his power. Not the other way round. That order is crucial. Some people pray: 'Lord, I am so weak in this particular area. Please give me power, Lord, and strengthen me to overcome.' In a way it is a legitimate prayer. But Jesus says, 'Be obedient, – *then* I'll give you strength and power.' We have to co-operate.

So our prayer now can be, 'Lord, I promise that today I'm going to do something about this. Please strengthen me with your Spirit as I co-operate with you by my obedience.' It is not the form of words that matters, it is the understanding of God's priorities. This makes all the difference. God's power comes to us in the context of our obedience to him.

Four descriptions of the Holy Spirit

In John 14, in the context of dedicated living, Jesus gives four different descriptions of the Holy Spirit.

In verse 16 the Spirit is described as the Counsellor. The Greek word *parakletos* is even better translated as a companion, one who comes alongside us. He is to us as a friend.

In verse 17 he is the Spirit of truth. The Holy Spirit is the revealer of truth. So naturally the Spirit will help us at the point where we desire to put God's truth into action.

In verse 18 Jesus says: 'I will come to you.' In the context, Jesus is not referring to his second coming but is saying that the Spirit who is to come will be the Spirit of none other than Jesus himself.

And in verse 23, to be even more explicit, Jesus says, 'We will come to you.' That is the Father and Jesus. The Holy Spirit is in very reality the Spirit of God.

Put that teaching together, and what do we have?

The Holy Spirit is alongside us as our companion and friend
Where we go, he goes. In our joys, he is there; in our sorrows, he is there. He is there alongside us in our work. He is there as we search for a new job. He is there when temptation strikes, or when human strength fails. In the deepest sense, he is our companion. He is there to help us face the challenges life brings.

He is there in the hospital ward. He is there when we die. He is our companion.

The Holy Spirit is the Spirit of truth

This means he is uniquely able to guide us in the ways of God, which for most of us, at least sometimes, can involve struggle. He knows the Maker's instructions inside out and backwards. He wrote them. There is no one better to keep us up and running. He is the Spirit of truth.

The Holy Spirit is the Spirit of Jesus

When Jesus says, 'I will come to you,' it means that, because he is the Spirit of Jesus, the Holy Spirit understands our weakness, sensitivity and frailty. Jesus shared our human experience for thirty-three years. He understands the struggles, both yours and mine. 'For we do not have a high priest who is unable to sympathize with our weaknesses, but we have one who has been tempted in every way, just as we are – yet was without sin' (Heb. 4:15). We are speaking of the God who has total inside working knowledge of the conditions we work under as human beings.

The Holy Spirit is the Spirit of power

Jesus emphasizes this in verse 23, when he says the Father and the Son will come to the one who loves and obeys Jesus and his word.

What kind of power has the Father demonstrated? His power is demonstrated in creation – the Father made all things. What kind of power has Jesus demonstrated? His power is demonstrated in redemption. What does the Holy Spirit bequeath to us? He applies to our lives what in his love God the Father has accomplished through his Son. So now there is no condemnation for those who belong to Christ Jesus. 'The power of the life-giving Spirit has freed you through Christ Jesus from the power of sin that leads to death' (Rom. 8:2, New Living Translation).

This is what we mean when we speak of *almighty* God. The Father and Jesus will come in the power of the Spirit to the one who obeys Jesus' teaching. There is and can be no greater power available to us in the whole universe.

Obedience releases the power of God through the Holy Spirit
Have you ever felt unable to find strength to overcome the issues before you? There is the daily challenge to live in a way that is honouring and committed to Jesus Christ. It involves our thoughts, aspirations and goals; what we say and how we say it; our actions and activities; the way we use our money – in fact our whole Christian service.

What does Jesus say to us today on this matter?

Right living depends on a right relationship to Jesus. A right relationship implies obedience in our lifestyle. Obedience itself releases the power of God through the Holy Spirit. According to Jesus' teaching, there is an order: love, obedience and power. If, from love for Jesus Christ, we respond with obedience in the issues which challenge our over-comfortable lives – even though this may be a struggle for us – God will respond with the strengthening might of his Holy Spirit.

Where is God challenging you to obedience and to generosity toward others? 'I command you to be open-handed toward your brothers and toward the poor and needy in your land' (Deut. 15:11).

A kingdom without a king?
Over the years there has been some theological blurring of the edges over the relationship of social action to the kingdom of God. From a biblical perspective this is what has to be borne in mind: the kingdom is a community ruled over by a King. King and subjects belong together. Therefore if Christ the King is not present through his people, acts of mercy, however valuable, cannot be called kingdom acts, for a kingdom without a King runs counter to the biblical witness. All great qualities of human kindness reflect something of the image of God. Such qualities

are common to all. Yet the unredeemed cannot do the work of God, however worthwhile their work may be – it is different in kind. Nonetheless, the charitable actions of the general community provide a challenge. How much more should followers of Christ be concerned for the responsibilities of the kingdom, and the passionate concerns of the King himself?

This implies a need for repentance from the self-satisfied ways of a largely middle-class culture, which spells anything but freedom for large numbers who for reasons beyond their power are the alienated in our society and world. Where such changes happen in the heart, at the level of energy and motivation, then the Lord can exercise true transforming power through his people.

The message of Jesus for those who would embrace kingdom responsibilities is repentance within, not revolution without. The inner attitudes must change, if the wrongs are to be righted. Privilege equals responsibility in a world where God desires his reign to spread with healing grace to all mankind. There will come a day when the opportunity to help will come to an end. But, for the present, there remains only one question over which Jesus the King requires our response. *Will we be obedient?*

Summary Points

■ Jesus made a requirement of repentance.

■ The parable of the rich man and Lazarus illustrates the nature of kingdom responsibilities.

■ Such responsibilities include our use of money, talents and opportunities.

■ A right relationship to Jesus implies obedience of heart and life.

■ Obedience is enabled by the Holy Spirit.

■ For the kingdom to be present in social care and action, the work has to be done by Christians, subjects of the King.

For Reflection

Discuss the following example in relation to what you have learnt about the distinguishing marks of the kingdom.

Suppose some worthwhile social work was proposed among single mothers. The proposal was that work would be funded by local Christians, perhaps a group of churches. But the workers were all to be non-Christians. However valuable, could this work be described as kingdom work (or even Christian work)? What priority should it have on your or your church's giving and why?

The scriptures provide warnings to the rich (p.174).

'Better a poor man whose walk is blameless than a rich man whose ways are perverse' (Prov. 28:6).

Avoiding the more gross examples of dishonesty, given that most of us are rich in comparison with the truly poor, what kind of subtle elements of perversity do you need to be warned of? Can you think of scriptures which give insight into this?

The scriptures provide counsel to the rich (p.175).

> 'Command those who are rich in this present world not to be arrogant nor to put their hope in wealth, which is so uncertain, but to put their hope in God, who richly provides us with everything for our enjoyment. Command them to do good, to be rich in good deeds, and to be generous and willing to share' (1 Tim. 6:17-18).

What does Paul mean, in relation to the security of wealth, 'not to be arrogant'?

In what way does Paul suggest the rich can put their hope in God?

What difference can this make to you?

Why does Paul use this strong expression: 'Command them to do good.' Why does he not just say 'encourage them'?

Meditate prayerfully on these key phrases:

- *put your hope in God*
- *be rich in good deeds*
- *be generous*
- *be willing to share*

Chapter 10

KINGDOM EXPECTATIONS

'Unless I go away, the Counsellor will not come to you;
but if I go, I will send him to you' (John 16:7).

In John chapter 16, Jesus speaks more comprehensively about the work of the Holy Spirit than in any other passage in the Gospels. This teaching encourages a clear perspective on the rule of God now and right expectations of the powers of the new age to come. How important this is for those committed to overcoming the dangers and discouragements of an era so often openly hostile to Jesus and fundamentally opposed to the will and rule of God.

Opposition and discouragement

The world of heartache is common to all. Christians have no immunity. Broken relationships, illness, bereavement, unemployment and other struggles are experienced by all, regardless of allegiance to Christ. Yet followers of Christ may face *additional* pressures. There may be opposition when standing up for kingdom values; discouragement when seeking to follow Jesus in a particular situation; even scorn when wanting to be an effective witness to family and friends, or colleagues.

Yet Jesus tells the disciples, 'God blesses you when you are mocked and persecuted and lied about because you are my followers. Be happy about it! Be very glad! For a great reward awaits you in heaven. And remember, the ancient prophets were persecuted, too' (Matt. 5:11-12).

So, clearly, we have to live with opposition and discouragement. The question is: How are we to face it? How can we cope with it day by day? What should be our expectations of the kingdom, and its power to overcome? This discouraging

situation is what Jesus anticipates when he speaks to the disciples
in John 16 about the Holy Spirit. The underlying truth is this:
God will always be bigger and more powerful than any human
situation of opposition and discouragement, however bitter or
vast that problem may seem to be.

Preventing breakdown

Jesus is concerned for the disciples' response to opposition and
discouragement: 'I have said all this to you to keep you from
falling away' (John 16:1).

From John 15:18 onwards, Jesus has been speaking to the
disciples of the inevitability of persecution; they will have to
face persecution in the immediate days ahead. When Jesus said
these words, he had just begun to speak to them of the promise
of the Holy Spirit. He describes him in John 15:26 as the
Counsellor, the Spirit of truth. Jesus' words in John 16:1 are
built on all this. The coming of persecution and the coming of
the Spirit are spoken of in the same breath. They are the pivot
of the whole passage, and we have to keep the two together.

The New English Bible puts Jesus' words in this striking
way: 'I have told you all this to guard you against the breakdown
of your faith.' According to Jesus, this is the way to prevent spiritual
breakdown, to guard against folding-up spiritually. None of us
is immune and all of us are vulnerable. But Jesus' teaching is
realistic, and contains two elements that are to be held together.
They form the overall balance and emphasis in Jesus' kingdom
expectations for living in the present world order.

Persecution, opposition and discouragement are all real. In
some shape or form, they will come to each of us. We must
expect them, face them, and not run away from them. That is
spiritual realism.

God the Holy Spirit is more powerful than any human or
devilish opposition. His work continues triumphant even when
from our human perspective the outlook looks bleak. The
Counsellor, the Holy Spirit, is not lacking in wisdom or power.
That, equally, is spiritual realism.

Four dynamics of the Spirit

The promise of the Counsellor

> I did not say these things to you from the beginning, because I was with you. But now I am going to him who sent me; yet none of you asks me, "Where are you going?" But because I have said these things to you, sorrow has filled your hearts. Nevertheless I tell you the truth: it is to your advantage that I go away, for if I do not go away, the Counsellor will not come to you; but if I go, I will send him to you (John 16:4-7).

Jesus mentions such facts because he is returning to the Father. It sounds spiritual – in practice it will mean Jesus will be forcibly arrested and put to death. The consequence is the disciples will be left to manage on their own – without Jesus' personal support. From his words, it appears the disciples are overwhelmed with sorrow. They love Jesus – they do not want him to go. Because of the hostility they have experienced they may be anxious about how they will manage without him.

Jesus' comment is extraordinary. 'I tell you the truth: it is to your *advantage* that I go away.' In what possible sense could Jesus going away be advantageous?

By dying on the cross and taking on to himself the penalty of the sin in our lives, Jesus is able to bring us alive spiritually. When we come into that relationship with him, the Holy Spirit comes immediately into our personalities. He strengthens and guides us. He starts working from inside us, rebuilding us as kingdom people, committed to God's service.

Unless we have received Jesus' forgiveness and turned away from wrong ways, the Holy Spirit will not be able to come to us; he is unable to come because, deep down, we are still antagonistic to God. That is the state of any person not committed to Christ. This is why Jesus says he has to go away; he has to die to make it possible to deal decisively with our basic antagonism to God.

Winning friends and influencing people

It is arguable that during his human life on earth Jesus' deeper influence is only measurable in hundreds, certainly not in many thousands. In the end only a handful of committed disciples remained. It was ultimately to their advantage that he went away. The coming of the Holy Spirit not only transformed their lives, but as a consequence of their testimony Jesus has found his way into the hearts of countless millions of lives all the way down the centuries. His cross is the way of forgiveness, and his Spirit is the way of strength and power for living for him in this world; it enables us to face any hurdle or issue which confronts our lives.

'It is to your advantage that I go away, for if I do not go away, the Counsellor will not come to you; but if I go, I will send him to you.' *Parakletos*, the Greek word translated *counsellor*, means a friend, companion, one who comes alongside us. What is the word-picture Jesus is using? It is a simple one. Where we go, he goes – right into the situation where it is tough, where there is opposition, where there is discouragement. 'I will send him to you.'

The ministry of the Counsellor

'And when he comes, he will convince the world concerning sin and righteousness and judgment: concerning sin, because they do not believe in me; concerning righteousness, because I go to the Father, and you will see me no more; concerning judgment, because the ruler of this world is judged' (John 16:8-11).

The first aspect of the Holy Spirit's ministry, according to Jesus, is to convict of sin. The word translated 'convict' is the Greek word *elencho*. It is the word used in the ancient Greek-speaking world to describe cross-examination in a law court, when someone is on trial. When someone who is guilty is cross-examined, one of two things can happen. If that person puts in a plea of not guilty, either the cross-examination can convict him outright of the wrong things he has done, or it can convince him of the weight of the evidence against him and the weakness of his own case. The result being a change of plea – from not guilty to guilty. *Elencho* has this double meaning of convict as well as convince.

The power of conviction

Billy McIlwaine from Northern Ireland was for many years a vicious terrorist who hated Roman Catholics. He believed the only good Catholics were dead Catholics.

In a Channel 4 interview on British television, he described how, with his marriage practically in ruins, and wanted by the police, he was regularly consuming three bottles of whisky a day. He lay in a hospital bed, with his cirrhosis of the liver so advanced that the consultant told his family he would be lucky to live even a few weeks. Billy McIlwaine said that facing death, he experienced one of those rare moments – his whole life flashed before him. He realized for the first time how bad his life had been. This bitter, hardened terrorist was convinced about his sin.

Dying in his hospital bed in Northern Ireland, Billy McIlwaine cried to God for forgiveness. And he prayed: 'Lord, if there is room in your heart to forgive someone as foul as I am, then I'll dedicate whatever life I have left to serving you, by loving those I have only sought to hate, despise and destroy.'[1]

He lived and went on to be a changed man, and gave his energies to Soldiers of the Cross, working for reconciliation between Protestants and Catholics in Northern Ireland. His transformation was clear. His marriage was restored, his health saved, and he began to love and show love to the people he once hated. Only the Holy Spirit can accomplish such a change.

So conviction is the first step for which to pray. When we are concerned for another person to become a Christian, we should pray that the Spirit will convince them of their need and

---

1. Reproduced by permission of Channel 4 television.

convict them of their sin. It is God, and God alone, who breaks down the barriers of indifference, resistance and sin. This is the first role of the Holy Spirit.

Salvation, from the beginning to the end, depends on God. We do have our part to play; but it rests ultimately on the Spirit's transcendent power, not on our unreliable human contributions. The first work of the Spirit is to convict of sin. Sometimes, as in the case of Billy McIlwaine, the work of conviction will take many years to come to fruition. But the Lord knows what he is doing. He never leaves anything to chance. He can get through to anyone.

The revelation of the Counsellor

'I have yet many things to say to you, but you cannot bear them now. When the Spirit of truth comes, he will guide you into all the truth' (John 16:12-13).

The reason Jesus sends the Spirit into our tangled human experience is to straighten us out so we can live full, enriched lives which are honouring to God. Hand in hand with Jesus' power at work in our hearts, is Jesus' word – his truth – at work in our minds.

To change a person's behaviour you have to influence mind and will. To be equipped with the powers of the new age, we need God's word as much as we need his Spirit. Here in Jesus' teaching we see that the two belong together. That is why Jesus says to the disciples that although he still has many things to say to them, the Holy Spirit himself will take over that role and guide them to perceive all the truth Jesus wants to make known to them, and to us.

In one sense this is Jesus' promise for the inspiration of the New Testament. The disciples already had Jesus' words. We know that the Gospels were compiled from collections of Jesus' sayings and reports of his actions made by the disciples. Yet here is a promise of further revelation. It is a promise geared to the writings and teachings of the apostles. The writings of the New Testament are guaranteed to tell unique truth – God's power to change us. It was Jesus who promised and guaranteed the inspiration of the New Testament. It was a promise to the apostolic authors: 'He will guide you into all the truth' (John 16:13).

The focus of the Counsellor

'He will glorify me, for he will take what is mine and declare it to you' (John 16:14).

The Holy Spirit has a spotlight ministry. He throws the focus entirely upon Jesus. Above the entrance to Broadcasting House, the home of the BBC in London, next door to All Souls Church, Langham Place, there is an impressive carving. It is of two figures, and depicts Prospero sending Ariel out into the world. Late at night a spotlight from the other side of the road, high up in the Langham Hotel, is focused on to those two figures and makes them vividly stand out. It is a shaft of light, cutting clear across Langham Place, causing attention to go straight to that carving of Prospero and Ariel. They are spotlighted for everyone to see and there is no missing them.

The Holy Spirit has a spotlight ministry. He focuses entirely on Jesus. He is the one who prompts us to glorify Jesus in what we say and think and do. He makes Jesus stand out in our understanding, in our desire to serve him, and in the way Jesus is perceived by others. He throws all the attention on to Jesus. It's a concern from the very heart of God, so to glorify Jesus should be our goal too – we also should long to throw the spotlight on him.

If we respond to the conviction that the Holy Spirit brings when we are in the wrong, if we obey the teaching that he has inspired and which itself comes from Jesus, then we are in a position to serve and honour Jesus with our daily lives – to glorify him. This is one way we spotlight Jesus day by day.

Jesus points out four dynamics concerning the Counsellor: the promise, the ministry, the revelation, and the focus. Jesus said that he mentioned these four dynamics to guard against the breakdown of faith. Faith is always going to be under pressure. The Christian life is always going to be difficult, for we cannot avoid struggles. But we have received the promise of the Counsellor. We are not alone. We have an incredibly powerful, strong friend and companion. No matter where we go, no matter what the turmoil, he goes too. He is there.

The ministry of the Counsellor goes on, unimpeded by human weakness or opposition. He is as able to convince and convict a terrorist, or anyone, however hardened or pained or disillusioned. God is able to make himself known even in the face of human resistance. He convicts in order to bless.

The revelation of the Counsellor is the means by which to face opposition and discouragement. Most, if not all, of the New Testament was written against the background of persecution, unbelief and opposition. The word of God, the revelation of the Counsellor, the Spirit of truth, is Jesus' way of strengthening us for a struggle that, with his resources, we can overcome. The Scriptures are vital to our strength.

The focus of the Counsellor gives us a goal. Whatever situation we are involved in, whatever challenge there is before us, one question is enough: Is my response glorifying to Jesus Christ? All we need is to decide that this will be our goal, and the Spirit will give us strength for it to become reality. As always, the struggle will be over motivation. To glorify Jesus is the Spirit's entire concern – and he will make it happen. The spotlight must go on to Jesus, and away from ourselves.

There are two truths to hold together which will help to guard against the breakdown of faith. The first is a right understanding of kingdom reality. There are bound to be times of difficulty, discouragement and opposition. In a real sense, they are opportunities to face up to our commitment to the King and to grow in his grace. The second truth to appreciate is that even during such difficulties we are not on our own. There are powers for the new age. God is God. His power is mightily at work within us. We should be sure to use the resources he has made available to us. The Counsellor, the Spirit of truth, is both with us and in us. Holding on to these two truths means that in opposition and discouragement we can face the issues and overcome.

The signs of the new age
Kingdom people are called to face the struggles of existence, but with a new power to overcome, a power which is itself released through obedience to Christ; for the wisdom of the King, and his plans for us, will always transcend the horizons of our human perspectives. Overcoming in the present depends on our view of the future. In communities where there is high unemployment, the unlikelihood of change often brings a depressing erosion in resolve. Hope is an essential human dimension. Without hope, there is no future worth aspiring towards, only a promise that the next step may be as dark as those which have gone before. We have a deep psychological need to trace the rainbow through the rain.

The apostle Paul writes that the followers of Christ were saved in hope: 'But hope that is seen is no hope at all. Who hopes for what he already has? But if we hope for what we do not yet have, we wait for it patiently' (Rom. 8:24-25). That hope in which we are saved is seen vividly in the ministry of Jesus, and is most graphically presented in the signs of the kingdom.

John records seven miracles of Jesus which are signs pointing both to who Jesus is, and to the nature of the kingdom he is inaugurating. 'Jesus did many other miraculous signs [Greek: *semeia*] in the presence of his disciples, which are not recorded in this book. But these are written that you may believe that Jesus is the Christ, the Son of God, and that by believing you may have life in his name' (John 20:30-31).

The seven signs of Jesus' ministry which John records are a foretaste of the messianic kingdom. They portray the hope in

202 *Living By God's Master Plan*

which we are saved. The turning of water into wine (ch. 2), the healing of the Roman officer's son (ch. 4), the cure of the Bethesda cripple (ch. 5), the feeding of the five thousand (ch. 6), the walking on the water (ch. 6), the healing of the man born blind (ch. 9), and the raising of Lazarus (ch. 11) penetratingly illustrate the new powers of the age to come, and the supremely moving compassion of God towards the pain and alienation of the human condition. Nowhere is this combination of power linked with compassion more clearly portrayed than in the raising of Lazarus at Bethany.

Till death us do part

The death of someone dear to us releases powerful emotions within. In early days of bereavement, almost everyone finds death difficult to think about and speak of openly. Bereavement is a painful, disorientating experience. The prospect of our own death is the supreme crisis of our lives. In these circumstances, we all feel acutely the searing pain of loss and the power of the unknown.

Does the kingdom of God have anything relevant and distinctive to say in these situations? Does it make the kind of difference to cause us to face our mortality with a different perspective and hope?

Jesus faced this painful subject of death. He did not surround it with the usual conspiracy of silence. The issue comes to the fore in John's Gospel in the sign or miracle often described as the raising of Lazarus. It is about a death in the family.

The relevance of the situation

'Now when Jesus came, he found that Lazarus had already been in the tomb four days. Bethany was near Jerusalem, about two miles off, and many of the Jews had come to Martha and Mary to console them concerning their brother' (John 11:17-19).

Stage one in the investigation of the events at Bethany is to establish the relevance of this situation in relation to our own needs today. Does this event speak to our own experience? Is it relevant? Or is it light years away from our world, our anxieties, our pain, our fears? Such an event, however moving, will be of no use to us today if it is a dusty piece of ancient literature, and that alone.

Jesus responds to a situation of bereavement and grief. There has been a death in the family. Lazarus, the brother of Martha and Mary, has died. Funerals took place sooner than they do in our colder climates. When Jesus arrives, the funeral has already taken place; Lazarus has been in the tomb four days.

Jewish families are supportive in bereavement. The special expression used by Jews is 'to sit shivvas' which means the most bereaved members of the immediate family are consoled, brought food, and looked after by a circle of friends and relations who come and visit. They sit with the bereaved for several days after the death. Sitting shivvas actually refers to the mourning stools which are brought for the bereaved to sit on at this time, while others provided help and support in various practical ways. This process of mourning and support is exactly what was going on at Bethany: 'Many of the Jews had come to Mary and Martha to console them concerning their brother' (John 11:19).

This Jewish way of helping is supportive. The bereaved members of the family are not expected to say or do anything in particular. There is an expression of grief and authentic identification and sharing of pain. Jews have a great deal to teach Gentiles about grief, family support and friendship in these difficult times.

The immediate relevance of this situation in which we find Jesus is that it speaks directly to our own experience of the fragility of life. We do not need much imagination to feel the sense of pain and loss this bereavement has brought to the family of Lazarus.

When the two sisters send the message to Jesus that Lazarus is sick (John 11:3), the sense of urgency and fear behind their words is almost tangible – exactly the same emotions we feel and encounter today.

It is not difficult to emotionally identify with the bereaved sisters, Martha and Mary. But at a deeper level an identification needs to be made with Lazarus, the person who has died. Our lives are very fragile. The fact is we just do not know how long we have to live.

We can unwittingly be complacent about the future and take it for granted. There are no guarantees of any kind, and there is a built-in precariousness about life. Jesus is speaking to a relevant situation, the sort of situation in which we may find ourselves – emotionally and practically. It is an issue we all have to face. It is not just other people's death we have to cope with, most of all it is our own.

Facing the issue

The second stage in understanding the sign of Lazarus involves the way Jesus changes and challenges our perspectives on the subject of death.

The climax of the conversation between Martha and Jesus comes when Jesus says: 'I am the resurrection and the life; he who believes in me, though he die, yet shall he live, and whoever lives and believes in me shall never die' (John 11:25-26). These are remarkable words; by them, Jesus changes our perspectives on death.

(1) The perspective changers

There are many important instances in history where individuals, by their words, actions or discoveries, have dramatically changed the way we see things. In 1530, Nicolas Copernicus was the man who discovered that the sun was the centre of the solar system. It was revolutionary; it literally changed perspectives. In 1628, William Harvey discovered the circulation of the blood. It is hard to imagine how important that one single discovery has been in the developments in modern medicine and health care. There are many more striking examples. Wilhelm Rontgen discovered X-rays. Isaac Newton discovered the laws of gravity. In our own day, more than any other, Bill Gates has stimulated access to the world wide web. These are all people who have changed our lives and re-orientated the way we see things.

New ways of seeing mean we change our perspectives. This is also true of the story of the raising of Lazarus. Jesus' words to Martha change our perspectives on human mortality, giving us a new way to see the whole subject of death.

What is really behind what Jesus is saying? We must be specific and find out to what he is actually referring.

(2) Making assumptions

When we find ourselves in conversation, there are certain things we take for granted. We make assumptions, there is always something behind what we say. Talk to anyone who loves the theatre: if you mention Broadway or the National to them, they will immediately know what you mean. The same will stay with those who love the great music classics. But to the uninitiated, Rach 3 may sound like a shelf at the supermarket, though to a pianist it is unmistakable. Rach 3? Rachmaninoff's third piano concerto. Like Tchaik 1. Or even Rach Pag!

When there is a common understanding behind what we say, we call this a frame of reference. We do not need to spell out every single detail, because certain assumptions are common to us and our listeners. So what was the frame of reference behind what Jesus said? What were the assumptions he made about his hearers' background knowledge?

A verse in Hebrews affords us a theological glimpse behind the scenes. It is a summary verse of much New Testament teaching and provides the frame of reference for us on the subject of death and judgment: 'Man is destined to die once, and after that to face judgment' (Heb. 9:27).

When Jesus says, 'Whoever lives and believes in me shall never die,' the whole verse is inexplicable unless something else, an unspoken but implied wider frame of reference, lies behind his words. What he cannot be saying is you will never physically die if you believe in him. Jesus never taught physical immortality – that is mythology, not Christianity. So what is he talking about? Does the verse from Hebrews 9 give us the frame of reference we need?

The implication of what Jesus is saying is about spiritual death, not physical death. It is to do with judgement. In speaking to a godly Jewish person like Martha, the assumption which Jesus would make was that she would know the scripture teaching that after death comes judgment. Hebrews 9:27 suggests that it was a basic part of the Jewish Christian understanding that death is followed by judgment.

Jesus' words alter our perspectives on death because they force us to face our accountability to God. We may fear the physical aspects of death, and most of us do. Yet there is, as Jesus clearly implies, the possibility of eternal death – a spiritual death more to be feared than physical death.

When we die, and our lives are played back to us and we see ourselves as we really have been in our many weaker moments, we will have to agree before God that we are guilty. After death there is the judgment; we are accountable to God.

But Jesus offers a way out – a lasting solution to the problem of death. Jesus claims he is God's unique way out. This is all tied in with his own death and resurrection. Jesus died willingly and sacrificially by Roman crucifixion. It was God's own solution to the problem of death – understood in the widest terms.

Jesus' sacrifice took both physical and spiritual death seriously. His death is a payment for sin. It means that when we stand before God at the judgment, if we have responded to Christ now, our account will be marked 'paid in full'. That is the nature and power of forgiveness. If we live and believe in him, we shall never die, because Jesus' resurrection broke death's stranglehold – he is the resurrection and the life. He enables us to face the judgment. Jesus simply holds out his love.

(3) A lesson about the love of God

'When Jesus saw Mary weeping, and the Jews who came with her also weeping, he was deeply moved in spirit and troubled' (John 11:33).
> 'Jesus wept' (John 11:35).

When someone close to us dies, we feel it deeply because we loved them. If there had not been any love, there would not be much sense of loss. That is why it is right to express our grief. It is an expression of our love and the sadness we feel. What does this incident say to us about the love of God?

The real mistake when thinking about God is to think of him in the abstract, as an idea or force or even as stern and unapproachable. God is not like that – he is personal.

At Lazarus' tomb, Jesus shows us the unimaginable – God shedding tears. The picture of Jesus weeping, baring his own pain and compassion, demonstrates not only that God cares and understands. It also reveals that God has made Jesus available to us, to help us as we contemplate and face death. Real love is always more than a feeling, it ends up with action: it always wants to do the utmost to help and put things right. Jesus did not simply weep, he acted in power and changed the situation.

(4) Jesus demonstrates his power

'Then Jesus, deeply moved again, came to the tomb' (John 11:38).

Jesus lifted up his eyes and said, 'I thank you that you have heard me. I knew that you hear me always, but I have said this on account of the people standing by, that they may believe that you did send me.' When he had said this, he cried with a loud voice, 'Lazarus, come out.' The dead man came out, his hands and feet bound with bandages, and his face wrapped with a cloth. Jesus said to them, 'Unbind him, and let him go' (John 11:41-44).

It is difficult to imagine a more dramatic event. Graveyards can be bleak places. Jesus, himself deeply upset, was surrounded by other bereaved people. Yet what they witnessed when Jesus acted so decisively must have been absolutely extraordinary. The raising of Lazarus was a one-off miracle. It sprang from Jesus' concern and compassion for Martha and Mary. But much more than that, it was a piece of tangible evidence, a sign that Jesus is able to do what he says he can do.

If you go to an opera house to hear an opera or go to a theatre to hear a musical, as the house lights go down the orchestra or the band will always play some kind of an overture, a kind of prelude to give you a taste of what is to come. The overture is not the opera or show itself, but it does give you a feel of what is on the way. It moulds your expectations. It is a curtain-raiser – the sure sign something better is poised to happen.

The raising of Lazarus is just such a curtain raiser. John says these miracles of Jesus are meant to be signs, pointers to who Jesus actually is. They lift the lid on what the coming kingdom of God will be like.

The raising of Lazarus points backwards to give evidence of who Jesus is; but it also points forwards to show us what Jesus can do. Jesus' own resurrection is the final guarantee of eternal life. The raising of Lazarus is a prelude, an overture, a curtain-raiser, a sign. It is something which points us powerfully to who Jesus is, and what he can do in the full face of death.

It is not a morbid thing to speak of death. The really morbid thing is to be unprepared for death.

We learn from these aspects that Jesus alters perspectives on death. But Jesus' own reaction of pain and compassion, speaks to us also, not of a God who is distant or uncaring, but of a God who loves us, sheds tears for us, and who has, in response to our own mortality, put into action the most remarkable rescue plan the world has ever seen.

The whole incident in John 11 has, then, been recorded in

order to prompt us. It is true we sometimes need a jolt to help us see things more realistically, and to do what is necessary. On this issue only we can take responsibility for ourselves, as no one else can face death for us. We have to ask ourselves whether we are facing up to that. Jesus' teaching, no matter who we are, leads us to be certain of one fact about death. One day we will all look back; then we will realize that placing our trust in Jesus was the most important choice of our whole life.

Signs and wonders today

As recorded in the Gospels, Jesus' miracles are signs of God's power and compassion and his anointing of Jesus as the Messiah. They are signs of all that characterizes the hope which the kingdom embodies, and demonstrate how God's rule properly responds to the deepest longings and pains of the human heart.

> Miracles are a foreshadowing and promise of coming universal redemption and the fullness of the kingdom. Casting out demons signals God's invasion of the realm of Satan and Satan's final destruction (Matt. 12:29; Mark 3:27; Luke 11:22ff; John 12:31; Rev. 20:7ff). Healing the sick bears witness to the end of all suffering (Rev. 21:4). Miraculous provisions of food tell us about the end of all human need (Rev. 7:16ff). Stilling storms points forward to the complete victory over the powers of nature that threaten the earth. Raising the dead announces that death will be forever done away with (1 Cor. 15:26).[2]

The issue is a broad and complex one. Are these signs of grace embedded purely in the historical reality of the past, speaking powerfully of future glory still yet to be revealed? Or is there, in some measure great or small, a sense in which those signs may be properly expected to be manifested today, as part of the present reality of the kingdom which Jesus has inaugurated?

---

2. John Wimber, *Power Evangelism* (Hodder & Stoughton, 1985) p.98.

Ways of seeing

Expectations of kingdom grace today can be rightly formulated
only by lining up our faith, hope and expectations for the present
with an accurate picture of the expectations the Bible gives us
for such life today. Do we understand God aright? Are we clear
about the kind of world in which we live? What is our view of
the purposes of the kingdom? What is the attitude of faith within
ourselves? What does Scripture itself direct? These questions
all involve various ways of seeing God, the world, the kingdom,
and our own attitudes and goals. There is little point to kingdom
privileges and responsibilities in the kingdom of God if it is not
at all clear where God himself fits into the picture. What
constitutes a right vision in such things?

The real absence

The rationalist world-view pictures God as being manifestly
absent from this world. Absent either because he does not exist
– the view of atheistic rationalism – or absent because, as the
Creator who has made all things, like an absentee landlord he
has left the world to get on with its own business. This is a form
of rationalism which has seeped into the church ever since the
deists first propounded it in the eighteenth century. Both views,
the non-Christian and the quasi-Christian, boil down to the same
conclusion: God is absent from this world. We are on our own.
In Arthur Koestler's phrase, 'God has left the receiver off the
hook.' Do not expect any response from the beyond.

World-view determines expectations. What do we say to the
assertion of the absence of God? It depends on fundamental
assumptions about the world in which we live.

There are two possible ways of seeing the world. Ever since
the birth of modern science through the pioneering work of
Newton, Galileo, Copernicus and others, all Western thinkers
have been agreed on the basic nature of the universe in which
we live. There is a uniformity of natural causes in this world.
When an apple falls from the tree to the ground, we expect it to
happen that way next time too, and not to fall upwards! There

is a uniform set of expectations built into the natural pattern of cause and effect. However, the issue for us revolves around whether the system in which these causes function is a closed or an open one. Is the world like a house with all the doors and windows locked and bolted, where no one can get in from outside? This is the position of the rationalists; however the world got there, no one is going to be allowed to tamper with it now it is here. Or is the world, like that house, a self-contained system, but one where the means of access is open, where no one has bolted anything against intruders, and God can introduce elements of change when and wherever he desires to do so?

The biblical position must be the latter, the open system; on the basis of the incarnation alone, this view makes the most sense. Rationalists should also agree, on the basis of the following consideration, that it is the position of the greatest reasonableness. It is one thing to observe and agree upon the uniformity of natural causes; it is a very great leap of faith, indeed an assumption without sufficient cause, to then assume that just because something has happened in one way before, it must, by right, happen in precisely the same way on every subsequent occasion. Of course there is an element of predictability built into our lives – otherwise we would never trust an aeroplane even to take off. But at the same time, it is going beyond the evidence to say there is no possibility of outside intervention which will change the course of events, should God decide to.

To believe in an open system is not so much the position of faith; in fact, the closed system view reflects a certain kind of misconstrued faith, when it races ahead of any empirical evidence and by its arbitrary exclusions demonstrates itself to be anything but scientific. The open system is an attitude of openness. It says these possibilities may happen; it does not rule them out from day one.

Jesus' incarnation, the incarnation of the Creator King and God as man, is a powerful pointer to the open-system view. If God was able to enter the human arena then – historically, personally, visibly and tangibly – there is no reason in principle why he should not have now an involvement in the lives of individuals and the affairs of this world; and indeed the whole universe, both before and beyond that time. There is a biblical continuum from the initial statement of Genesis in Genesis 1:2, where the Spirit of God is described as 'hovering over the waters', to the magisterial announcement of Revelation 21:3, 'Now the dwelling of God is with men....' The real presence of God in our world must mean that we are expected to be open to the working of that same Holy Spirit today.

The now and not yet of the kingdom

Jesus' miracles have a way of illustrating the truth of his claims and at the same time pointing ahead to the future – an authenticating and eschatological dimension.

As signs they tell us about the compassion of God and his kingly sovereignty over all world affairs – the human as well as the social, the political as well as the natural. They also authenticate the Messiahship of Jesus, in that the Messiah reflects the attributes of divine kingly sovereignty. They further illustrate the eschatological dimension, bringing forth a glimpse and foretaste of the shape of things to come. The signs point mainly beyond our time to the times as yet to be fulfilled. But in an important sense, we now live in the presence of the future, because the kingdom of God, though still unfolding, has a present reality as well as a future dimension.

Jesus' claims about the arrival of the kingdom of God were unambiguous: 'If I drive out demons by the Spirit of God, then the kingdom of God has come upon you' (Matt. 12:28); 'The kingdom of God is not coming with signs to be observed; nor will they say, "Lo, here it is!" or "There!" for behold, the kingdom of God is in the midst of you' (Luke 17:20-21). In one breath, Jesus clearly taught that the kingdom of God was a present reality, identifiable with himself. Yet he was at pains to present the grand plan of God as a fact both dynamically present in his own person and for the present age, and also as future hope still to be revealed. The parables of the marriage feast, the tares, the talents, and the wise and foolish virgins also make this clear; as do specific sayings such as Matthew 7:21-23 and 8:11-12, which give a definite future dimension to the kingdom as well.

The tension between the now and the not yet is, for us, a creative tension. On the one hand we can and should be open to the powerful working of God's Spirit to transform us inwardly, to guide our circumstances, and to bring God's gracious answers to our prayer requests. Nothing less can be expected: 'For the LORD is the great God, the great King above all gods. In his hand are the depths of the earth, and the mountain peaks belong to him. The sea is his, for he made it, and his hands formed the dry land' (Ps. 95:3-5). At the same time the grand plan of the kingdom is still unfolding. We should pray in all circumstances (Phil. 4:6); when sick, we have the right to ask the elders of our church to pray for healing (Jas. 5:13-16); there is no area of our lives, our society or our world which we should not bathe in prayer (1 Tim. 2:1-2). All, however, must be subject to the wisdom of God, who alone knows his best purposes for us (Rom. 11:33-36; Prov. 3:5-12).

Two defective views of God distort the careful balance the New Testament draws between the present and the future of God's Master Plan. Both are sub-Christian, and both inspire damaging extremes.

1) God stripped of his regal power. This is the God with whom it is comfortable to get along. He makes no particular demands on us. It is OK to go to him when you are in trouble, not that it makes any material difference, but the thought may make you feel better. If we recoil from this, reflect that many people who are apparently committed to the gospel of Christ hold views which effectively have the same outcome. They do not expect God to actively unsettle their comfortable existence, at least not in ways which would mean that he made his power and will most actively known.

2) God as genie in the lamp. This is the opposite extreme. Rub the lamp hard enough and the genie appears to do your will. Some of us tend to treat prayer like this. We tell God what he should do; for example when we pray for healing, we are clear that sickness does not represent the will of God; we have no doubt that, because this is what we want, it must be what he wants.

But there is always a provisionality about the New Testament promises on prayer. Jesus has made us a conditional promise: 'You may ask me for anything in my name, and I will do it' (John 14:14). This is *an unlimited invitation* to bring all our needs to God and submit them to the mind of Christ. But it is *a limited promise,* for it is linked to Jesus' wisdom and will. He will do whatever accords with his supreme purposes. This must be the reason for the expression 'in my name' – it means 'according to the mind of Jesus'. It is not a simple statement about the mediation of Christ. Praying in the name of Jesus means more than that. It disfigures Jesus' meaning to regard this statement as a blank cheque. We violate the nature of our relationship with God as children to the Father if, ignoring the family relationship, we do not acknowledge that our Father knows best.

God can and does heal. But we should never claim healing at the expense of the wisdom of God. As our Father, we should bring all our needs to him. No prayer ever goes unanswered. We must learn to accept the answer God gives back, for this is the way of growth in discipleship. From his supreme vantage point, God's ultimate wisdom is always best for us.

Even the most committed Christians can slip into neo-paganism when it comes to prayer. It is easily possible to view God as a glorified genie in a lamp – one who may be released and summoned by impressive-sounding formulae and spells. Make no mistake, God is not bound. Nothing is beyond his power; nor is anything beyond his mind and wisdom to comprehend. Never underrate him – but never overplay your relationship to him either. Let us always have great expectations of a God who deals wisely and graciously with us according to his power revealed in the resurrection, according to the mind of Christ, and 'according to the plan of him who works out everything in conformity with the purpose of his will' (Eph. 1:11).

Kingdom come

Let Paul, who was no stranger either to the painful realities of discipleship, nor the powerful workings of the Holy Spirit, have the last word about the grand plan of the kingdom of God. A kingdom already come, yet still to be fully realized:

I consider that our present sufferings are not worth comparing with the glory that will be revealed in us. The creation waits in eager expectation for the sons of God to be revealed. For the creation was subjected to frustration, not by its own choice, but by the will of the one who subjected it, in hope that the creation itself will be liberated from its bondage to decay and brought into the glorious freedom of the children of God.

We know that the whole creation has been groaning as in the pains of childbirth right up to the present time. Not only so, but we ourselves, who have the firstfruits of the Spirit, groan inwardly as we wait eagerly for our adoption as sons, the redemption of our bodies. For in this hope we were saved. But hope that is seen is no hope at all. Who hopes for what he already has? But if we hope for what we do not yet have, we wait for it patiently.

In the same way, the Spirit helps us in our weakness. We do not know what we ought to pray for, but the Spirit himself intercedes for us with groans that words cannot express. And he who searches our hearts knows the mind of the Spirit, because the Spirit intercedes for the saints in accordance with God's will (Rom. 8:18-27).

Summary Points

■ Jesus taught the disciples how to respond when mocked, persecuted and lied about.

■ His key resource was the provision of the Holy Spirit.

■ Jesus' miracles are signs of the kingdom.

■ The raising of Lazarus points both to who Jesus is and what he can do in the face of death.

■ The signs indicate the creative tension between 'the now' and the 'not yet' of the kingdom.

For Reflection

God blesses you when you are mocked and persecuted and lied about because you are my followers. Be happy about it! Be very glad! For a great reward awaits you in heaven. And remember, the ancient prophets were persecuted, too (Matt. 5:11-12, p.193).

Work out two ways in which you could apply Jesus' words. Either make up a case study or use a real life situation. Then, first, explain and apply Jesus' words in a plausible-sounding but shallow way, which will trivialize the suffering and pain someone might be going through. Then, second, in a thoughtful, spiritually-minded way, provide a richer perspective by which that person may be helped. Then review what you have learnt as a result.

It is not a morbid thing to speak of death. The really morbid thing is to be unprepared for death (p.208).
　　Why do you think this statement is true, and what is its

importance (a) for the Christian and (b) for the non Christian?

Using the incident of the raising of Lazarus, what points would you bring out to show a non-Christian how Jesus Christ has the answer to death?

Jesus' miracles are signs of God's compassion and power, and his anointing of Jesus as the Messiah (p.209).

Should we therefore expect to see signs and wonders today, and if so where, and to what extent?

Chapter 11

THE MASTER PLAN

'Let us offer to God acceptable worship, with reverence and awe; for our God is a consuming fire' (Heb. 12:28-29).

We live in the light of the return of the King. Jesus has promised to return to the earth as Judge of the living and the dead, and to usher in a new world order. When he comes, the kingdom comes – in complete fulfilment. Until that time, 'We must go through many hardships to enter the kingdom of God' (Acts 14:22).

Jesus' return is the pivot of history. All time converges on this climactic moment of the King's saving dealings with this world. The pledge is made, but when he comes, what will the new world order be like, and how should we live in the light of what is to come?

A new heaven and a new earth
Evolutionary optimists say our world will get better and better, 'World without end.' Tomorrow's world technologists envisage a Utopian dream of a happier, safer, cleaner world where swords will be beaten into microchips. Yet environmental pessimists say the future is bleak. Many are fearful that mankind may destroy the planet before he has a chance to improve it. 'In the end life is only triviality, just for a moment. And when the end comes. Then nothing' (Bertrand Russell).

Eschatology is the shorthand term used to describe the fiction, theory and facts about the last things of this world. But biblical eschatology is more realistic than the outlook of evolutionary optimists, and more challenging than the prognostications of environmental pessimists. The Bible's teaching about the end of the world is not about coming to a full stop. It is about a new world – a world renewed which involves both continuity and discontinuity from life as we know it now. In his apocalyptic vision, John wrote: 'I saw a new heaven and a new earth; for the first heaven and the first earth had passed away' (Rev. 21:1).

What kind of reality?

'I thought a Christian goes to heaven when he dies, so why is there going to be a new heaven and a new earth? What's wrong with the old heaven, anyway? And why do we need a new earth if we are going to heaven?' That is what immediately comes into some people's minds when they first encounter this subject. The Bible does not normally speak of 'going to heaven when we die', though it certainly means that. Its concept of life beyond death is of a much richer, exciting, dynamic and stimulating environment than simple talk of heaven may bring to mind.

The poet, Laurie Lee, justifiably criticizes the popular images of heaven as 'too chaste, too disinfected, too much on its best behaviour'. In similar vein, Walter Rauschenbusch, the American social theologian, wrote in 1917: 'In the present life we are bound up with wife and children, with friends and work mates, in a warm organism of complex life. When we die, we join – what? A throng of souls, an unorganised crowd of saints, who each carry a harp, and have not even formed an orchestra!'

Both criticisms are based on caricatures which are uncomfortably close to the distorted pictures drawn from older hymnody and Victorian preaching. However, to communicate convincingly today, we need better Bible teaching on heaven and the new world, for the new heaven and the new earth are a most exciting prospect.

There are several reasons why the Bible speaks of a new heaven and a new earth, rather than 'going to heaven when you die'.

Dream on...

In Genesis 28:12 we meet Jacob, the son of Isaac: 'Jacob dreamed that there was a ladder set up on the earth, and the top of it reached to heaven; and behold, the angels of God were ascending and descending on it!' This was one of those Old Testament dreams given by God as a means of revelation.

What does the dream mean?

The dream has a New Testament fulfilment. Right at the beginning of his public ministry, Jesus says to the sceptical Nathaniel: 'Truly, truly, I say to you, you will see heaven opened, and the angels of God ascending and descending upon the Son of man' (John 1:51). That is the first major teaching emphasis of Jesus in John's Gospel. But to what is he referring?

Jesus is making a reference to Jacob's dream. So right at the start of the Bible, and right at the beginning of Jesus' ministry, this point is underlined. Heaven, which is the home or realm of God, and earth, which is the home or realm of man, are to be brought together. Heaven and earth are to be reunited. In the symbolism of Jacob's dream, it is as if a ladder or bridge will be set up between God and man, between heaven and earth. Clearly, Jesus is saying, 'I am that bridge.'

The picture of the angels coming and going is of a future but permanent interaction between God and man, between heaven and earth. While Jesus is the bridge – between divinity and humanity, between the life of heaven and the life of earth – he is also the one who has inaugurated, by his death and resurrection, the coming of the new world order. The new heaven and the new earth will not be two separate realities, they will be a unity between God and man. The new world is one where God and man are together.

This is more earthly than the caricatures of a harp-twanging heaven, and yet more heavenly than the Utopian dreams of a high-technology, computer-crazed earth. That is the reality of the biblical prospect. The life of heaven and the life of earth will be drawn together in a single new reality, for which the most common biblical description is 'a new heaven and a new earth'.

The importance for the present

Why do we have to think about all this now? Do we not have enough issues to face in the present without anticipating what the future will hold? For many of us, our relationships, studies, work or simply paying the bills is quite enough to think about. If we are involved warmly and enthusiastically in our churches, perhaps in Christian service, do we need to think about a future so far ahead? The answer is to do with purposefulness.

Creatures with a purpose

How you prepare yourself when you set out on a journey depends on what your destination will be like. If we head for the sun for our summer holidays, we may think about buying some lightweight clothes or a new camera or some suntan oil. We make preparations. Why? Because there is a purpose involved and an end in sight. This perspective can shed light on our humanness too. In this, as in some other respects, we are distinctively different from the animals with whom we share so many biological similarities: we have a teleological nature – we are creatures with a purpose.

When I was an undergraduate, and before I became a Christian, I was immensely concerned about the question of purpose. Many of us ask, 'What is it all about?' At that time, when I was a musician and an active composer, my answer to that question was divided. I did not believe in God, but I was aware that through music and the arts generally one could perceive something beautiful and purposeful at the heart of things. Yet the philosophy which I read at university told me another story. The French existentialist left-wing philosopher, Jean Paul Sartre, was particularly influential in the early seventies. And what he said about purpose stuck fast in my mind. He said: 'It was meaningless that I was born, it is meaningless that I live, and it will be meaningless when I die.' How can this contradiction be resolved? Our heart tells us one thing – our head, another.

The biblical teaching on the new heaven and new earth provides the answer to that heart/head dilemma. Jesus has done everything for us. When he created an eternal home for us – it was not to be a rest-home, but a place of creative activity. The fact he has done this lends ultimate meaning to our lives. We are going somewhere; we have a destiny – a purpose. This affects the sense of meaning which we have in the present. When life goes well, we all have a sense of purpose. It is when we come up against obstacles like pain, loss and suffering that our sense of purpose gets knocked off centre.

The apostle Paul gives us a reminder which sets us on the right course: 'I consider that the sufferings of this present time are not worth comparing with the glory that is to be revealed to us' (Rom. 8:18). For him, the coming 'glory' was obviously a significant perspective-changer.

Glorious things of thee are spoken

Do you keep a stock of glorious moments – the secular as well as the spiritual? If you like Sibelius, it might be the end of his fifth symphony. If you like the theatre, it might be the memory or a recording of Gielgud's rendering of the Hamlet soliloquies. If you love the countryside, it might be a wonderful view or a particular sunset. You might even have a favourite brand of special chocolate which is glorious. Such human titbits are a tiny taster of a far greater magnificence, for which the Bible's word is glory. Think of anything you consider really marvellous, multiply it an infinity of times over, and you begin to approach the quality of what Paul is speaking of as 'the glory to be revealed'.

The glory that is to be revealed to us is from God. True glory is always a reflection of him. So sufferings, however painful they may be, do somehow pale into insignificance when viewed from an eternal perspective and compared with the glory to come. 'Man is born to trouble as surely as sparks fly upwards' (Job 5:7). With a sense of the gloriousness of the place and the person for which we are bound, and a sense of purpose inspired by the vision of the coming new world, we can find a new and encouraging perspective, no matter how tough the obstacles of pain and suffering.

There is an important balance to be maintained here. The pain and the awfulness of suffering is in no way minimized or written off by any of the apostolic writers. Real suffering is set in a context which transforms and redeems it. This is part of the glorious majesty, part of the work of Christ the King. God recognizes the reality of the present fallen world's hard edges – its pains and suffering – but he does more than that. He has acted decisively to remedy the situation.

By the incarnation and the cross, he has directly experienced the worst the world can offer, but he has gloriously triumphed over it. His victory has a dual aspect. It is decisive, but from our perspective it has a large promissory dimension: the victory has been won; we can experience that now. On the other hand, although the kingdom of God has been inaugurated, what we currently experience is only a glimpse of the glory that will finally be revealed to us.

In the Creator's image

'The glory and honour of the nations will be brought into the heavenly city. Nothing that is impure will ever enter it' (Rev. 21:26).

This interesting and key verse in Revelation is saying something about creativity in the widest sense. We are made in the image of God the Creator. The God who in Genesis 1 affirmed the goodness of the world he made will not write off everything that has been glorious and honourable in the history of the world and mankind. There is a sense in which all that has been good and creative in individual lives and all that has been good in the arts and the sciences will be there in the new heaven and new earth. Or at least there will be a *transformation* to an even greater glory of all that has been best and good in every aspect of our lives, from the least of us to the greatest. 'The glory and honour of the nations will be brought into the heavenly city.'

Matthew Henry, the great devotional Puritan writer, comments on this verse: 'Whatever is excellent and valuable in this world shall be there enjoyed in a more refined kind, and to a far greater degree – brighter crowns, a better and more enduring substance, more sweet and satisfying feasts, a more glorious attendance, a truer sense of honor and far higher posts of honor, a more glorious temper of mind, and a form and a countenance more glorious than ever were known in this world.'

Yes, everything matters. Everything we do, to a greater or lesser extent, is significant for eternity. That is what Jesus suggests in the parable of the talents. In the new heaven and the new earth, nothing impure will enter in. We will leave all that behind – but nothing worthwhile will be wasted.

Is there something which you feel is badly under-appreciated? The honour and the glory of all peoples, all that is best, big or small, will find its place of appreciation in the new heaven and the new earth. This is why it is important to dwell on these realities now. It lends an extra dimension of purpose to our lives, because everything good matters – right through to eternity.

What will it be like?
The New Testament interest in the things of the new world is not concerned with detail. The New Testament emphasis was once somewhat obscurely put to me as 'theological and soteriological, rather than cosmological'. In everyday language, that means there is not much geographical information given about the new heaven and new earth. There is not much point in speculating about what it will all look like and feel like.

Those who are scientists may like to attempt to predict the physical basis and processes of a renewed and perfected world. The Bible seems to say there will be both continuity and change. The real point, however, is that God will be right at the visible centre of our lives. This will be as the climax of the whole work of salvation.

I heard a loud voice from the throne saying, 'Behold, the dwelling of God is with men. He will dwell with them, and they shall be his people, and God himself will be with them;

he will wipe away every tear from their eyes, and death shall be no more, neither shall there be mourning nor crying nor pain any more, for the former things have passed away (Rev. 21:3-4).

What is heaven going to be like? It is going to involve a powerful presence and a positive absence.

The powerful presence

The powerful presence is God himself. He will dwell with his people. In saying what that is going to mean or be like, it is difficult to get much further than that basic statement. It will be remarkable, an experience of unending glory.

When Claire and I became engaged, a friend said to me, 'I expect you can't imagine anything more marvellous than spending a lifetime in Claire's company, can you?' I thought then, 'No, you're right.' And I am glad to say he is still right. When two people are in love, all they want to do is spend time in one another's company.

If human love can give us such a sense of glory, how much *more* glorious it will be when we are in the presence of God. How glorious to grasp how wide and long and high and deep is the love of Christ! How glorious this love so amazing, so divine, so rich, deep, generous and warm. To be rooted and established in such love, surely, will be our deepest experience of glory. And the commencement of these unending days of glory is already written on God's calendar. We will surely know the powerful presence of our loving God.

The positive absence

The positive absence means the absence of tears, death, mourning, crying and pain. This is to do with God's loving fatherly presence with us, and the power of the cross. It is moving. In the new world, there will be no more pain. We may shed tears for the suffering that goes on in our world. Suffering is not something 'out there', very often it is in our own lives, in our personal experience, or in the life of someone we care for. Suffering has so many faces: loss of loved ones, long protracted disabling illness, psychological and emotional pressures, painful memories and coming to terms with our lives.

In the new heaven and the new earth there will be no more pain and no more suffering. There is going to be an end to it. It is not that we will be anaesthetized to it all, but we shall be transformed – we shall live for ever in the presence of our loving, caring, heavenly Father. That is why Paul is able to say in Romans 8:18: 'I consider that the sufferings of this present time are not worth comparing with the glory that is to be revealed to us.'

Suffering can be transformed by glory. If you know that the journey's end is in sight, if you know the happiness which awaits you, it gives you courage to keep going, with joy along the way – whatever your circumstances.

Journey's end

Paul, when writing to the Thessalonian Christians, is unable to give a timetable for the second coming; instead, he uses picture language to emphasize its unpredictable occurrence:

> Now, brothers, about times and dates we do not need to write to you, for you know very well that the day of the Lord will come like a thief in the night. While people are saying, 'Peace and safety', destruction will come on them suddenly, as labour pains on a pregnant woman, and they will not escape (1 Thess. 5:1-3).

When will Jesus return? When will the judgement be? Will life get better or worse before or after he comes? When he does come, will that be an end to life as we know it altogether? If we only had the times mapped out, how much simpler it would all be! Or would it? It is understandable why we should like to know a precise timetable for the end times.

Jesus, like Paul, emphasized that the day of the Lord – the

Old Testament term of expectation now seen as the return of Christ – would come not only unexpectedly, but that its date is impossible to calculate. 'No-one knows about that day or hour, not even the angels in heaven, nor the Son, but only the Father' (Matt. 24:36).

In the light of these statements concerning the unexpectedness and incalculability of the second coming, it is odd that some claim Jesus and Paul expected these events to happen during the lifetime of the early disciples. These texts clearly illustrate that they were at pains *not* to commit themselves to time-tabling, since only God the Father knows the date he has set.

Conversely, such sects as the Jehovah's Witnesses have looked red-faced to the outside world, having confidently predicted the end of the world on at least five occasions – for the years 1874, 1914, 1915, 1975 and 1976. Several times it was a case of quick re-calculations all round.

Even that master of calculation, John Napier, the inventor of logarithms, managed to get it wrong, calculating the date of Christ's return any time between 1688 and 1700. Naturally, an authority such as his was closely followed and admired. Consequently his commentary on the book of Revelation had quite a vogue, with twenty-three editions and several translations before the world's predicted deadline. After 1700 it did not seem to sell so well!

The reason Jesus was reticent about times and seasons is that kingdom people are meant to remain passionately active on the King's behalf right up to his return. We can give him no better welcome than that. The unknown hour is designed to keep us on our toes. Timetabling the kingdom will inevitably affect our intensity of performance on the King's behalf. None the less, for many years Christians of the finest credentials have taken on the task of glimpsing behind the scenes, and have come up with some fascinating observations.

The discussion largely revolves around the understanding of Revelation 20, where John describes a period of a thousand years, a time when Satan is bound, preventing him from deceiving the nations any longer. At the end of that thousand year period, Satan is released. Having deceived the nations once more, this time for a short period, he is finally defeated. Thereafter follows the judgement and the new heaven and new earth. The period of a thousand years is referred to as the millennium, and there are four main views as to what it means.

Premillennialists see Jesus' return as preceding this thousand-year period. It bases this view on a strictly chronological appraisal of the arrangement of the book of Revelation. Since Revelation 19 describes the second coming of Christ, it would appear obvious that Revelation 20 describes a thousand-year period after that event.

But is Revelation a strict sequence of historical events? There are three sets of visions – the seven seals (6:1–8:5), the seven trumpets (8:6–11:19) and the seven bowls (15:1–16:21). The most natural reading of them is that they are indeed historical events, but looked at from different standpoints. The three groups are parallel accounts of the same period. Each time the writer backtracks, adds another layer of colour, and changes the perspectives from which the events are viewed.

Premillennialists see the world in decay, with Jesus returning after a period of tremendous turmoil and suffering such as described in Mark 13 and 2 Thessalonians 2. During the thousand year rule which follows, Christ's power will be finally and fully asserted on earth.

Postmillennialists, as the term suggests, see Jesus returning after the millennium. It is tremendously optimistic, seeing the present age as giving way to Christ's thousand-year rule of triumph through his people.

Amillennialists reject belief in a future literal thousand-year rule. They see Revelation 20 as a picture of this present age, with Satan bound and no longer able to deceive the nations, with the gospel enabled to spread, according to the promise to Abraham, to all peoples. The people of God enjoy the present reign of Christ, with the powers of the kingdom already revealed, yet wait for the consummation of things with the actual historical coming of Christ at his second coming.

Dispensationalists have a scheme of the future which was largely unknown until J. N. Darby of the Plymouth Brethren movement popularized it in the nineteenth century. The approach of seven different dispensations in the way God deals with man – innocence, conscience, human government (commencing with Noah), promise, law (from Moses to Christ), grace (the age of the church) and kingdom (the millennium) – and the sequence of eight covenants which, according to the Scofield Reference Bible, accompanies it, appears to be a careful and reverent handling of Scripture. However, it implies that God treats men and women in different ways in different periods, and it does violence to Scripture's own view of itself as a unity and a witness to the one unfolding plan of salvation.

All four views have this in common: they are anxious for the concerns of Christ and the coming of his kingdom. Premillennialists and postmillennialists have high expectations of what Christ can and will achieve on this earth. They share a strong and vital view of the strength and power of Jesus. Yet the adherents of premillennialism, committed as they see a vision of steep decline before the return of Jesus, can lack grit and resolve in social responsibility. Likewise, postmillennialism can appear over-optimistic concerning what can be achieved before Christ's return. In my view, amillennialism seems to be the position which is fairest to the intention of Scripture, though we still have to live with some unanswered questions.

Christians are bound to differ. Although we are all subject to Scripture, our minds are fallen, so none of us has a monopoly on truth and our interpretations of specific scriptures can be at considerable variance. We have to decide what are primary and what are secondary issues of faith. In the end, theologically, although it has many implications, the interpretation of the millennium rule of Christ is a secondary issue. The reason is clear. *Jesus declined to give us a timetable.* We should not therefore try and create one, but instead be circumspect and discreet in our pronouncements. One thing is absolutely certain, none of us can evade our responsibility to live in the light of this momentous event, whatever be the day or hour of its coming.

In the light of the future, how should we live in the present?
In 2 Peter 3:14, speaking of the new heaven and the new earth, Peter says, 'Since you wait for these, be zealous to be found by God without spot or blemish, and at peace.'

We need to relate this hope and expectation for the future to our present situation. Despite moves towards world peace at the close of the twentieth and beginning of the twenty-first centuries, there is still a terrible potential for destruction in our world today. The good news of Jesus is that the forgiveness of his cross and the re-creative power of God through the Holy Spirit can restore a measure of order, meaning, freedom, dignity and responsibility to a world which needs hope.

We have to learn to relate our hope for the culmination of history, the return of Jesus and the new world which he will inaugurate, to our concrete duties within history now. There are several ways in which the purpose and motive of the new world spur us on.

We are spurred on to evangelism because the new world will contain multitudes from all the nations. We have an important part to play in taking that gospel to all peoples.

We are spurred on to social action because the new world will be a place where righteousness dwells. If right action is to be the primary characteristic of the kingdom to come, then we must work out our duties in this present manifestation of the kingdom.

We are spurred on to love life. The references in Revelation and Isaiah to the wealth and the honour of the nations teach us to be richly involved with all that is best in the arts and sciences.

We are spurred on to love peace. If, in the new world, as both Isaiah and Micah say, 'they shall beat their swords into ploughshares, and their spears into pruning hooks ... neither shall they learn war any more' (Isa. 2:4; Mic. 4:3), does that not mean we should pursue peace and aim to be peacemakers in every possible way? 'Every possible way' will include personal relationships – at home, at work, in church, in society and internationally.

The prospect of a new heaven and a new earth is an immense encouragement to us, providing us now with clear purpose and leading one day to the fullest glory. But there is also a challenge to kingdom people who are destined to share in this new order. That challenge involves the inter-relationship between belief and behaviour. It means making the kingdom visible through our lives as we wait for the grand consummation of all things.

Live in awe

A certain kind of understanding about God, the kingdom, and the final outcome of history, should inspire a certain kind of lifestyle. This is all the more important when it is considered that the issue of belief and behaviour is one where Christians all over the world are at their weakest.

It is where the crack shows most clearly: there is a tendency for a gap to open up between belief and behaviour. The way we live so often denies in practice what we believe in theory. Unfortunately, in these situations, the critics of Christianity have a field-day. It is not just the media who observe and comment, it is the people closest to us; they are the ones who watch us. The people in our office or work place, the non-Christians at home, those of our friends who are not Christians – they are all watching us. They may want to know if there is something in what we believe and what we say we stand for. But we can be sure about one fact. They can smell a phoney a mile off. It is our responsibility to close the gap between behaviour and belief, and to bring integrity of lifestyle to what we proclaim about Christ and our commitment to him. Our witness to the good news of the kingdom depends on it.

The writer to the Hebrews shows that the Jewish Christians of the first century were as guilty as we are of hypocritical, sub-standard Christian living. By consequence, their witness – like ours – was becoming tame, eroded and ineffective. The writer makes his diagnosis not upon the basis of their laziness or apathy (though such attitudes were involved); instead, he sees the major failing to do with something deeper.

The major failing is to do with a blunted vision of God, a way of seeing God which does less than justice to the full truth about him. It is failing to live in awe. If our sense of the awe of God diminishes, so too will our sense of inspiration to serve him. Our vision of God, our sense of awe – which includes our love, our gratitude, but also our sense of his surpassing greatness, his majesty and his splendour – shapes the tie-up between behaviour and belief and affects our witness.

The writer to the Hebrews urges us, 'Let us offer to God acceptable worship, with reverence and awe; for our God is a consuming fire' (Heb. 12:28-29). The worship referred to there, as the context makes clear, is to do with lifestyle, the way we live before God. The New Testament often used the word 'worship' in this wider sense. It does not refer to the singing of hymns or a church service. It is making the strong point that the whole of our lives are of interest to God – that everything we are, and everything we do, can and should be part of our worship.

Our God is 'a consuming fire', so we must offer to him acceptable worship, with reverence and awe. Is this the way we would normally choose to describe God? Why does the writer use such vivid language? What impact is it meant to make upon us? To say our God is a consuming fire is a strong description. We should ask why. We need to go further into the teaching in Hebrews 12.

Three responsibilities

Responsibility for yourself
It is easy to become despondent, especially when things do not go our own way. We hardly need reminding of this, because it is so obvious. But the danger with despondency is that it can produce inertia within us. And when inertia sets in, we can begin to lose our direction, our energy and our sense of purpose.

Even when the things which go wrong in our lives are small and relatively trivial, it is easy to end up feeling so tired and despondent that you want to pack up and do precisely nothing. Most of us feel sorry for ourselves, even if it is all fairly inconsequential. If we let them, our emotions do exert a very powerful influence over us.

The real danger with despondency is that it brings with it this eroding aspect of inertia. It saps our vision of God and his purposes for us. We look inwards instead of outwards and upwards, and gradually we grind slowly to a halt. The enthusiasm, inspiration and zeal we have had all comes to an end. It is more than feeling sorry for ourselves. When inertia sets in, we become ineffective at the very point there is most potential for growth.

Whether our troubles are relatively trivial and slight, or whether they are disquieting and a tremendous burden, the danger of despondency is the same. It leads to inertia. It is precisely to those who are going through this experience of despondency, that these words in Hebrews 12 are addressed: 'Therefore lift your drooping hands and strengthen your weak knees, and make straight paths for your feet, so that what is lame may not be put out of joint but rather be healed' (Heb. 12:12-13).

Every problem, difficulty and struggle for us as Christians carries within it the potential for growth; what is lame can be put out of joint, but alternatively it can be healed. So we have to guard against despondency. Whether our troubles be light or burdensome, none of us is ever going to be immune from trouble of one kind or another. We cannot avoid it. We have to learn to face it and accept it. As the first part of Hebrews 12 suggests, God permits such things, not to hurt us, but to aid us in our growth in maturity as his children.

The first responsibility is for ourselves: not to sink into despondency and its consequence of inertia, but to keep our vision clear and our commitment strong.

Responsibility for our relationships

Attention is now immediately drawn to relationships, for it is in our closest relationships we experience and contribute to our most stretching and upsetting conflicts. This is why we have to take hold of our responsibility in this area. We are to 'strive for peace with all men, and for the holiness without which no one will see the Lord' (Heb. 12:14). In the original Greek, the word for 'strive' is a strong and active expression. Notice, too, an important theological link between peace and holiness. Holiness means becoming more like God. It implies committing ourselves to his will, to his ways of doing things. It is desiring to become more like Christ. How then do holiness and peace link up, especially in relationships?

Picture a problem in a relationship of some kind. Imagine there is somebody who continually annoys you, maybe from the family or work – someone who goads you, and whose attitudes or actions are to you like a red rag to a bull.

What can you do about it? Perhaps you have tried to improve matters between you, but the arguments, or the anger within you, gets the better of you. You tried and you failed ... and failed ... and failed again. It is dispiriting. Such failures may make you despondent. Worse still, inertia can set in. Then we simply learn, through continuing discouragement, to accept the aggravation as a normal part of our life. There must be an alternative. What is the way forward?

The clue from this Bible passage is the link between peace and holiness. When we strive for holiness in our lives, bringing our lives into willing conformity with God's purposes, then a practical way of peace is more possible.

One cause of conflict between us is that under the surface of our lives lurk all kinds of sensitivities. This is our emotional baggage which we have carried around with us since childhood. Underneath the surface, everyone is sensitive. The problem comes when someone steps on one of our most cherished inner pains.

This happens when those inner sensitivities become

threatened by the words or actions of others, or simply by what they stand for, or even by association with the memory of words, attitudes or actions of things now past. What happens is we rush to the defence of our sensitive inner selves. We wave our own words around like offensive weapons, and then the sparks fly upwards. Acrimony is the order of the day. No one is immune. As Christians, how can we counteract this weakness within ourselves?

There is a way forward, and it is to do with holiness. When we give up our lives to Christ, and more and more seek for holiness, we give God a chance to heal these inner sensitivities of ours by actually letting him into our bruised inner selves. It is like removing a plaster, exposing a wound to the fresh air and letting it heal in the open. It is something we must do – to open our lives fully to God, and let him touch our painful inner parts where there is resentment and hurt – the areas where there is need for change. This may have to do with attitudes and expectations, or it may relate to our need to fully forgive another person.

Our relationships matter, especially those relationships with people who have wronged us. The first work is to put right the wrong attitudes within ourselves. We cannot nurse anger for ever, for it will get the better of us in the end. Jesus' forgiveness enables us to forgive those who have hurt or wronged us. As Christians we are being scrutinized; people do look to the way we handle our relationships, and it is at this point that they may question whether Christianity works or not. It is as basic as that. This is the way to live and please God; it is the way others show the powerful reality of Christ's kingdom and the new world to which we are called.

Knowledge of this equation between peace and holiness is important. Furthermore, we can point to another principle: the quality of our relationships with each other is dependent on our relationship with God. If holiness comes first, you will be enabled to pursue the way of peace in your dealings with others. Neglect God and his righteousness and your relationships suffer.

Holiness keeps us on course. It enables us to work at peace in our relationships. It liberates us inwardly, because we are making room for God in our lives.

Responsibility for others

We have a responsibility for one another. The overall concern of Jesus when he spoke of his second coming was that his subjects should be ready for him when he comes. We do have to close the gap between behaviour and belief. And we have a responsibility for each other, to help one another know the grace of God in our lives: 'See to it that no one fail to obtain the grace of God; that no "root of bitterness" spring up and cause trouble, and by it the many become defiled; that no one be immoral or irreligious like Esau' (Heb. 12:15-16). This is the wider responsibility towards all Christians, and especially towards the members of the churches of which we are members.

There is an awful Christian syndrome. It goes something like this. You bump into another Christian at church. You smile broadly, out comes the conditioned reflex: 'How are you?' 'Fine!' is the sometimes less than honest reply. One goofy grin later, off you both go again, happily singing your respective choruses under your breath, your lives not having touched.

The excesses of sincerity can be just as bad.

'How are you?' (The eyes are fixed on yours.)

'Er, very well thank you.'

'But how are you really?'

They are both just caricatures. But unfortunately in any social situation, and especially in churches, extremes are always present. They range between shallow insincerity or nosy paternalism.

How much do you care about other people in your church? How much do you care about other Christians in your place of work or study? Do you care at all? Are you concerned about how other Christians are doing? Whether they are under pressure, struggling, discouraged or despondent, is not our role to encourage other Christians? We will not achieve this by hearty slaps on the back, for such encouragement is meant to come in two distinctive ways: by love and by prayer.

Everyone needs to be loved, listened to and encouraged. In order to love a person you have to give time to them. So we must not skimp on the quality time we spend with people. Sadly it is possible to be charging around, spreading ourselves as thinly as can be, not really allowing ourselves time to connect in a real way with each other's lives.

We have three responsibilities: to ourselves, to our relationships, and to other Christians – especially those within our local church. Neglect any of them, and the cracks begins to open between behaviour and belief. So let's beware the sin of diversification. Don't do too much. Don't become too busy. Don't spread yourself too thin. If you do, what happens next proceeds inevitably and predictably. First, you will suffer. Then, your relationships will suffer. And then, the church will suffer. For the world to see the changed lives which Jesus Christ makes possible, we need to work at all three responsibilities. We cannot afford to let them slip.

The two worlds
We often speak about someone being highly motivated, goal-orientated and having real direction in life. Such focus makes all the difference in the end. When I was a music student, I used to be fascinated by the piano writing of Franz Liszt. Liszt was the greatest piano virtuoso of the nineteenth century – probably of all time. His piano writing, particularly the works known as *The Transcendental Études*, is the most ingenious, creative, virtuosic and technically demanding work in the whole of the piano literature. In a word, it is stupendous.

Liszt was one of the most goal-orientated artists of the nineteenth century. He was a pupil of Karl Czerny, the man who wrote all the five-finger exercises. Czerny himself had been a pupil of Beethoven. One day the young Franz Liszt heard the legendary violinist Paganini. Paganini was so remarkable as a violinist, people used to say he was in a league with the devil!

He was a phenomenon. In his field, there has never been a virtuoso like him.

Liszt was so bowled over by Paganini's playing, he resolved there and then to turn his back on the past, the world of Beethoven and Czerny, and to re-create on the piano the fantastic virtuosity and ingenuity and brilliance that Paganini had displayed on the violin. He worked at it all his life. Among other works, the remarkable *Transcendental Études* ('after Paganini') were the result. They are truly staggering. Liszt knew what he wanted to do. He had his goals set out. He knew where he was going.

In a spiritual sense, we need to have our goals mapped out too. We need to know where we are going. Hebrews 12 describes two possible worlds to work towards. One is the past; the other is the future.

The point here is that the Hebrew Christians did not have any goals mapped out. They did not have that sense of working towards a future which is entirely in the purposes of God. That, by contrast, is the point of verses 22 to 24: 'You have come to Mount Zion and to the city of the living God ...' This means we have been incorporated into God's kingdom, we are part of his people, and we are working towards a goal. Lose sight of the goal, and you immediately loosen the relationship between belief and behaviour. Those three responsibilities of self, relationships and others do not matter so much if you have nothing to work towards, and there is no future seriously to consider.

So which world are you working towards? Are you taking the risks of faith which are a necessary part of working towards the future with God? Or are you more preoccupied with the past? Our priorities need a regular check-up. Again, if you let yourself get too busy, your vision can get stifled.

One consequence

'Thus let us offer to God acceptable worship, with reverence and awe; for our God is a consuming fire' (Heb. 12:28-29).

Fire in Scripture is often a visual aid which illustrates God's holiness; think, for instance, of the fire of the burning bush, or the fire of Sinai. What is your vision of God? Do you have before your mind the blazing heat of God's holiness, his justice, his righteousness and his love? He burns so much with care for us that he sent Jesus Christ to die so we could become his children. Do you realize it is this God, the consuming fire, whose child you are? This God cares passionately about you, about the way you live, about the way your treat yourself, about your relationships and about other Christians.

Our God is a consuming fire. He burns with ferocious anger when that crack opens up between behaviour and belief, because it means we have lost our vision of God, of the future and of our part in it.

There are three responsibilities, two worlds and one consequence. 'Thus let us offer to God acceptable worship, with reverence and with awe.' Why? Because we are God's kingdom people. The God who reigns has acted out of love and mercy to bring us into an everlasting covenant relationship with himself. Our responsibility is to live for his glory; that means sowing the seed of the word, which itself depends on the integrity of our witness to the King. This integrity is measured by the extent to which our discharge of our kingdom responsibilities reflects the King's own passion for justice and mercy. Effective communication of the gospel of the kingdom depends on this. We are called to be holy, to reflect the holiness of the God who loves us. It means that, as a kingdom people, we are called out to be different.

What part are you playing in the difference? Is all this true of you? Go back to your vision of God. We need to live in awe. Our friends, our families, those we work with all watch us – they can smell a phoney a mile off. Have you a blunted vision of God? Remember our God is a consuming fire. For the sake of the purposes of the kingdom which is unfolding with glory, whose full reality is soon to be consummated, we are under an obligation. As we move towards the future, before a watching world, we are the heralds of the kingdom of God. We must, therefore, narrow the gap between behaviour and belief.

For the grand unfolding Master Plan of the kingdom of God to touch the lives of our generation and any generations which remain, we must be the King's faithful witnesses. The question is as pointed today as when it was first addressed to the disciples: When the Son of Man comes – when Jesus the King returns to usher in the fullness of the kingdom – *will he find faith on the earth? (Luke 18:8)*.

Summary Points

■ The Bible speaks of a 'new heaven and a new earth' rather than going to heaven when you die.

■ Glory is a perspective changer.

■ Since 'the glory and honor of the nations will be brought into the heavenly city' everything we do which is of value matters for heaven.

■ In heaven there will be the powerful presence of God himself, and the powerful absence of suffering, pain and evil.

■ Jesus declined to give a timetable for his return; so should we!

■ As we await the consummation of the kingdom we must close the gap between belief and behaviour, and live in awe.

For Reflection

'In the end life is only triviality, just for a moment. And when the end comes. Then nothing' (Bertrand Russell, p.219).

How does the new heaven and the new earth answer Russell's rationalistic pessimism?

Think of anything you consider really marvellous, multiply it an infinity of times over, and you begin to approach the quality of what Paul is speaking of as 'the glory to be revealed' (p.223).

How does your stock of glorious moments help you to think of the glory to be revealed?

In a spiritual sense, we need to have our goals mapped out. We need to know where we are going (p.239).

In the light of what you have learned in this chapter, spend some moments praying about your goal to live for Jesus and the kingdom.

Appendix – A case study

ASSESSING CONTEMPORARY CLAIMS OF THE COMING OF THE KINGDOM

The Toronto Blessing

The coming of the new millennium has undoubtedly kindled a worldwide interest in what is widely, though vaguely termed, spirituality. While only a generation ago all forms of organised religion had declined to a marginalised place in public life, a new and living chord of hunger for hope has been touched with the dawning of the new age.

Leading the way, or responding to the spirit of the age, all kinds of public figures rehearsed their concern for the spiritual. While Princess Diana consulted horoscopes, Prince Charles preferred to become a defender of faiths (rather than *the* faith – a traditional role for the British monarchy). The England Football manager (symbolically tough and earthy), Glen Hoddle, enlisted the services of a faith healer for the England squad, and publicly speculated about theories of Karma and reincarnation (for both of which he was widely criticised, and eventually removed!). Former Soviet countries, only recently so pleased to open their doors to all the civilizing influences of the West, found they had to close them fast again – the profusion of cults and 'isms' spawned by the new age proved to be too much to handle.

The informal New Age movement has certainly encouraged a readiness to explore spiritual claims in and from all quarters of the globe. But the New Age mind is uncritical and inclusive. Hence, for the objective onlooker, the sense of religious chaos. However, a major dynamic and inspiration for New Age thinking has certainly been the coming millennium. This inspiration has equally affected many in the more organised religious sector, especially in relatively mainstream Christianity. On the back of a highly materialistic age, this wave of interest and concern has touched many Christians. This is especially the case with those who have been concerned to be ready when the Lord comes. Some (guided by theological conviction and certain styles of biblical exegesis) have come to see the millennium as having a special significance for the unfolding plan of God in redemption.

So in the last decade leading up to the new millennium, from a specifically Christian perspective perhaps the most highly publicised, controversial and influential movement, claimed to be 'uniquely of God', started near Toronto airport – the now famously titled *Toronto Blessing*.

Within months of reportedly wild phenomena, hotel rooms all around the area were packed out. Visitors from all parts of the globe joined a virtual stampede to the Airport Vineyard Church. Everyone wanted to check out the visible and audible wonders of what the Holy Spirit was doing in 'refreshing' Christians with his love and grace. Reports were astounding. Once the media decided here was prime headline material, what some called modestly 'This present move of the Holy Spirit' became more widely and proudly known as 'The Toronto Blessing'.

The following text is an unedited account of my own reaction to the so-called Toronto Blessing when I visited the Airport Vineyard Church for a major conference of Christian leaders in October 1995. It was originally written only for private circulation among my friends and for my church. At the time, although a number of papers and journals urged me to publish, I did not do so, for the issue was controversial. I did not wish to join with arguments on either side of the debate. My concern was that loving unity and face-to-face discussion is a better way of making headway in understanding and commending the truth about God and his ways.

Christians did get very heated on the matter as the experience and teaching emphases of the Toronto Blessing spread far wider than what was going on near the airport. I had to remind myself then, as today, that the Holy Spirit's supreme desire is that we should win the world for Christ. We can spend much time and energy in the wrong kind of debate. We *are* called to be discerning and resist error. However, keeping emotionally calm as we do is something we do not always achieve! To assess a move of the Holy Spirit and get hot under the collar, is surely not the fruit the Spirit would normally want to inspire.

Now that the impact of the Toronto Blessing has both gone international *and* begun to wane, this may be a time when we can be allowed some historical perspective. So I venture into print! However God may or may not have used Toronto, many of the lessons that can be drawn, and particularly the interpretative tools I have employed here in analysis, I believe are of significant value.

In assessing any contemporary claims of kingdom fulfilment, the Bible and its expectations are our No. 1 resource. There are, however, other approaches to be borne in mind which support the biblical critique of such movements. Thus some aspects of the *method* behind this case study may be needed long after Toronto is forgotten. There are likely to be other pretenders to the kingly throne, and other requirements may press in upon us to assess contemporary claims of the coming of the kingdom.

He who stands firm to the end will be saved. And this gospel of the kingdom will be preached in the whole world as a testimony to all nations, and then the end will come.... At that time if anyone says to you, 'Look, here is the Christ!' or, 'There he is!' do not believe it. For false Christs and false prophets will appear and perform great signs and miracles to deceive even the elect – if that were possible (Matt. 24:13-14, 23-24).

THE TORONTO BLESSING – AN AUTHENTIC MOVEMENT OF THE HOLY SPIRIT?

Reflections on the *Catch The Fire Again* Conference held in Toronto, Canada, October 4-8, 1995

The mighty winds of Hurricane Opal that swept through Toronto last week were mere tropical gusts compared with the power of God thousands believe struck them senseless at a conference of the controversial Airport Vineyard Church. At least with Opal they could stay on their feet.

Not so with many of the 5,300 souls meeting at the Regal Constellation Hotel. The ballroom carpets were littered with fallen bodies; bodies of seemingly straightlaced men and women who felt themselves moved by the phenomenon of the Holy Spirit. So moved, they howled with joy or the release of some long buried pain. They collapsed, some rigid as corpses, some convulsed in hysterical laughter. From room to room come barnyard cries, calls heard only in the wild, grunts so deep women recalled the sounds of childbirth, while some men and women adopted the very position of childbirth.

Men did chicken walks. Women jabbed their fingers as if afflicted with nervous disorders. And around these scenes of bedlam were loving arms to catch the falling, smiling faces, whispered prayers of encouragement, instructions to release, let go....

'I think this is an international movement of God that has potential to rescue the planet,' said John Arnott, senior pastor at the Airport Vineyard.

On Sunday 8th October 1995, 1.6 million readers of the *Toronto Star* newspaper will have read Leslie Scrivener's report of just one evening's meeting of *Catch the Fire Again* – a conference hosted by the pastors and people of Toronto's Airport Vineyard Church, now famous for the strange and controversial manifestations known as the 'Toronto Blessing'.

Because of the extraordinary interest expressed in the conference, the venue was changed at the last moment to a nearby hotel, the huge Regal Constellation, which could cope with the five and half thousand conference participants. Pastors and church leaders from every continent were present, many wearing headsets for the simultaneous translation facilities. Some expressed a feeling akin to the gathering of the nations – church leaders and representatives from all over the globe gathering for an exceptionally special meeting to receive from God.

There are always dominant themes in any large conference, and in Toronto delegates were repeatedly told that the Holy Spirit is preparing his people for revival; that the 'refreshing' of the Spirit, which is said to come from the manifestations described so accurately in Leslie Scrivener's report, are rapidly moving on to the 'Harvest Time' – a period understood as a wholesale world-wide turning to Christ.

On the Sunday morning the *Toronto Star* report appeared, one of the Vineyard Pastors actually went public in a prophecy which had been hinted at throughout the week. This was a significant climax to the growing intimations of the previous days' claims.

The date and time
On the Sunday morning in the Airport Vineyard Church at 272 Atwell Drive the whole Vineyard pastors' team, along with their wives (very North American), were brought to the front of the church. They were then prayed for – 'soaked' in Vineyard language – and most (predictably) fell to the floor, groaning or laughing. And then it was revealed. The Holy Spirit had prepared the date and time of the Harvest. It was very close.

The date and time had in fact been revealed to the speaker.

(Which is what I had expected, given the gathering of the leadership in the manner described.) However, the prophetic minister on this occasion said he didn't think it was wise at this point to tell everyone the date and time publicly. 'Maybe it wouldn't be good for all of you to know.' But make no mistake he said, it is coming, soon and very soon.

As you may imagine, this news sent shock waves through the church. Many were slain in the Spirit, including David Ruis, the gifted worship leader who couldn't get off the floor to continue leading the worship. But when someone else stepped into the breach, the celebrations continued, way past the Sunday morning lunch hour. Nobody seemed to mind ... you don't, do you. Not when you're one step away from the millennium rule of Jesus Christ.

The spreading fire

There is no doubt that heady claims are made for what is happening through the ministry of the Toronto Airport Vineyard Church, and that its influence is spreading rapidly. For the past twenty-one months, night after night, 1,000 or so visitors have come each evening to receive the Toronto blessing. Since January 1994, a cumulative figure of about 650,000 have come to Toronto, including 20,000 Christian leaders and 200,000 first time visitors from every country and denomination.

Life magazine named the Toronto Blessing as the top tourist attraction of last year. In Britain John Arnott claims that one out of six churches has 'received the blessing'. On the evidence of this one conference there is no sign that the movement is abating. Quite the opposite.

How did it all start?

In January 1994, a preacher called Randy Clark from St. Louis, Missouri, was prayed for by Rodney Howard-Browne, in some people's eyes a highly controversial South African evangelist. Randy Clark immediately observed, 'My hands are burning, they're on fire.' Rodney Howard-Browne said to him, 'Go to your church and lay hands on anything that moves.' And he did.

The following evening, Randy was to speak at the Vineyard Church near the Toronto airport. By 11.00 p.m. eighty per cent of the congregation were on the floor, laughing and crying. And so was born 'The Toronto Blessing'. And so it grows and grows.

What is going on?

I went to the conference asking God to keep my heart and mind wide open to what he wanted to teach and say to me. I am grateful for friends who prompted me to prepare myself in this way. It's far too easy to criticise what you find a threat or a challenge or when what you see and hear discomfits you. To be frank, to be immersed for days on end in a five star, club class version of the Toronto experience is exhausting even for out and out enthusiasts. I've needed space to reflect on what I saw and heard. So since coming back, I've tried to clear my head, be really prayerful, look carefully at the Bible, and ask one simple question – What is going on here?

Different people answer that in different ways.

Some just dismiss everything without question. They may not like Rodney Howard-Browne, so anything which goes back to him can't be any good. Or they can't find the manifestations in the Bible. Or even find the Bible in Toronto. The Spirit without the Word writes the whole thing off. For some.

Some others, the enthusiasts, say it's the Holy Spirit. As I heard one of the conference leaders pray from the front: 'Lord, we tried doing church without you. It was no fun. Thank you that this – this is all of you.'

For me the issue is, does the answer to the question – What is going on here? – have to be all or nothing. My first response to that is to look simply at what the average visitor to the Vineyard sees and experiences and takes home to share with others, and then to ask how it all adds up from a biblical point of view.

Snapshots of the Conference

Each day the Conference had three long sessions. Afternoons were given over to workshops where some discussion took place, but morning and evening were on a larger scale and reflected closely what normally happens in the Vineyard meetings night after night.

We would start off by standing to sing. This is a very loud experience. (If you're used to pop concerts you'll be at home in this one.) We'd sing choruses, often with very brief words, to the accompaniment of a small band. Excellent musicians, very highly amplified indeed – even by my super decibelic standards. Choruses were often repeated many, many times. This is anathema to some Christians, of course. I don't mind too much, but I think this needs to be monitored.

I will say that the criticism that repeated choruses has to be mindless is ill founded. There is a view that repetition concentrates the mind on a specific thought or the emotion that thought engenders. That's true and reasonable, even if it isn't your personal cup of tea. Personally I found this style of worship sometimes mantra-like and then quasi mesmeric. I am not saying anyone got hypnotised. I don't know if they did – (I doubt it) – but the overall effect was hypnotic. Not the best way to keep the old critical faculty fresh and receptive. But maybe some like me are far too cerebral anyway. Anyway, it didn't hurt for a few days. But I'm not sure whether this is wise long term.

This was the effect on me. After standing for an hour or more of very loud music of this kind (there were occasional soft spots too – but these were even more mesmeric and mantra-like), I became increasingly sensed-up to my inner feelings. So were those around me.

Manifestations

This wasn't the time to fall down (the chairs were still in place) but day after day, night after night some did collapse 'early', panting onto the seats. Lots made funny sounds. A few spoke in tongues. Some roared like lions, some laughed, some just danced in the Spirit (very nice sometimes), there were those who jumped up and down, some shook bits of their anatomy, some bent deeply from the waist, some rolled or thrashed on the floor, a lot jerked or did funny walks. There was in fact an awful lot of jerking. It looks like the Toronto version of wearing a fish badge, you do a kind of involuntary jerk to show you're under the blessing ... or something.

At several points during these first parts of the meetings I thought people were ill, like the man next to me who I thought was having a heart attack. It turned out to be a spiritual heart attack, but how was I to know? 'Are you alright?' I said, rather concerned and trying to be a kindly neighbour. 'Yeah,' he said, 'It's only the Lord. But it's really great.' And that's the interesting thing. There's a lot of good which seems to come out of these manifestations.

By the way, here's my confession, I didn't manifest. I would have been quite happy to. (I think ... certainly if it was of God.) But I didn't. Still John Arnott says he doesn't manifest much either. But he also says the manifestations don't matter. Now that's worth an extra thought. John Arnott appears a very sincere, fatherly sort of chap. But on this point I disagree with him strongly. The manifestations do matter hugely. In fact, the helpers keep on praying with you till you fall over. They don't condemn you if you don't. But most do end up falling anyway. The Toronto Blessing without the manifestations wouldn't be anything to write home about, and it would be more honest to admit it.

After the worship, there's usually testimony – a very relaxed time, a cross between a talk show and a revival meeting. It is so relaxed that on the first day, Ken Gott, a visiting British speaker and the leader of the (then) four hundred strong Sunderland Christian Fellowship, known in Canada as Britain's Toronto, arrived drunk on the platform ... drunk 'in the Spirit', that is. Ken was supposed to be interviewed as a main speaker. But he came up the stairs laughing, bending and twitching, and ended up on the floor with another bunch of leaders and speakers who also couldn't get a clear word out. What a muddle, I thought.

Explaining it all

John Arnott did have an explanation for Ken's wacky behaviour.
(They described it as wacky, not me.) And this is a major
apologetic you hear in various forms to explain these
manifestations, and to crown the implicit plea that everything
should be done decently and in order. So John Arnott said, 'The
Holy Spirit's work may look messy and weird to you. Of course,
it is. But who cares when you see the fruit afterwards. Paul's
conversion was messy, wasn't it. But who minded when they
saw the fruit?'

Maybe that's a fair comment. But is the apostle's experience
on the road to Damascus the measure and norm for everyone?
And is being unable to speak on the first day of a conference in
a hotel in Toronto directly comparable to the conversion
experience on the Damascus Road of the apostle to the Gentiles?
By his use of the Bible, John Arnott thinks it is. I don't. But
John Arnott is right to focus on the fruit and not just the
manifestations themselves. However, as I'll mention in a
moment, the two really belong together.

More snapshots

The pattern for these testimony times has an interesting feature.
It's to do with something called soaking. Each time, the person
who has spoken is prayed for by the team until they keel over.
They are then 'soaked' in the blessing through prayer, which is
often done through fanning, and other signs made with the hands,
as well as petition. This soaking is a key Vineyard concept.

Then follows something akin to preaching. In my experience
this was rarely biblical. A Bible passage or verse may have
occasionally been referred to, but you'd be hard pressed to say
this was real Bible teaching. At one point I asked the opinion on
this of a highly intelligent and well schooled American missionary
working in northern Iraq. What did he feel about the place of the
Bible? 'Who needs teaching when I can get to know Jesus better?
I don't want to be taught if I can bask in his presence.' I found this
a fairly standard response from those I asked on this matter.

However this response shouldn't be dismissed too quickly. Why? Because this person told me he had been spiritually dried out before he came to the conference. Lots of people attend for the same reason. And he said he was refreshed. Deeply so. And he meant it. I believe him. I was really thankful to God that one of his workers in such an isolated situation should be so encouraged. But as they say, the end doesn't necessarily justify the means. My experience, sinful and weak that I am, is that God often does wonderful things in spite of me, rather than because of me.

So what's going on?
Well, you see what's going on in section three of the morning and evening meetings. And these are the long bits. Everyone is asked to clear and stack the chairs (in piles of ten please) and then it's time to receive. Now they are careful to say, don't let anyone pray for you who is not one of our ministry team. They even wrote to me before I came to say this.

They said then it was 'because some people might be present who do not share our values'. But I think that the issue may go deeper. They believe the blessing is passed on normally only by those who have received it. Just like Rodney Howard-Browne to Randy Clark, and Randy Clark to John Arnott. A kind of apostolic succession. It's a sort of sacramental way of thinking.

So many will get in the prayer line, and that's what will happen. At this point they will have already appealed for 'catchers' (you need to be strong – but it's a great way to learn how to do this ministry, says John Arnott) and the catcher stands behind, and the prayer minister stands in front, and most people fall over in a couple of minutes. Then they're left on the floor, to thrash or rest or whatever, until it's time to get up again.

We were told the (non Christian) Regal Constellation staff were quite used to seeing bodies all over the place. For me, it was always strange, really odd, but I'm very conventional. However, I was not prejudiced about this. It doesn't offend me. I quite like lying flat on my back as it happens. But in this case,

I had a serious intention. I did want to know what was happening in people's lives, especially those affected by manifestations. So I made it my business to ask. (There were lots to choose from....)

In some of the people clearly some great things have happened. Some others, of course, have been disappointed. And this points to the fact that such an experience is neither automatic, nor always beneficial. But let's concentrate on the good and positive.

People talk about this sense of refreshing. They talk about a sense of falling in love with the Holy Spirit or with Jesus. Many times, there's a good effect on a marriage, a feeling of greater effectiveness in ministry, a closer, more real, sense of God. Sometimes some kind of healing or deliverance may be felt to have taken place.

So what's going on? As I have said, I believe the manifestations are important to the Vineyard. If it wasn't for the manifestations, people wouldn't come in the numbers they do. On the other hand, as John Arnott says, the focus should be on the fruit.

Wiring it all up

I want now to ask what is the connection between the manifestations and the fruit?

Here's my stab at a first draft answer. Bear in mind that I write this not a week after the end of the conference, and I feel that after such an in depth exposure to the Toronto claims, some degree of personal processing is necessary. So please forgive me for what I have got wrong.

Worship and the gospel

First I think I have discerned what I'll call for now a kind of justification by experience.

Justification by faith is right at the heart of the gospel. John Arnott understands this well. On one occasion I heard him explain the gospel beautifully clearly in these terms. Justification is God's declaration that you are in a secure relationship with him, by virtue of Jesus' death on the cross as a full and sufficient payment for your sins. As the old hymn has it, 'Ransomed, healed, restored, forgiven.'

So Christians traditionally reflect Paul's language in Romans 5:1, when we speak of justification by faith. We accept what God has already done for us. We enter this relationship under a pre-paid scheme. Faith is like us exchanging a free voucher for entry into God's everlasting family and kingdom.

Now I want to say that I was particularly impressed by some things I saw in Toronto. I have, for instance, seen at Toronto a greater warmth of individuals apparently responding to the love of God in an outward, overt way than I think they have ever done before. It was very warm enthusiastic worship. It would definitely put some people off. But this kind of response is what I mean by justification by experience. The intoxicating nature of these meetings night after night (in this case day after day as well), opens up some hearts in a way they haven't been opened before or for a long time.

It seems to me that all the elements in their worship combine to bring this effect: of helping some to deeply recognise their justification by God – by experience. It's akin to what has been described over the centuries as entering into assurance. And maybe that's what it is. But the comprehensive effect seems to work first through the emotions and not through the mind. Assurance usually works the other way round.

John Arnott often speaks (rightly) of knowing the Father-heart of God. And this is what many take home. God's amazing fatherly care and acceptance of us through the blood of his Son. This comes through the songs, and is in a sense teaching gospel truth (just as songs and hymns have always taught gospel truth). However, it seems to take the place of much teaching – this is a serious weakness; but it also seems to open hearts up – which is a desirable strength.

Carpet burn

The second element I have noticed is a profound life change in many of the people I met, where a form of psychological and spiritual healing takes place. This goes beyond the normal talk of refreshing and joy that the Lord has brought many through the Toronto Blessing. (By the way the Vineyard Church are slightly amused that a British newspaper called this move of the Holy Spirit 'The Toronto Blessing'. The Vineyard are more modest in the way they describe it.)

So what happens to people when they fall to the floor? For some people this is learned behaviour. Pentecostals have been doing this for years, and it's hardly new. Some people fall in worship because this is the thing to do – in the same way that some Anglicans like to look deadly serious throughout divine service! Following such expectations isn't necessarily hypocritical, though it can be. The Lord surely looks on the heart, which is where the real action is.

However, some people who fall to the floor apparently do so entirely non volitionally. Whether this is the Lord 'making them fall down' is not really the issue. I suspect not in most or all cases. But that weakening of the limbs and that giving way to what the Lord wants to do in an individual's life has had some profound, and in some cases highly beneficial, consequences which are difficult to dismiss.

Some people when they fall say they 'rest in the Lord'. Others may 'thrash' around in varying degrees of animation. Some will remain carpeted for many hours. Well, you may say, Evensong was never like this. And you're right. It does sound odd; it looks odd and is odd. But nonetheless some speak of a significant measure of release and inner healing. (Some speak of physical healing too, but that doesn't concern me at the moment. I do believe God does sometimes heals us physically, but it doesn't take special kinds of prayer to ask him. This however is special in style and it seems to me the 'style' does contribute quite a lot.)

Primal scream

Over the years I have written widely on the relationship of secular techniques of counselling and Christian pastoral counselling practice. I was keen to dig beneath the surface at Toronto to ask what was happening at the level of the mind. So with these antennae activated, I went scurrying around on the carpet at the Regal Constellation Hotel, and what did I find?

A few years ago, there was a lot of excitement in clinical circles because of a clinician called Arthur Janov, who became famous with his book *The Primal Scream*, and the therapeutic method which went with it. The basic idea was as old as the Freudian hills, and was all about bad experiences in the birth canal (did you have one?) and a dinky method of resolving the angst which was an unwelcome hanger-on in your adult life. So the big scream – the primal scream – was the answer. Thrashing around on the floor in a quasi drunken state, you let it all out. You went back to your nascent moments – and relived it all. Got it all off your chest. If you're Freudian, a kind of abreaction.

For some this has seemed to be just the job. We all know the value of a good cry – even a good moan. Whatever Janov's psychological imprecision (is it really possible to remember let alone relive the birth experience?), he did have some success in releasing otherwise pent up emotions which seemed impervious to other forms of therapy.

I have seen people undergoing this form of therapy, and in several cases what I saw on the Canadian carpet, and what people described was happening to them, reminded me strongly of just this Janov approach.

But there is a significant difference. Here the release is 'before God'. Here's a consciousness that the Lord can and will heal our hurt hearts. So many North Americans talk of their parental hurts. (We're hardly immune either.) Maybe for some, what they describe as a profound encounter with God is a kind of sanctified therapy. It's just a theory. But that's how it seemed to me. In the jargon, as I say, a form of abreaction. That's not to dismiss what's happening, just to try and understand.

Expecting the harvest

However when people get up off the carpet, as the Vineyard pastors insist, it's the fruit which matters. And there are many claims of a closer walk with God, transformed lives, greater zeal for evangelism. All good stuff indeed. But I don't think this is purely to do with carpet burn. It does have to do with heightened expectations. Which is the third element I noticed.

I guess many of us are pretty fed up with some aspects of the world as it is these days. In fact if you live in North America the signs of moral decline are even more horribly obvious than they are in Europe. So the experience of an apparent new move of the Holy Spirit, with special manifestations and talk of a world wide turning to Christ (the much spoken of 'harvest') and the Lord's imminent return, really fuels the fires of spiritual expectation. This is a dominant element and result of the Vineyard ministry.

Indeed we should expect the Lord's return. It will be glorious and awesome. But there is a sense in Toronto that the Lord has waved down the flag at the finishing line, and the final race is about to begin. At last we're all going to see the action. Well, when expectations are heightened in this way, hyped up some would say, depending on how we are made, some of us may become a little uncritical in the way we process what and how we're taught. Like my friend who said, 'Who needs teaching when I can get to know Jesus better?'

I personally am very worried by the absence of real Bible teaching in what I saw at Toronto. This was after all a major conference for pastors. Most of the time the Bible was ignored. A couple of times a passage was read. Once or twice there was some attempt at Bible teaching (by John Arnott and Ron Allen). I have to say with genuine respect for John Arnott, what he made of the so-called visions of Abraham, Jacob, Moses and David was not what I think the Bible makes of them. Not to put too fine a point on it.

The Bible is definitely not the controlling factor in what is taught and practised at Toronto. This of course represents a major change in 2,000 years of Christian practice from 2 Timothy 3:16 onwards. Since the Holy Spirit inspired the Bible, it seems incongruous if he should now be prompting his people to effectively ignore or mishandle it.

Holy hysterics?

What about the manifestations? Yes indeed, what about them?! They are certainly noticeable. From the moment I saw Ken Gott and other speakers 'drunk in the Spirit' unable to say their piece at the beginning of the conference, I knew everything I had been told (or most of it) was true about Toronto. It was happily chaotic. Lots of snorting sounds. Animals braying. Roaring, tweeting. Plenty of shaking, falling, and loads of people had the jerks. It's pretty odd, and quite funny really. More fun than your average Cathedral Mattins, and there's a lot of laughter too.

Honestly, I thought it was a mad house at first, and wondered whether I could get an earlier flight back. But I got used to it. I thought I might enter into party mode and cluck like a chicken, but my integrity wouldn't have it. The whisper in my ear (from the memory pack in my brain) was they've just got the hysterics. That's all it is. But my experience tells me the story in a slightly different way.

Non pathological epidemic hysteria is not a mental disorder, and it doesn't have to be wild, noisy and wacky, but it does affect groups of people where there is a certain set of circumstances. This can be where there are heightened expectations; a particular world view, philosophy or theology; strong leadership; audio or visual elements with some kind of mesmeric effect; and some kind of openness, however modest, to go with the flow.

This doesn't mean that what is happening in Toronto, and in the churches influenced by Toronto, is 'mere' psychological phenomena. But the possibilities of such reactions are certainly mechanisms built into our human and social make-up and I believe are probably at work here. Certainly the neurological elements cannot be denied. Laughing results from the brain's temporal lobe; jerking and twitching from the motor centres; falling, drunken walking, and inability to move from the brainstem. These pre-wired neural circuits need stimulus.

Some may argue that they are supernaturally stimulated. I don't rule this out. But it seems to me that the more usual explanation for most people is more mundane. Good old epidemic hysteria. Not at all 'a fit of the hysterics', but as I've explained the response of the brain to certain sets of stimuli. Which of course, as God invented the brain and all our responses, he can use, and maybe he is using in Toronto, and anywhere he wishes.

By saying this I am trying to point out that these claims about the Holy Spirit's manifestations are not at all like the claims of possession which are observed in some pagan religions. We are 'in Christ' not 'possessed by Christ' or the Holy Spirit. At the same time, there is an important question as to the nature or origin of these manifestations. Are they the Holy Spirit 'coming upon' an individual (hence the danger of seeing this as a possession-like syndrome); or are they an individual's own response to God? I'll come back to this in a moment.

Signs of revival

There is some emphasis in Toronto that these manifestations are similar to the manifestations of historical revivals (if that is what they were) as reported by writers like Jonathan Edwards and others. But just because people have behaved oddly like this before doesn't tell us anything really. Neither does it invalidate things. But the comparison does tell us that at least the animal sounds are new. But so what?

Well, they're only glorified snorts (if you see what I mean). However, one girl I heard from across the hall did do an amazing line in something which sounded straight out of the Amazon jungle. But for the most part they don't sound like your average camcorder sound effects tape.

It is all pretty odd, I have to say. But the good bit is that in these meetings everyone seemed hugely happy, relaxed and flexible. None of your po-faced church going here. If we could have that chunk of the Toronto Blessing it would certainly do us all good....

So the big question: is this the Holy Spirit? Or to put it the way we often speak of, 'Is it of God?'

Going with the flow

My answer to this is a question of flow. Which way is the flow going? Is this God to man or man to God? Is this God showering down his blessing, causing all these sweet people to behave in such odd and unusual ways? Or is it a human (and maybe real) response to God?

I have thought about this constantly. For me it is the question. I have prayed about it, thought about it, talked about it, and above all searched the scriptures. At the moment, I really think this is man to God. That's the way the flow is going.

Some of it undoubtedly is fleshly. (Christian jargon for human beings playing games, putting it on, and not really in touch with God, though they may have convinced themselves they are.) I saw lots of this. But that's hardly unusual. We all wear our masks, and sometimes the heart is very deceitful and leads us to play games with religion, play at being spiritual, when our heart for God is not really in it. So London, New York, Cape Town, or anywhere else, is no different to Toronto in this respect.

I don't want to criticise wrongly, because I also saw in Toronto a devotion to Christ which to me seemed very genuine (in some cases wonderfully so). But I remember that sincerity is not the touchstone of authenticating truth. The road to heresy has been paved with many smiling faces. I should also say, regretfully, that it seems to me there is quite a deal of manipulative leadership in the whole Toronto movement. Not all of it is, but some belongs to the tradition of the loudest style of Bible bashing we have come to expect from a few in North America.

In this case they thump the Holy Spirit rather than the Bible. I was reminded several times of the prophets of Baal calling down the fire till they were hoarse and exhausted. I don't mean to sound rude or offensive. But these otherwise lovely people do shout at the Holy Spirit. 'More fire, Lord, send down the fire, Lord, now, Lord, do it, Lord.' It may be sincere (I'm sure it usually is), but it is capable of working everyone else up into a frenzy. Mind you, maybe it would be good if we could all get just a little more enthusiastic for the things of God sometimes. Wouldn't it?

The Holy Spirit super highway

It is salient to remember that this all started with Rodney Howard-Browne. He has a classic Pentecostal background, and those who have taken all this up are of a similar persuasion. Put that together with modern communications: a church situated minutes from a major airport; TV and radio coverage; newspaper reports; videos and music CDs. The so-called revivals of the past never had such a head start. But the form of it, the theological emphasis, the manifestations, the whole presentation is sourced in one man, Rodney Howard-Browne. So whatever may be God's part in it all, the way it looks, the whole presentation has a very human origin, and that is the man who flamboyantly describes himself as 'The Holy Ghost bar tender.' Rodney Howard-Browne describes his ministry thus: 'I serve the new wine and invite them to drink.'

So my answer to the question what is going on here is: I don't fully know. But some of what I think I can comprehend I have outlined above. I am not at all convinced that we should drop everything (literally) and get Torontoed. Not at all. But I am convinced that we should not automatically write off everything we don't like to see, or can readily critique from our Bible position, and thus miss the challenge which a part of the body of Christ issues to us. That challenge has a lot to do with real, full, loving, energetic devotion to Christ.

Concerns

Yet at the same time I am concerned by what I saw. Some believe Toronto is going down the road of becoming a cult. I don't believe they have run that course just yet, but I agree there is a danger, particularly in a church so uncontrolled by God's Word. On the other hand there is an enormous openness to God, a willingness to open up lives to be transformed and used for the sake of the kingdom, and a spontaneity of joy and true devotion to Christ.

For all they talk about evangelism, they are not hugely active in making Jesus known. They regard this move of the Spirit as a refreshing for believers. The emphasis on feeling good, 'the feel good factor', is very Western, North American, and twentieth century. To my mind, however, when the Holy Spirit came at Pentecost he came not for this kind of refreshing, but that we should be witnesses (Acts 1:8) and get on with the premier task of world evangelisation. The Holy Spirit is also the one who wants to make us more like Jesus. To be the agent of sanctification in our lives.

And finally

I stood in the Regal Constellation hotel in a room with 3,000 others (another two thousand in the over flow!). Most of them were on the floor, I was still standing. I looked around as many were laughing, groaning, thrashing, wobbling, and squawking, and I said to God, 'Lord, when I get back home to Bromley, will you be there as well as here? Can you be with me in the mundane as well as in these heady, noisy times of worship and praise? Do I really need to receive some special anointing passed on by special people from Rodney Howard-Browne via Randy Clark via John Arnott via one of the commissioned team in the prayer queue?'

And then I remembered Jesus' words in Matthew 28:20: 'I am with you always, to the very end of the age.' Whatever good there is in Toronto, and I don't rule out some long-term good, it does strike me that the Toronto claims are highly overblown. Particularly that the Spirit of Jesus is at work in a more unique way there than anywhere else in the body of Christ. On so many counts, it really doesn't pass the Bible's own tests. That is, if you take the Bible seriously.

If you go into any supermarket, pick off the shelves whatever catches your fancy, sweet things, savoury, a wide array, bring it home and empty your bags, no doubt you'll have quite a store of good things. But put them all into one pot, and casserole for an hour or two, and you may find the effect to be quite odd or even quite sour.

There are undoubtedly some good ingredients at Toronto. And by looking at the strongest ingredients (like the emphasis on fruit) you may think everything is fine. But put everything together and ask what's the total picture, the final mix, and I think you get a less tasty result. Take the whole spectrum – the Spirit without the Word, the prophecies, the manifestations, and a lot more that I haven't taken space to describe – and I have to say (quite regretfully) what comes out of the pot as the final mix is a strange and volatile mixture.

To me, it doesn't look at all like what the Bible leads me to expect will be the work of the Holy Spirit. But that said, the Toronto work is there. It won't go away (for some time at any rate). And I still think we shouldn't be destructively critical. We'll all know people who will be thanking God for the good things coming out of the Airport Vineyard. I thank him too. But let's also pray for Toronto, and the growingly large number of churches influenced by them.

When you have finished reading this, perhaps you will pray that God the Holy Spirit will graciously lead them into all truth and harness their undoubtedly wonderful enthusiasm and joy for an increasingly mature and effective witness and mission.

I have to remember that I am a sinner with a capital S, and God wants to change me so he can use me too. And while we who have been called to be pastors and teachers have the responsibility to teach right doctrine and refute error, we also have to remember that God wants us to be moulded by his will and purposes, so we can help our churches make Jesus known.

In this I know the Lord wants me (and you) to be holy, to put Jesus first, and open my life fully to the ministry of the Holy Spirit. And that, for all the mind blowingly wonderful and strange things which went on, is actually what the ministry at Toronto really impressed upon me last week.

I want to be more in step with the Spirit; more changed and empowered by him; more holy; more concerned for the glory of God; more active for the progress of the gospel of the kingdom; more expectant of Jesus' longed-for return; more ready when he comes. Going to Toronto touched my heart in all these ways, and for that I'm truly thankful. There are problems with this movement, but the zeal, devotion and sense of expectation should be recognised. I'm praying that the Lord will channel all that's truly right, good and from him in the Toronto Blessing (and that means there's a lot of weeding to do), so that the true movement of God in the gospel, in all his churches around the globe, will indeed be released in its full potential to rescue the planet. Whenever it is, that harvest is surely coming.

Subject Index

Abraham 10, 33, 34-7, 40, 44, 45, 57, 62, 63, 94, 107, 108, 175, 176, 178, 180, 181, 229, 259

Ahijah 74

Airport Vineyard Church 244, 247-65

Allenby, General 48

Amos 81, 181

Antiochus IV Epiphanes 48-9, 82

Archelaus 87, 88, 89

Arnott, John 249, 252, 253, 254, 255, 256, 259, 264

Assyria 17, 18, 47

Atonement 52-3, 65

Babylon(ian) 17, 18, 19, 24, 48, 74

Blood (as sacrifice) 51-3, 65

Boulanger, Nadia 84

Circumcision 54-7, 65, 93

Clark, Randy 249-50, 254, 264

Community 29, 30, 111, 140, 147, 148, 155, 168, 189, 190

Copernicus, Nicolas 204, 210

Covenant 10, 15, 29, 30-41, 43, 44, 45, 48, 51, 53, 54, 56-8, 60, 63, 68, 72, 93-4, 99, 107, 108, 116, 230, 240

Cyrus 18, 19

Czerny, Karl 238-9

Darby, J.N. 230

David 33, 41, 43, 44, 45, 46, 47, 49, 53, 54, 59, 65, 67, 71, 75, 86, 108, 259

Dobson, James 38

'Doomsday' 177

Egypt 13, 37, 39, 44, 47, 48

Elijah 13, 21

Elizabeth 59, 60

Estrangement 31, 34, 40, 45, 117

Ezekiel 15

Ezra 93

Galileo 210

Gamaliel 82

Gates, Bill 205

Geldof, Bob 150

Gott, Ken 252-3, 260

Grace 10, 34-5, 37, 40, 45, 57, 58, 60, 61, 103, 107, 108, 115, 116, 117, 118, 122, 124, 127, 141, 148, 154, 164, 167, 182, 209, 210, 230, 244

Harvey, William 204

Henry, Matthew 224-5

Herod Antipas 50, 75, 96

Holiness (of God) 25, 37, 38, 40, 45, 53, 60, 61-2, 66, 240

Holiness (of man) 65, 143, 155, 235-7

Howard-Browne, Rodney 249-50, 254, 263, 264

Isaiah 15, 17, 18, 19, 20, 21, 22, 23, 24, 25, 26, 49, 53, 67, 71, 76, 77, 81, 147

James 122, 181

Janor, Arthur 258

Jehovah's Witnesses 228

Jeremiah 15, 39, 51, 54, 57, 74, 107

Jeroboam 74

Jerusalem 18, 19, 29, 31, 49, 72-5, 77, 78, 80, 81, 82, 83, 85, 86, 90, 91, 96, 119, 130, 139, 148, 202

Joel 132-3

John the Baptist 59, 75

Joshua 47

Josiah 48
Judas Iscariot 82
Lazarus 173-6, 178, 180, 191
Lazarus (of Bethany) 202-8, 216, 217
Lee, Laurie 220
Lewis, C.S. 143, 179
Liszt, Franz 238-9
Luke 73, 85, 138-45, 146, 148, 157, 172
Luther, Martin 119-21, 125, 127
McIlwaine, Billy 197-8
Martha and Mary 202-8
Mary (mother of Jesus) 58-64, 65, 66, 140
Megiddo 47-8
Mercy 34, 40, 45, 56, 61, 62, 63, 172, 189, 240
Messiah 9, 10, 41, 43, 46, 49, 50, 51, 59, 63, 65, 67, 68, 71, 72, 73, 75, 76, 77, 80, 81, 83, 90, 91, 96, 137, 147, 157, 209, 212, 217
Micah 81
Millenium 9, 58, 229-30, 243-4
Moses 10, 13, 33, 37-40, 44, 45, 54, 55, 56, 57, 79, 93, 107, 108, 180, 182, 230, 259
Napier, John 228
Napoleon 48
Nebuchadnezzar 74
Newton, Isaac 205, 210
Noah 33, 34, 35, 40, 45, 56, 108, 230
Paganini 238-9
Palestine 9, 10, 47, 49, 60, 67, 81, 91, 98
Paul 13, 26, 40, 41, 42, 57, 66, 70, 82, 102, 115, 116, 117, 120, 123, 124, 129, 136, 138, 149-67, 168, 182, 192, 201, 215, 223, 227-8, 242, 253, 256
Peter 130-7, 141, 144, 145, 146, 231
Pharaoh Neco 48
Pharaoh Ramses II 13
Pharisees 60, 73, 75, 76, 77, 78, 79, 80, 84, 85, 91, 107-14, 119, 172, 173
Philistines 47
Pilate 96, 119, 120
Pompey 49, 96
Prophets 10, 15, 57, 60, 62, 66, 73, 74, 75, 78, 80, 81, 108, 171, 172, 180, 181, 182, 193, 216
Rauschenbusch, Walter 220
Reconciliation 31, 34, 45
Reign/rule of God 9, 10, 11, 13, 14, 15, 19, 20, 24, 25, 26, 29, 30, 40, 53, 58, 61, 69, 98, 99, 137, 148, 168, (God who reigns) 171, 178, 193, 209, 229, 240
Rontgen, Wilhelm 205
Sadducees 77, 108
Simon the Zealot 82
Solomon 47, 74
Stoics and Epicureans 13
Strauss (family) 33
Tiglath Pileser III 47
'Toronto Blessing' 244-5, 248-66
William the Conqueror 177
Williams, Charles 179
Worship 25, 60, 61, 68, 155-6, 219, 233, 239, 240, 249, 251, 256, 257, 264
Zaccheus 85, 86
Zealots 50, 77, 82-3, 86, 91, 171, 172
Zechariah 81
Zedekiah 74

Scripture Index

Genesis
1 224
1:2 212
3 31
4:4 52
9:8-17 34
9:12-16 56
12:2 35
17:3-5, 7 34
17:4 35, 36
17:7 36
17:11 57
28:12 220
50:20 45

Exodus
19:5-6 38
19:6 50

Leviticus
11:45 38
17:11 52

Deuteronomy
4:7 107
6:4 79
6:4-5 55
6:4-9 79
6:6-9 78
7:1-4 93
7:6 94
11:13-21 79
15:11 189
30:1-5 55
30:6 55, 57

Joshua
12:21 47

1Samuel
13:14 41

2Samuel
7 43
7:10-11 44
7:12 44
7:13 44
7:14 45
23:1 41

1Kings
4:12 47
11 74
18 21

Ezra
9 93
9:2 93

Job
5:7 223

Psalms
14:1 115
16 132
23 27
95:3-5 213
118:24 80
118:26 79-80
137:4 48
139 126
139:24 126

Proverbs
3:5-12 213
3:34 122
28:6 174-5, 191

Isaiah
1:18 53
2:4 231
2:11-12 80
9:6-7 67
9:7 49
40 15, 27
40:5 19
40:10-11 20
40:10-31 15-17
40:18 20
40:19 21
40:21 21
40:22-3 22
40:25 22
40:26 23
40:27 24
40:28-31 24
40:31 13
53 92
53:1 42
53:5-6 53, 71
59:2 83, 92
60:3 49

Jeremiah
7:28 107
17:9 108, 126
27 74
27:12-15 74
31:31-2 39
31:31, 33 53, 54

Ezekiel
18:32 178
34:12-14 27
34:23, 31 27
36:26 47

36:26-8 51
37:4 60

Amos
3:7 81

Micah
4:3 231
6:8 172

Zechariah
9:9 29
9:9-10 81

Matthew
5:10 156
5:11-12 193, 216
5:17 57, 66
7:21-3 213
8:11-12 213
10:4 82
10:22 102
12:28 212
12:29 209
13:44 70
15:13-14 107
16:18-19 148
16:19 10
21:1-16 46
21:5 29
24:13-14 245
24:23-4 245
24:36 228
28:20 264

Mark
1:14-15 95, 105
1:15 9, 67, 93
1:40 151
2:1-12 77
2:27 76
3:18 82
3:27 209
4:3-9 97
4:11-12 69, 98
4:14-20 100
4:26-9 103
7:6-7 77
13 229

Luke
1:1 139
1:1-4 138
1:2 140
1:3 141, 142
1:4 139, 144
1:30 59
1:33 59
1:35 59
1:46-7 60
1:46-55 58
1:48 61
1:49 61
1:50 62
1:51-3 63
1:51-5 62
1:54-5 63
4:18-19 68
4:21 68
6:15 82
11:20 42
11:22f 209
12:32 107, 124
13:31 75, 77
13:33-5 75
15 125

15:2 111
15:3-7 111
15:7 112
15:8-10 112
15:10 112
15:11-32 112, 114
16:13 171
16:16 171
16:19-21 173
16:22-3 175, 176
16:24 178
16:25-6 178
17:20-1 84, 212
17:21 53, 60
18:8 241
19:1-10 85
19:1 87
19:11 85
19:11-27 85, 87
19:14 88
19:35-40 73
19:37-9 85
19:38 78
19:39 78

John
1:2 122
1:51 221
2 202
3:3 61
4 202
5 202
6 202
6:44 103
8:31-2 70
8:32 144
9 202

10:11 27
10:14-16 27
11 202, 208
11:3 203
11:17-19 202
11:19 203
11:25-6 204
11:33 207
11:35 207
11:38 207
11:41-4 207
11:57 76
12:31 209
13:23 176
14:14 214
14:15 183, 184, 186
14:16 186, 187
14:17 187
14:18 187
14:21 184
14:23 184, 187, 188
15 116
15:18f 194
15:26 194
16 194
16:1 194
16:4-7 195
16:7 193
16:8-11 196
16:12-13 198
16:13 199
16:14 199
18:36 82
20:30-1 201

Acts
1:3 172
1:6-8 148

1:7 11
1:8 264
1:13 82
2:13 131
2:14-15 130
2:14-36 130
2:17-18 132
2:17-21 132
2:19-21 133
2:22 134
2:22-3 134
2:23-4 45
2:25-8 132
2:32 136
2:36 134, 137
2:43-7 148
5:36-7 82
14:22 219
17 157
17:5 158
21:38 82

Romans
1:3 41
1:17 120
1:18 83
3:10 115
3:23 29
5:1 256
5:2 116
7:7 39
7:15-25 26
7:21-4 40
8 117
8:1-2 121
8:1-17 65
8:2 188
8:14 116
8:14-17 115, 125
8:15 117, 123

Romans, cont.,
8:15-16 123
8:16-17 124
8:18 223, 227
8:18-27 215
8:24-5 201
8:34 42
9:4 68
11:33-6 213
12:1 150

1Corinthians
12 116, 149
12:27 149
15:26 209

2Corinthians
8:2-3 182
8:9 182

Galatians
3:7 64
3:24 40

Ephesians
1:11 214
3:10-11 61
3:14-15 27
3:14-21 27

Philippians
2:6-8 135
4:6 213

Colossians
1:25, 28 102
2:2-3 70
2:11-12 57
4:14 138

1Thessalonians
2 157
2:1-2 159
2:1-12 159
2:3-4 162
2:4 162, 163
2:7 165
2:8 165
2:9 165
2:10 165
2:12 166, 167
5:1-3 227

2Thessalonians
2 229

1Timothy
2:1-2 213
6:17-19 66
6:17-18 175,
  192

2Timothy
1:11 129
2 116
3:16 70, 260

Hebrews
2:10 124
4:15 188
9:11-14 52
9:27 205, 206
12 233-4, 239
12:12-13 234
12:14 235
12:15-16 237
12:22-4 239
12:28-9 219,
  233, 239
13:20 27

James
1:22 181
4:6-8 122-3
5:13-16 213

1Peter
1:1-2 106
2   116
2:9 168
3:15 106, 141
5:4 27
5:5 61

2Peter
1:10-11 106
3:14 231

1 John
1:7 122
3:1 115

Revelation
1:18 10
4:3 56
5:5 10
6:1-8:5 229
7:16ff 209
8:6-11:19 229
11:15 12, 105
12:10 122
15:1-16:21
  229
19 229
19:9 176
19:17 176
20 228-9
20:7ff 209
20:12 177
21 31
21:1 220
21:1-3 31
21:3 212
21:3-4 225-6
21:4 209
21:26 224
22:16 41